TREASURES OF GRACE

Great Fast

EXPANDED EDITION
LINKING THE READINGS & SERMONS

VOLUME 1

A deep-dive commentary on the Liturgical readings
From the Ninevites' Fast to the Second Sunday

Archdeacon Banoub Abdou

Foreword by His Eminence Metropolitan Youssef

Translated by St. Mary & St. Demiana Convent

THE PARTHENOS PRESS

Treasures of Grace—Great Fast (Expanded Edition)—Linking the Readings & Sermons: Volume 1
Compendium by Archdeacon Banoub Abdou
Translated by St. Mary and St. Demiana Convent

Designed by St. Mary and St. Demiana Convent.

Published by:
The Parthenos Press
101 S Vista Dr, Sandia, TX 78383
theparthenospress.com

Cover art: Michaelangelo's "Adam." As much as a human is reaching up to God, so much more is God reaching down to the human.

CONTENTS

Foreword

Annually, there are five *Katameros* books in the Coptic Orthodox Church. *Katameros* (καθ᾽ ἡμέραν) is a Greek word found 45 times in the Holy Bible that means "from day to day" or "daily." Thus, *Katameros* refers to the allotted liturgical readings according to each day. Each book serves a specific season: The Great Fast, Holy Week, Holy Fifty-Days, Annual days, and Annual Sundays. The church was very purposeful in her choice for each day's readings. In his work, published in 1958, Archdeacon Banoub Abdou (1900–1967) attempted to shed light on this wisdom.

The readings for each liturgical day begin with the chanting of the Gospel on the previous evening during the Evening Raising of Incense (that is, Vespers). Each Gospel reading is always accompanied, or rather preceded, by the chanting of the psalm (usually only one verse or a couple of verses). The next morning, another Psalm–Gospel pairing is chanted during the Matins Raising of Incense. Before this Psalm–Gospel set, a unique feature for the Great Fast is the reading of the prophecies. Later, during the catechesis (the Liturgy of the Word), a passage from the Pauline Epistles (the 14 epistles written by Saint Paul) is followed by the Catholic Epistle (a select passage taken from James–Jude), which is then followed by a passage from the Book of Acts. The Acts is followed by the Synaxarium, the chronicles of the saints (not addressed here). A third Psalm–Gospel set concludes the catechetical readings. Another unique feature on the Sundays of the Great Fast is the "Sunday Evening Raising of Incense," where another Psalm–Gospel set is chanted.

In his compendium, Archdeacon Banoub Abdou begins each day "Linking the Readings" where he gives an overall summary linking all the day's readings, highlighting the connecting themes between the prophecies, Gospels, and the epistles. Next, he goes deeper to focus on each in more detail. He first treats the prophecies (during the Ninevites' Fast, each day, only one prophecy is read from the book of Jonah).

Next, he addresses the Gospels; the psalm usually expands upon the accompanying Gospel. He groups and treats all the Psalm–Gospel sets before finally turning to the Epistle readings, which is a slight variation from the order followed during the Divine Liturgy. The Archdeacon then includes a sermon on each of the Gospel readings. *Linking the Readings* (previously published), the cliff-notes version, did not include these sermons, but covered the span of the whole Fast. The First Volume of this trilogy covers the readings from the Vespers of the Ninevites' Fast until the Second Sunday of the Great Fast. The Second Volume covers the readings from the Third Sunday and the Fourth Sunday. The Third Volume covers the readings from the Fifth Sunday until the Seventh Sunday.

The *Katameros* for the Great Fast incorporates (and begins with) the readings for Jonah's Fast, or rather the Fast of the Ninevites. One might ask what this fast has to do with the Great Fast, but first let us address the idea of fasting and why the Great Fast is so significant. When God created Adam and Eve in the Garden of Eden, they (and their descendants) lived as strict vegans and so they each lived hundreds of years. After the flood, when *new* items were introduced into the human diet, the lifespan began to decrease, and the human nature changed from gardener to hunter. In fasting, we are seeking to return to not only the diet, but also the obedient life Adam lived in the Garden of Eden. In fasting, we are exerting self-discipline by saying "No" to ourselves. We are depriving ourselves of something we want, remembering the times we took or did something we should not; we are *making up* for our sins. This is what the Ninevites did, they repented from their sins by abstaining from all food (not just eating strict vegan food), and in three days God relented and did not destroy their city (Jonah 3).

The church always arranges for this three day fast to begin two weeks before the Great Fast, as a prelude, because, as the Lord said, "As Jonah was three days and three nights in the belly of the great fish, so will the Son of Man be three days and three nights in the heart of the earth"

(Matthew 12:40). Jonah's "burial" in the belly of the great fish is symbolic of Christ's burial in the tomb of earth for three days, and the acceptable repentance of the Ninevites is reminiscent of our repentance throughout the Great Fast. Henceforth the Great Fast is the "Fast of fasts"!

Archdeacon Banoub Abdou's work, originally published in Arabic under the title "Knooz El Neima," is a vast compendium. This English translation by Saint Mary and Saint Demiana Convent in Georgia is neither literal (rendering a rigid read), nor figurative (losing the intended meaning). However, it is a comfortable medium, carrying the meaning and spirit of his words and simultaneously an enjoyable read for the fluent English speaker. We would like to extend our deepest thanks to all who joyfully labored in the translation process, to bring this book to the light; may the Lord reward them with the heavenly in place of the earthly. All the credit goes to the Archdeacon's depth in expounding on the Scriptures, and any mistakes are to be blamed on the translator.

The purpose of this book is to aid the Coptic reader understand why the church in her wisdom chose those specific passages to be read on each day during the Great and Holy Fast, and to aid every reader dive deeper into the meanings within these select Biblical passages and muse over the beauty of God's word and its amazing linearity throughout the Holy Bible.

May the Lord use this work to enrich each Holy Bible reading and each reader during the Great and Holy Fast.

Metropolitan Youssef
Saint Mary and Saint Demiana Convent
January 7, 2023
Nativity Feast

SALVATION THROUGH FAITH IN CHRIST THE MASTER'S RESURRECTION[1]

NINEVITES' FAST - MONDAY
THE CALL TO REPENTANCE
(Calling sinners to repentance)

Linking the Readings:

All the readings of this day center on one theme: **Calling sinners to repentance**

The prophecy speaks of **God calling sinners to repent**, as He sent Jonah to the people of Nineveh (whose evil had risen to heaven) to call on them to repent.

The Vespers Gospel centers on the **Savior urging sinners to repent**, as He answered those who came to inform Him of the Galileans whose blood Pilate mingled with their sacrifices: "Unless you repent you will all likewise perish"; the Matins Gospel centers on **His mercy to sinners if they request forgiveness**, as shown by His saying that He gives good gifts to those who ask of Him; and the Liturgy Gospel centers on **cautioning the penitents against relapsing to sin**, as He spoke of the evil spirit that returned to the person who relapsed from his repentance bringing along seven other evil spirits.

The Pauline Epistle **urges penitents to offer their bodies unto holiness**, after having previously offered them to uncleanness and lawlessness; the Catholic Epistle centers on **the destruction of the impenitent**, describing them as "wandering stars for whom is reserved the blackness of darkness forever"; and the Acts reading speaks of **church expansion through the entry of penitent converts into the faith**, as Peter baptized

---

[1] Resurrection from the dead, of which Jonah was a type.

many, causing increased fellowship, "and the Lord added to the church daily those who were being saved."

PROPHECY

Prophecy   Jonah 1:1–17

God calls sinners to repent: God called Jonah, the son of Amittai, to go to the people of Nineveh (whose wickedness had risen to Him) to call them to repent. Jonah instead fled from the face of the Lord to Tarshish on a ship. God sent a great storm against the ship causing its near submersion. When the mariners learned that the storm was because of Jonah, they reluctantly tossed him into the sea (heeding his advice) in an attempt to avoid drowning. God prepared a great fish to swallow Jonah, where he remained [in prayer] for three days and three nights.

PSALMS AND GOSPELS

Vespers Psalm   Psalms 95:1–2

As sinners rush to repent, according to the Lord of Glory's call in the accompanying Gospel reading, this psalm shows their joy in receiving the forgiveness of their sins: "Oh come, let us sing to the Lord! Let us shout joyfully to the Rock of our salvation. Let us come before His presence with thanksgiving; let us shout joyfully to Him with psalms."

Vespers Gospel   Luke 13:1–5

The Savior urges sinners to repent, as He told those who came to inform Him of the Galileans whose blood Pilate mingled with their sacrifices: "Unless you repent you will all likewise perish" (v. 5).

Matins Psalm   Psalms 103:1, 8

The beginning of the psalm encourages sinners who tame their souls with fasting and prayer to bless God's Holy Name. The second part explains the reasons to bless His Name, which are that the Lord is compassionate and responds to their prayers, as shown in the Gospel reading. The psalm says, "Bless the Lord, O my soul; and all that is within me, bless His holy name! The Lord is merciful and gracious, slow to anger, and abounding in mercy."

Matins Gospel   Matthew 7:6–12

The Gospel speaks of God's mercy to prayerful sinners who ask Him to forgive them and accept their repentance: "If you then, being evil, know how to give good gifts to your children, how much more will your Father who is in heaven give good things to those who ask Him" (v. 11).

Sermon: Call to Repentance
This sermon, written by Pope Youannis of Alexandria, is read immediately after the Matins Gospel. In it, he directs the attention of the faithful to God's plenteous mercies, to the Lord's continual seeking for their return to Him with all their hearts, and for them to initiate repentance as did the people of Nineveh. Next, he shows them that when the evils of the people of Nineveh had increased, God sent them Jonah to warn that their city will be overturned after 40 days. When the king heard this, he ordered his people to avoid all evil, wear sackcloth, and sleep on the ground until their repentance is accepted. Their repentance

11

was indeed accepted when they humbled themselves before the Almighty. Jonah's knowledge of God's mercy was the most probable reason he ran away from His presence, to avoid seeming like a liar before the Ninevites when God has mercy on them and forgives them. The Holy Patriarch goes on to explain to the congregation that God does not cling onto His wrath to the end of time and does not wish the death of the sinner. He encourages sinners to resemble the people of Nineveh in their fasting and humility, to win the mercy of the Lord. Next, he reminds the people neither to appear sad like the hypocrites when fasting, nor to do evil to anyone, so they may gain the kingdom of heaven.

Liturgy Psalm   Psalms 130:3–4

Since on Judgment Day people will give an account for every idle word spoken, and anyone who relapses from repentance has a more evil end, the psalm speaks on behalf of sinners who have committed these sins and humbled themselves before God. It confesses that if He does not forgive them, they will perish, because He alone is the God of forgiveness, and they depend on His mercy: "If You, Lord, should mark iniquities, O Lord, who could stand? But there is forgiveness with You, that You may be feared."

Liturgy Gospel   Matthew 12:35–45

The Savior cautions penitents against the results of relapsing to sin, as He illustrated by the fate of the person who relapsed from repentance: ultimately, the evil spirit returns to him "and takes with him seven other spirits more wicked than himself... and the last state of that man is worse than the first" (v. 45).

EPISTLES

The Pauline Epistle   Romans 6:17–23

U rging penitents to offer their bodies unto holiness: Paul thanks God

for the faithful, because although previously enslaved to sin, they obeyed, from their hearts, the form of doctrine delivered to them. "For just as you presented your members as slaves of uncleanness, and of lawlessness leading to more lawlessness, so now present your members as slaves of righteousness for holiness," revealing to them the result of either choice: "What fruit did you have then in the things of which you are now ashamed? For the end of those things is death. But now having been set free from sin, and having become slaves of God, you have your fruit to holiness, and the end, everlasting life" (vv. 19, 21–22).

The Catholic Epistle   Jude 1:1–13

D estruction of the impenitent: Jude charges the faithful to stand fast

in the faith which was once for all delivered to the saints, warning against false teachers who creep in only to divert them from the Lord's grace unto lewdness. He gives some examples: destruction of the Israelites who left Egypt yet did not believe; the angels who did not keep their proper domain; Sodom and Gomorrah; and those who perished in the rebellion of Korah—describing the destruction awaiting all those "wandering stars for whom is reserved the blackness of darkness forever" (v. 13).

The Acts   Acts 2:38–47

C hurch expansion through the entry of converts into the faith: Peter

the apostle charged his listeners to repent and be baptized in the name of the Lord Jesus for the remission of their sins. They joyfully accepted his words and were baptized, and that day three thousand persons joined the church, and they shared everything in common, being all with one accord: "And the Lord added to the church daily those who were being saved" (v. 47).

Vespers Gospel
Luke 13:1–5
Encouragement to Repent
See Sixth Week Monday Liturgy Gospel of the Great Fast.

Matins Gospel
Matthew 7:6–12
God's Gifts to those who Pray
See First Week Sunday Vespers Gospel of the Great Fast.

Liturgy Gospel
Matthew 12:35–45
Danger of Relapsing from Repentance

DANGER OF RELAPSING FROM REPENTANCE

Overview

During Christ the Master's second circuit of ministry in Galilee, they brought to Him one who was demon-possessed, blind, and mute to heal. He cast out the demon and cured the person and so the scribes and Pharisees resumed attacking Him, accusing Him of casting out demons by the power of Beelzebub, the ruler of the demons. The Lord of Glory immediately discredited their accusation, laying the foundation for some of His teachings. In the pericope dealing with the last part of the Savior's teachings to the scribes and Pharisees, He revealed that the heart of man is the key to his guidance or error. Those who err must be judged, and their end will be worse than their beginning.

Mystery of Guidance or Error

> 35 A good man out of the good treasure of his heart brings forth good things, and an evil man out of the evil treasure brings forth evil things. 36 But I say to you that for every idle word men may speak, they will give account of it in the day of judgment. 37 For by your words you will be justified, and by your words you will be condemned.

35 – The Lord of Glory blatantly pointed to the scribes and Pharisees' jealousy, the source behind them accusing Him of using witchcraft; they could not speak of goodness while they were evil (since out of the goodness of the heart the mouth speaks). He went on to explain that the heart of man is the underlying cause to his guidance or error: "A good man out of the good treasure of his heart brings forth good things, and an evil man out of the evil treasure brings forth evil things." Every vessel reveals its contents.

36 – The Lord did not want to pass over their false accusations without revealing their punishment on judgment day, so He expressed a general standard: "For every idle word men may speak, they will give account of it in the day of judgment."

37 – He showed the reason: "For by your words you will be justified, and by your words you will be condemned." The word a person speaks originates from his beliefs; his conscience judges him as righteous or evil.

J udgment against Unbelievers

> 38 Then some of the scribes and Pharisees answered, saying, "Teacher, we want to see a sign from You." 39 But He answered and said to them, "An evil and adulterous generation seeks after a sign, and no sign will be given to it except the sign of the prophet Jonah. 40 For as Jonah was three days and three nights in the belly of the great fish, so will the Son of Man be three days and three nights in the heart of the earth. 41 The men of Nineveh will rise up in the judgment with this generation and condemn it, because they repented at the preaching of Jonah; and indeed a greater than Jonah is here. 42 The queen of the South will rise up in the judgment with this generation and condemn it, for she came from the ends of the earth to hear the wisdom of Solomon; and indeed a greater than Solomon is here."

38 – The scribes and Pharisees did not cease accusing the Master (after He rebuffed their accusations of exorcising the demons by Beelzebub), but retorted stubbornly. Trying to test Him, they asked for a miracle to increase their faith in Him—as if the multitude of miracles they had witnessed from Him were not enough to convince them to believe in Him. Perhaps in making this request, they replicated their ancestors' stand against Moses; they would not accept the law, except after he performed several miracles before them.

39 – The Lord of Glory, who knew the hypocritical state of their heart, called them an evil generation because they run after vanity and commit evil. He said they seek "after a sign, and no sign will be given to [them] except the sign of the prophet Jonah." A skeptic might ask how to reconcile between this saying and the several signs He indeed did before them thereafter. The response would be He wanted to clarify that if a sign would draw people to the faith, then He would not delay, but if a sign were requested to tempt Him, then He would refrain. When

the devil said, *"If* You are the Son of God, throw Yourself down" (Matthew 4:6), He refrained.

40 – He gave the sign of Jonah as bearing the greatest similitude between Himself and this prophet. Jonah remaining in the belly of the great fish three days and three nights and coming out alive is a strong symbol of the death of the Lord in the tomb and His rising on the third day.

41 – The Savior continued giving the Pharisees parables of Gentile nations who returned to God for the simplest reasons, while the children of Israel continued in their hardness of heart and blindness. He said the people of Nineveh would rise up on the day of judgment and judge this generation. They believed at the call of Jonah and repented, even though Jonah is a weak fallible prophet, while the Jews rejected the teachings of Jesus, the One who surpasses Jonah's call as the light of the sun surpasses the light of a lamp.[2]

42 – He said the queen of Sheba (the queen of the South) will rise up in the judgment and judge them because her firm faith carried her to endure the hardships and dangers of the journey to hear the wisdom of Solomon, who, despite his great wisdom, remained a fallen human, whereas the Jews objected to Jesus, who is immeasurably greater than Solomon.[i] In this same manner, Paul the apostle directed his epistle to such Jews: "And will not the physically uncircumcised, if he fulfills the law, judge you who, even with your written code and circumcision, are a transgressor of the law?" (Romans 2:27). This is also clear in the parable of the Good Samaritan (Luke 10:25–37).

---

[2] The call of Jonah the prophet. The book of Jonah mentions: "And Jonah began to enter the city on the first day's walk. Then he cried out and said, 'Yet forty days, and Nineveh shall be overthrown!'" (Jonah 3:4–5). The 40 days reportedly represent the 40 years that passed between the crucifixion of Christ and the destruction of Jerusalem.

Their Fate

> 43 When an unclean spirit goes out of a man, he goes through dry places, seeking rest, and finds none. 44 Then he says, "I will return to my house from which I came." And when he comes, he finds it empty, swept, and put in order. 45 Then he goes and takes with him seven other spirits more wicked than himself, and they enter and dwell there; and the last state of that man is worse than the first. So shall it also be with this wicked generation.[3]

43 – The Savior showed the scribes and Pharisees that He cast out the demon from the demon-possessed, blind, mute person by the finger of God (not by the power of Beelzebub, the ruler of demons, as they had blasphemously claimed), and that this man was a type of the sinner who repents and secures safety from the demons. He then showed the sordid fate awaiting such a person if he goes back on his repentance and sells his soul to the demon once more: "When an unclean spirit goes out of a man, he goes through dry places, seeking rest." *He goes searching for a person devoid of the spirit of the law to overtake his heart.* When the Lord had asked the demon where he came from, he answered, "From going to and fro on the earth, and from walking back and forth on it" (Job 1:7). Peter the apostle said he is "like a roaring lion, seeking whom he may devour" (1 Peter 5:8). If he "finds none [a soul to rest in]... he says, 'I will return to my house from which I came...'"

44 – "...And when he comes, he finds it empty, swept, and put in order." The evil spirit returns to find that this individual (whose heart he had previously possessed) had failed to follow the way of the Lord and had returned to his first life, and so is a renewed fitting dwelling place for the evil spirit because this person neither obeys the truth nor avoids evil.

---

[3] See Luke 11:24–26.

45 – "Then he goes and takes with him seven other spirits more wicked than himself, and they enter and dwell there; and the last state of that man is worse than the first." By reneging his repentance, he adds evil to evil, and his fate becomes eternal condemnation. The Savior gave just such a warning to the man laid at the pool; after He healed him, He commanded him, "See, you have been made well. Sin no more, lest a worse thing come upon you" (John 5:14).

The condemnation of those who renounce their repentance is plainly declared by the Apostles Paul and Peter. The first said, "For it is impossible for those who were once enlightened, and have tasted the heavenly gift, and have become partakers of the Holy Spirit, and have tasted the good word of God and the powers of the age to come, if they fall away, to renew them again to repentance, since they crucify again for themselves the Son of God, and put Him to an open shame" (Hebrews 6:4–6). He also said, "For if we sin willfully after we have received the knowledge of the truth, there no longer remains a sacrifice for sins, but a certain fearful expectation of judgment, and fiery indignation which will devour the adversaries" (Hebrews 10:26–27).

The second apostle said, "For if, after they have escaped the pollutions of the world through the knowledge of the Lord and Savior Jesus Christ, they are again entangled in them and overcome, the latter end is worse for them than the beginning. For it would have been better for them not to have known the way of righteousness, than having known it, to turn from the holy commandment delivered to them. But it has happened to them according to the true proverb: 'A dog returns to his own vomit,' and, 'a sow, having washed, to her wallowing in the mire'" (2 Peter 2:20–22).

The Savior's words that the evil spirit returns to the individual from whom he came out, bringing along seven even *more* wicked demons, teach us that evil spirits have varying abilities to defraud and deceive. However, the power granted to them by God is limited; they cannot force a person against his will. Whoever cries out to God against them, putting on His whole armor, will doubtless conquer. John Chrysostom likens the devil to a dog that does not stray from its master's table as long as the master throws something to it; if it loses hope of any gains, it leaves.

This parable, given by the Savior about the one who repented then reneged, applies to the Jewish nation. After the coming of the prophets to them, after all the troubles, the tribulations, and the captivity, when He who is full of glory came to them, they paid Him no heed; therefore, the Roman emperor Vespasian and his son Titus overpowered and destroyed them. Josephus the historian documented this fulfillment while writing about the destruction of Jerusalem.

Some exegetes see that the individual from whom the demon was exorcised represents the people of Israel, who took delight in killing the prophets, in worshipping idols, and in committing sins. Moses' God-given laws exorcised the evil spirit. The evil spirit roaming in places where there is no water is indicative of his going to nations that have no laws. As for his return to the children of Israel, it is indicative of their lack of any virtue, their killing of the prophets, and their intent on killing the Savior. The wretched fate is an allusion to their captivity and death by the Romans, as Josephus again documented.

NINEVITES' FAST - TUESDAY
LISTENING TO THE GOSPEL

Linking the Readings:

All the readings of this day center on one theme: **Listening to the Gospel**

The prophecy speaks of **God listening to the repentance of sinners**, as He listened to the prayer of Jonah while he was in the belly of the great fish and ordered the fish to vomit him onto land, so that he may cry out to the people of Nineveh as He had ordered Jonah.

The Matins Gospel speaks of **God's patience with them** (perhaps they will hear His voice), as the landowner was patient with the unfruitful fig tree, giving it one more year; and the Liturgy Gospel focuses on the **Savior urging sinners to listen to the Gospel**, as He said that He had lit His lamp and placed it on a lamp stand so that all those who enter can see the light.

The Pauline Epistle speaks of the **importance of listening to the Gospel**, as the Apostle said that he preaches the Gospel to everyone, admonishing so that he "may present every man perfect in Christ Jesus"; the Catholic Epistle tells sinners they must **refrain from evil**; and the Acts reading **calls out to them to repent**, as shown by Paul the apostle explaining that God "commands all men everywhere to repent," and some of those who heard him believed.

PROPHECY

Prophecy   Jonah 2:1–10

God listens to the repentance of sinners: This prophecy mentions the prayer that Jonah offered up to God from the belly of the great fish, in which he declared that he was surrounded by floods and covered over by billows and waves. When his soul grew faint, he remembered God's mercy and prayed to Him, promising to fulfill his vows. God listened to his repentance and commanded the great fish to vomit him onto dry land to call on the Ninevites.

PSALMS AND GOSPELS

Matins Psalm   Psalms 103:14–15, 9–10

The psalm's beginning hints at what comes in the Gospel reading regarding the landowner's patience for one more year on the unfruitful fig tree, and concludes by begging God not to deal with sinners according to their sins, but according to His mercy: "For He knows our frame; He remembers that we are dust. As for man, his days are like grass; as a flower of the field, so he flourishes. He will not always strive with us, nor will He keep His anger forever. He has not dealt with us according to our sins, nor punished us according to our iniquities."

Matins Gospel   Luke 13:6–9

This Gospel passage speaks of the Savior's patience with His people's sins (perhaps they will repent), as shown by the vinedresser asking the landowner of the unfruitful fig tree: "Sir, let it alone this year also, until I dig around it and fertilize it. And if it bears fruit, well. But if not, after that you can cut it down" (vv. 8–9).

Sermon: Encouragement to Obey God
In this sermon, by Patriarch John of Constantinople, the saint encourages the faithful to take to heart Jonah's threats to the Ninevites with the destruction of their city. He reminds them that the great fish swallowing Jonah was symbolic of the death of the Savior for their sake; therefore, they should obey His commandments. Then he explains to them that

when Jonah felt distressed by his surroundings in the belly of the great fish, he prayed to God who answered his prayers. Thus, it is good for them to entreat God in tribulation, and He will save them; He will have mercy on them and will not treat them according to their transgressions. Then he reminds them of the story of the fig tree unfruitful for three years—symbolic of the years of youth, adulthood, and old age—to say they should bear fruits of righteousness and faith all their lives. He concludes his sermon by asking them to live in virtue so that they may gain mercy from God.

Liturgy Psalm   Psalms 85:2–3

This psalm refers to what follows in the Gospel in that the Ninevites repented at Jonah's call to repent, and so God relented from the wrath of His anger towards them, as the Savior pointed out in the Gospel: "If then your whole body is full of light... the whole body will be full of light." And so, the psalm says, "You have forgiven the iniquity of Your people; You have covered all their sin. You have taken away all Your wrath; You have turned from the fierceness of Your anger."

Liturgy Gospel   Luke 11:29–36

The Savior urges sinners to obey [the light of] the Gospel, which is set as a lamp shining before them: "If then your whole body is full of light, having no part dark, the whole body will be full of light, as when the bright shining of a lamp gives you light" (v. 36).

EPISTLES

The Pauline Epistle   Colossians 1:21–29

Importance of listening to the Gospel: Paul reveals to believers that the Savior reconciles us in the body of His flesh through His death, only if they continue in the faith and do not move away from the hope of the Gospel, for which he is a minister, showing that the purpose of the call of the Gospel is "that we may present every man perfect in Christ Jesus" (v. 28).

The Catholic Epistle   1 Peter 4:3–11

Refraining from evil: Peter begins to address the sinners, urging them to refrain from evil: "For we have spent enough of our past lifetime in doing the will of the Gentiles—when we walked in lewdness, lusts..." Then he alerts them that, "the end of all things is at hand; therefore be serious and watchful in your prayers," and commands them: "If anyone speaks, let him speak as the oracles of God. If anyone ministers, let him do it as with the ability which God supplies" (vv. 3, 7, 11).

The Acts   Acts 17:30–34

The call to repentance: This passage relays part of Paul's address to the Athenians at Areopagus: "Truly, these times of ignorance God overlooked, but now commands all men everywhere to repent," further clarifying to them that the Almighty has appointed a day in which He will judge the world with righteousness "by the Man whom He has ordained. He has given assurance of this to all by raising Him from the dead." Although some of the listeners mocked him when he mentioned the resurrection from the dead, others believed his words (vv. 30, 31).

Matins Gospel
Luke 13:6–9
The Fruitless Fig Tree
See Fifth Week Wednesday Liturgy Gospel of the Great Fast.

Liturgy Gospel
Luke 11:29–36
The Lamp of the Gospel[ii]

THE LAMP OF THE GOSPEL

Overview

During Christ the Master's second circuit of ministry in Galilee, they brought to Him one who was demon-possessed, blind, and mute to heal. He cast out the demon and cured the person and so the scribes and Pharisees resumed attacking Him, accusing Him of casting out demons by the power of Beelzebub, the ruler of the demons. The Lord of Glory immediately discredited their accusation, laying the foundation for some of His teachings. Among those listening to Him was one woman who was so moved by His words that she raised her voice praising Him, but He rather praised those who obey the Word. In this pericope, the Savior first speaks of praising those who live by the word and then judges those who are negligent in fulfilling it. He concludes by showing that the heart, which is the eye to the body, is the one that draws people to follow or reject the Word.

Judging the Careless[iii]

29 And while the crowds were thickly gathered together, He began to say, "This is an evil generation. It seeks a sign, and no

sign will be given to it except the sign of Jonah the prophet. 30 For as Jonah became a sign to the Ninevites, so also the Son of Man will be to this generation. 31 The queen of the South will rise up in the judgment with the men of this generation and condemn them, for she came from the ends of the earth to hear the wisdom of Solomon; and indeed a greater than Solomon is here. 32 The men of Nineveh will rise up in the judgment with this generation and condemn it, for they repented at the preaching of Jonah; and indeed a greater than Jonah is here."

29 – The scribes and Pharisees did not cease accusing the Master (after He rebuffed their accusations of exorcising the demons by Beelzebub), but retorted stubbornly. Trying to test Him, they asked for a miracle to increase their faith in Him—as if the multitude of miracles they had witnessed from Him were not enough to convince them to believe in Him. Perhaps in making this request, they replicated their ancestors' stand against Moses; they would not accept the law, except after he performed several miracles before them.

The Lord of Glory, who knew the hypocritical state of their heart, called them an evil generation because they run after vanity and commit evil. He said they seek "after a sign, and no sign will be given to [them] except the sign of the prophet Jonah." A skeptic might ask how to reconcile between this saying and the several signs He indeed did before them thereafter. The response would be He wanted to clarify that if a sign would draw people to the faith, then He would not delay, but if a sign were requested to tempt Him, then He would refrain. When the devil said, "*If* You are the Son of God, throw Yourself down" (Matthew 4:6), He refrained.

30 – He gave the sign of Jonah as bearing the greatest similitude between Himself and this prophet. Jonah remaining in the belly of the great fish three days and three nights and coming out alive is a strong

symbol to the death of the Lord in the tomb and His rising on the third day.

31 – The Savior continued giving the Pharisees parables of Gentile nations who returned to God for the simplest reasons, while the children of Israel continued in their hardness of heart and blindness.

He said the queen of Sheba (the queen of the South) will rise up in the judgment and judge them because her firm faith carried her to endure the hardships and dangers of the journey to hear the wisdom of Solomon, who, despite his great wisdom, remained a fallen human, whereas the Jews objected to Jesus, who is immeasurably greater than Solomon.[iv]

32 – He said the people of Nineveh would rise up on the day of judgment and judge this generation. They believed at the call of Jonah and repented, even though Jonah is a weak fallible prophet, while the Jews rejected the teachings of Jesus, the One who surpasses Jonah's call as the light of the sun surpasses the light of a lamp.[v]

In this same manner, Paul the apostle directed his epistle to such Jews: "And will not the physically uncircumcised, if he fulfills the law, judge you who, even with your written code and circumcision, are a transgressor of the law?" (Romans 2:27). This is also clear in the parable of the Good Samaritan (Luke 10:25–37).

Mystery of Guidance and Error[vi]

33 No one, when he has lit a lamp, puts it in a secret place or under a basket, but on a lampstand, that those who come in may see the light. 34 The lamp of the body is the eye. Therefore, when your eye is good, your whole body also is full of light. But when your eye is bad, your body also is full of darkness. 35 Therefore take heed that the light which is in you

is not darkness. 36 If then your whole body is full of light, having no part dark, the whole body will be full of light, as when the bright shining of a lamp gives you light.

33 – The Savior continued warning the Jews, in vain, of their pending condemnation because He lit the lamp of His teachings before them, neither hiding it—as they had falsely accused Him, asking Him for a sign from heaven—nor placing it under a basket (by not showing them any heavenly proofs), but placed it on a lampstand so "those who come in may see the light." He gave us His teachings not only to be convinced of their validity, but that we also may take them as a light and creed for our actions; whoever does not live by them will be condemned by them on the last day. Consequently, the Master will demand us to show and live these teachings because they were not written in the book to be hidden away, but to be studied and to enlighten.

34 – The Lord of Glory unfolded the mystery of revealing the truth to some people (such as the people of Nineveh and the queen of Sheba) and the mystery of hiding it from others (such as the Pharisees of that generation) by saying, "The lamp of the body is the eye." *If the eye is good, it gives light to the whole body, and if the eye is ill, darkened, and unable to see, it will harm the whole body and prevent it from walking and moving.* Since, as the heart is to the soul, the eye is to the body, then He means that the one who opens the eyes of his heart to the heavenly light will be saved like the people of Nineveh and the queen of Sheba. Those who close their eyes will remain unstable with hazy thoughts and scattered hearts darkened by evil beliefs like the Pharisees.

35 – The Savior exhorts us to the need of being cautious over the gift within us—the eye of the soul—lest it be darkened by sin and lack of faith, leading to blindness of the heart and an evil life.

36 – He concludes by revealing that the soul, if not overcome by desires and deceptions, will be able to see the light of His teachings and increase in brightness over time until it reaches the perfect morning in heaven.

NINEVITES' FAST - WEDNESDAY
FORGIVING THE PENITENTS

Linking the Readings:

All the readings of this day center on one theme: **Forgiving the penitents**

The prophecy speaks of **God accepting the repentance of sinners**, as He accepted the people of Nineveh when they repented at the call of Jonah.

The Matins Gospel speaks of **God's compassion on them**, as He promised to give rest to all those who are weary and heavy laden, if they come to Him; and the Liturgy Gospel speaks of **the Savior forgiving their sins**, as He fed the multitudes with the seven loaves (satiation being symbolic of the forgiveness of sins) and telling the Pharisees who asked Him for a sign that He will not give them any sign, but the sign of Jonah the Prophet.

The Pauline Epistle speaks of **saving the penitents by grace**, as the Apostle told the believers that they were saved by grace through faith; the Catholic Epistle urges them **not to love the world**, as the apostle commanded; and the Acts reading orders **not to overburden them**, as James the apostle judged in speaking of those returning to God from the Gentiles.

PROPHECY

Prophecy   Jonah 3:1–4:11

God accepts penitents: This prophecy shows that after the great fish vomited Jonah the prophet onto land, he obeyed God's command and began to call to the people of Nineveh, warning them that their city will be overthrown after forty days. They believed, called a fast, and put on sackcloth; as a result, God relented from the evil He intended to do to them. God's mercy to them saddened Jonah, so God sent an unexpected plant to give him shade. Then it was struck by a worm and withered, which also saddened Jonah, so the Lord told him: "You have had pity on the plant for which you have not labored... And should I not pity Nineveh, that great city?" (vv. 4:10–11).

PSALMS AND GOSPELS

Matins Psalm   Psalms 103:13, 12

The start of the psalm refers to God's compassion on sinners by revealing His Gospel message to them and ends with the promise to give them rest, as mentioned in the Gospel passage that He will give rest to those who come to Him. The psalm says, "As a father pities his children, so the Lord pities those who fear Him. As far as the east is from the west, so far has He removed our transgressions from us."

Matins Gospel   Matthew 11:25–30

This passage speaks of the Savior's compassion on sinners who turn to Him: "Come to Me, all you who labor and are heavy laden, and I will give you rest" (v. 28).

Sermon: The Need to Abstain from Evil
In this sermon, Archbishop Peter of Antioch tells his hearers that if they do not place the kingdom of heaven and its glory in front of their eyes, they will not be able to labor for it. Moreover, if they do not place the punishments prepared for the sinners in front of their eyes, they will not be saved from these punishments. Therefore, he encourages them to increase in good deeds before they leave this world, and to enter from

the narrow gate that leads to eternal life. Then he gives them the example of the people of Nineveh who poured out their tears before God, rushing to true repentance, and thereby were saved through the Lord's grace.

Liturgy Psalm   Psalms 32:1, 5

The start of the psalm foreshadows the Gospel reading on feeding the multitude.[4] Then, speaking for the penitent sinners, the psalm confesses the Lord's forgiveness of their sins: "Blessed is he whose transgression is forgiven, whose sin is covered. I said, 'I will confess my transgressions to the Lord,' and You forgave the iniquity of my sin."

Liturgy Gospel   Matthew 15:32–16:4

This passage speaks of the Savior forgiving the sins of the penitents, as shown by satisfying the multitude with the seven loaves and the fish (symbolic of the forgiveness of sins [through the Eucharistic bread]). Afterwards, He tells the Pharisees who considered themselves satisfied: "A wicked and adulterous generation seeks after a sign, and no sign shall be given to it except the sign of the prophet Jonah" (v. 4).

EPISTLES

The Pauline Epistle   Ephesians 2:1–22

Salvation of penitents by grace: The apostle recounts that we were previously dead through sin (being by nature children of wrath) until

---

[4] The multitude who were satisfied by the seven loaves and few fish (a symbol of the forgiveness of sins).

God revived us in Christ Jesus and by [His] grace saved us through faith. He shows that we were created in Christ Jesus for good works, and charges us, having been brought near to Christ the Master, not to live as we have before, strangers and foreigners, "but fellow citizens with the saints and members of the household of God" (v. 19).

The Catholic Epistle   1 John 2:12–17

Charging them not to love the world: The apostle cheers believers (young and old) for their victory over evil, clarifying to them that true knowledge of God is in keeping His commandments and loving the brethren. Then he charges them: "Do not love the world or the things in the world," revealing this mystery, "If anyone loves the world, the love of the Father is not in him" (v. 15).

The Acts   Acts 15:12–20

Not overburdening the penitents: In resolving the dispute that arose between the faithful over circumcision, and after listening to Paul and Barnabas, James passes this decree: "Therefore I judge that we should not trouble those from among the Gentiles who are turning to God, but that we write to them to abstain from things polluted by idols, from sexual immorality, from things strangled, and from blood" (vv. 19–20).

Matins Gospel
Matthew 11:25–30
Preaching the Gospel[vii]

PREACHING THE GOSPEL

Overview

Christ the Master chose 72[viii] apostles (besides the 12 disciples) and sent them to preach to the Jews and the Gentiles around them. When they returned from preaching, they came to Him with great joy and began telling Him of their great success in their mission. They greatly rejoiced over their miracles (especially the demons' submission to them), since by doing this, they were able to free people from demonic bondage. It is natural for the Master to receive their success with great joy, because His soul does not rejoice except in fulfilling His sublime will. This pericope speaks of the Savior's joy over Gospel preaching, its eternity, and the consolation it gives to the soul.

Revealing the Gospel[5]

> 25 At that time Jesus answered and said, "I thank You, Father, Lord of heaven and earth, that You have hidden these things from the wise and prudent and have revealed them to babes. 26 Even so, Father, for so it seemed good in Your sight."

25–26 [21] – The Gospel mentioned the Savior crying more than once (He cried at the tomb of Lazarus and over Jerusalem and its pending destruction), but it never mentioned Him rejoicing except in this situation. He did not rejoice for earthly means, since He did not care for those, but for spiritual reasons towards which He directed all His thoughts. He rejoiced for the sinners attaining salvation, and for the weak and ignorant accepting the Gospel preaching, whereas the wise and prudent of Israel rejected it, as they were overtaken by stupidity and became blind to the truth, being stubbornly disobedient.

---

[5] This subsection is taken from the Second Sunday of Thoout Liturgy Gospel (Luke 10:21). The number in brackets refers to the verse in Luke.

Rejoicing in the Spirit, He said, "I thank You, Father." This thanksgiving was not to give thanks for a favor, but to declare the acceptance of the fated destiny. *Father, you have done well because those who are wise in worldly matters and the outer appearance of the law, such as the scribes, Pharisees, and those like them, assumed they were likewise wise in the spiritual matters, although they are completely ignorant. You have hidden the ministry of the Gospel from them, but You revealed it to those with good intentions—people like the 70 apostles—people who were viewed by others as naïve in wisdom and understanding and who considered themselves poor, blind, and needy.*

The apostle says, "But God has chosen the foolish things of the world to put to shame the wise, and God has chosen the weak things of the world to put to shame the things which are mighty" (1 Corinthians 1:27). Likewise, James the apostle says, "Has God not chosen the poor of this world to be rich in faith and heirs of the kingdom which He promised to those who love Him?" (James 2:5). The soul's confession of its condition is the first step towards goodness, and humility and obedience are the first steps towards knowing the means of salvation.

Someone might object: "If God hid His words from the wise and prudent, then what is their fault?" God did not mean this, but He created them free, capable of doing good or evil by their choice. For this reason, He hid these things from the Jews who would not listen to the truth from the prophets, knowing they would refuse to obey His words, and revealed them to those whose minds were kept from falsity. The Savior attributed this action to the Father's goodwill by saying, "So it seemed good in Your sight." This Divine utterance is the basis for the theological topic known in the church as *Election and rejection*.[ix]

Secret to His Success[6]

> 27 All things have been delivered to Me by My Father, and no one knows the Son except the Father. Nor does anyone know the Father except the Son, and the one to whom the Son wills to reveal Him.

27 [22] – Lest the disciples assume the might of the Savior is limited to exorcising demons, He disclosed to them that "all things have been delivered" to Him by His Father. This saying supports His equality to the Father in essence and in all divine attributes. If we search all the Holy Scriptures, we will not find any of the ancient fathers, prophets, saints, or apostles who dared to utter such words; this indicates that the speaker is truly God.

Abundant Biblical proofs show the authority given to Jesus. There is His authority over nations, over life, over judgment, over all creation, and His overall autonomy.

His authority over all nations is clear from the words of Daniel: "I was watching in the night visions, and behold, One like the Son of Man, coming with the clouds of heaven! He came to the Ancient of Days, and they brought Him near before Him. Then to Him was given dominion and glory and a kingdom, that all peoples, nations, and languages should serve Him. His dominion is an everlasting dominion, which shall not pass away, and His kingdom the one which shall not be destroyed" (Daniel 7:13–14).

His authority over life and judgment is shown in His own words: "For as the Father raises the dead and gives life to them, even so, the Son gives

---

[6] This subsection is taken from the Second Sunday of Thoout Liturgy Gospel (Luke 10:22). The number in brackets refers to the verse in Luke.

life to whom He will. For the Father judges no one but has committed all judgment to the Son" (John 5:21–22).

His authority over creation is clear in the words of the apostle: "Therefore God also has highly exalted Him and given Him the name which is above every name, that at the name of Jesus, every knee should bow, of those in heaven, and of those on earth, and of those under the earth" (Philippians 2:9–10).

Finally, His overall autonomy is clear in the words of the apostle that "God, who at various times and in various ways spoke in time past to the fathers by the prophets" (Hebrews 1:2). By saying, "All things have been delivered to Me," the Master is rebuking the listeners, declaring that they have been given to Him, yet they refused and rebelled against Him.

He continued that the Father alone fully knows the mystery of the incarnation of the Son. No one can know the truth of the Messiah—that He is the Son of God and the Son of Man—unless the Father reveals it. He adds, "Nor does anyone know the Father except the Son." This means no one is able to understand the Essence of the Father because the divine nature is limitless, and no limited being can understand the divine nature except through the Son. John the Evangelist wrote: "No one has seen God at any time. The only begotten Son, who is in the bosom of the Father, He has declared Him" (John 1:18). The Son is the One who reveals to humanity the Father—a merciful, compassionate, philanthropic God. Moreover, God wishes to reveal Himself to those who obey the truth and are not inclined towards vanity.

Comfort to the Souls

28 Come to Me, all you who labor and are heavy laden, and I will give you rest. 29 Take My yoke upon you and learn from

Me, for I am gentle and lowly in heart, and you will find rest for your souls. 30 For My yoke is easy and My burden is light.

28 – The Savior calls the burdened to Himself: "Come to Me, all you who labor and are heavy laden."[7] The sinners who return to Him find Him prepared to forgive their sins, to relieve their aching conscience and their fear of death and judgment, and to grant them peace and reconciliation with God. This call also includes those burdened by the Mosaic Law. Setting aside the obligations of sacrifices and bodily cleansing, and going to Jerusalem thrice annually—by accepting the law of the Gospel—they are relieved of these burdens.

29 – Calling them to Himself, He says, "Take My yoke upon you and learn from Me." He calls upon them to carry His yoke[8] —to obey His commandments—and to follow in His meek humble-hearted footsteps. This is sufficient to give them rest from the concerns of the world. What He and His disciples want most is for people to follow in His footsteps; He is the One who said, "For I have given you an example, that you should do as I have done to you" (Luke [sic John] 13:15). Peter the apostle says, "For to this you were called, because Christ also suffered for us, leaving us an example, that you should follow His steps" (1 Peter

---

[7] This call proves humans have complete free will, full power, and absolute freedom to choose good or choose evil.

[8] Yoke of Christ. The church arranged one of the priestly garments to be the sticharion, which resembles the one customarily worn by Aaron as commanded by God (Exodus 28). It has an opening at the top, is worn around the neck, and drapes down the front only to the ankles. Reserved for the priest and priestly leaders, it is worn as a sign of carrying the Yoke of Christ. A bishop's sticharion has pictures of the 12 apostles just as the 12 tribes of Israel were on Aaron's breastplate, as commanded by God. This is a reminder of the apostles, a sign that they are the foundation of the church (Ephesians 2:20), and that their names were etched on the walls of the New Jerusalem (Revelations 21:14). Their pictures are on a bishop's sticharion so he can follow their example in his words and works. Wearing the sticharion as a stole reminds the priest of the rope wrapped around the Savior's neck when He was captured (Al-Kharida Al-Nafissa (1:294) [Arabic reference]).

2:21). John the apostle also says, "He who says he abides in Him ought himself also to walk just as He walked" (1 John 2:6).

His meekness[9] and humility of heart, which He wishes us to imitate, are supported by many scriptural passages. Zechariah says, "Rejoice greatly, O daughter of Zion! Shout, O daughter of Jerusalem! Behold, your King is coming to you... lowly and riding on a donkey, a colt, the foal of a donkey" (Zechariah 9:9). Paul the apostle says, "but made Himself of no reputation, taking the form of a bondservant, and coming in the likeness of men" (Philippians 2:7). His humility is exemplified in asking forgiveness for those who crucified Him and asking us to imitate Him in forgiving those who wrong us.

30 – Someone might ponder how His yoke is light when He previously said, "Because narrow is the gate and difficult is the way which leads to life" (Matthew 7:14). He said His yoke is light because of the supporting grace received from uniting with the Righteous One. The way that leads to life is perilous with the greatest difficulties; this path demands us to leave our ego behind and forgive our oppressors. The Savior's intent might have been to compare the difference between the light yoke of the Gospel and the heavy yokes of the Mosaic Law. One who is eager to fulfill His law finds it light because it is full of virtues; unlike a person slack towards it, who finds it burdensome because he has no inclination to obey.

The yoke is light because Jesus Himself grants sufficient grace to help the believer bear it, as the apostle says, "I can do all things through Christ who strengthens me" (Philippians 4:13). The believers' love for Christ, along with hope in a great reward, keeps one from feeling the burden of the yoke. The apostle says, "For this is the love of God, that we keep His commandments. And His commandments are not

---

[9] Among the attributes needed in the shepherd of a church is meekness; his meekness is known to all like his Master who was meek and humble of heart.

burdensome" (1 John 5:3). Humanity bears this burden because it is the burden of resisting sin, the yoke of mourning, and the yoke of fulfilling our obligations—obligations we cannot accomplish without Christ's help.

Liturgy Gospel
Matthew 15:32–16:4
Feeding the 4,000 and the Pharisees ask for a Miracle[x]

FEEDING THE 4,000 AND THE PHARISEES ASK FOR A MIRACLE

Overview

After the Savior healed the daughter of the Canaanite woman, near the area of Tyre and Sidon (at the beginning of His third circuit of ministry in Galilee, after He moved from there and came alongside the sea of Galilee where He healed many who were lame, blind, and mute), He had compassion on the crowd who followed Him and fed them from the bread, as the Gospel records. This passage speaks about the Savior's love and compassion on the hungry crowds (who symbolize sinners seeking forgiveness), about Him feeding them from the seven loaves and the fish, and finally about Him refusing to give the Pharisees a sign other than that of Jonah the prophet, because they are, as He said, "A wicked and adulterous generation."

The Savior's Compassion

> 32 Now Jesus called His disciples to Himself and said, "I have compassion on the multitude, because they have now continued with Me three days and have nothing to eat. And I

do not want to send them away hungry, lest they faint on the way."

32 – After Mark the evangelist narrated the Savior healing many lame, blind, and mute near the sea of Galilee (as we have mentioned), he wrote: "In those days, the multitude being very great and having nothing to eat, Jesus called His disciples to Him and said to them, 'I have compassion on the multitude, because they have now continued with Me three days and have nothing to eat.'"[10] We have shown in the explanation of the Gospel of the five loaves and two fish which is read during the Liturgy of the fifth Sunday [of any Coptic month] that the Savior did the miracle of multiplication of loaves two times only. The first, narrated by Luke (9:12–17), we explained in that same place,[xi] and the second is the one mentioned here.

By comparing the two occasions, we see some variation. In the first, the disciples initiated the conversation by asking the Savior to "send the multitude away," but here they were silent because they had witnessed His ability in the first time, especially since the crowd had not yet reached the point of need. In the first time, the Savior did not start the conversation about the crowd, but here, the merciful and beneficent One started the conversation. By saying to His disciples, "I have compassion on the multitude," He is reminding them of the first sign. By saying, "I do not want to send them away hungry," He is indicating His ability and goodness, and also of the far distance between them and their dwellings. Here Mark adds, "Some of them have come from afar."[11]

---

[10] [Mark 8:1–2].
[11] [Mark 8:3].

Feeding the Multitude

> 33 Then His disciples said to Him, "Where could we get enough bread in the wilderness to fill such a great multitude?" 34 Jesus said to them, "How many loaves do you have?" And they said, "Seven, and a few little fish." 35 So He commanded the multitude to sit down on the ground. 36 And He took the seven loaves and the fish and gave thanks, broke them and gave them to His disciples; and the disciples gave to the multitude. 37 So they all ate and were filled, and they took up seven large baskets full of the fragments that were left. 38 Now those who ate were four thousand men, besides women and children. 39 And He sent away the multitude, got into the boat, and came to the region of Magdala.

33 – The disciples answered, "Where could we get enough bread in the wilderness to fill such a great multitude?" This indicates that they were not yet perfected—they were amnesic of the first sign—and that they were not close to any village, so that there was no reason to doubt the sign.

34 – Here the Savior asked, "How many loaves do you have?" They answered, "Seven, and a few little fish." They did not say (as at the first time) this small quantity is insufficient, because they were now more aware of His ability—although their memory might have lapsed at the beginning. This meager quantity shows their contentment and the simplicity of their life.

35 – The Savior gave orders for the crowd to sit down.

36 – He took the bread and fish, gave thanks, and gave [them] to the disciples to place before the multitude.

37 – When all the people were full, they collected the fragments, which filled seven baskets—the same number as the original loaves. These are beside the leftover fragments from the first miracle of multiplication (twelve baskets)—a visual reminder to them of the variance between the two times.

38 – Also notice the variation in number between the two occurrences; this time there were fewer people than in the first time.

39 – Then He dismissed the multitude, got into the boat, crossed the lake to the western side, "and came to the region of Magdala."[12] Mark gave the exact location by saying He "came to the region of Dalmanutha."[13]

Refusing the Request of the Wicked[xii]

1 Then the Pharisees and Sadducees came, and testing Him asked that He would show them a sign from heaven. 2 He answered and said to them, "When it is evening you say, 'It will be fair weather, for the sky is red'; 3 and in the morning, 'It will be foul weather today, for the sky is red and threatening.' Hypocrites! You know how to discern the face of the sky, but you cannot discern the signs of the times. 4 A wicked and adulterous generation seeks after a sign, and no sign shall be given to it except the sign of the prophet Jonah." And He left them and departed.

1 – Thereafter, the Pharisees and Sadducees asked the Savior for a sign from heaven. The desire behind this request was not to believe in Him but rather to antagonize Him. Theirs was not an honest request made

---

[12] The word Magdala means tower. Mary Magdalene hails from this village. Dalmanutha is a smaller village near Magdala.
[13] [Mark 8:10].

in good faith, but a deceptive attempt to catch Him in their snares, and make the people doubt Him. Perhaps, by specifying a sign from heaven, they sought a likeness to the halting of the sun and the moon during the days of Joshua when the Lord delivered the Amorites to the children of Israel (Joshua 10:12–14).

2 – Mark adds here that the Savior "sighed deeply in His spirit."[14] He showed His sadness over their blasphemy, obstinacy, and hardness of heart, since by this hardness they brought misery upon themselves. He asked, "Why does this generation seek a sign?" This reveals that they were not oriented toward faith with their request. Next, Matthew says the Savior, in His answer, reproached them for their ugly deeds by saying, "When it is evening you say, 'It will be fair weather, for the sky is red.'"

3 – "And in the morning, 'It will be foul weather today, for the sky is red and threatening.' Hypocrites! You know how to discern the face of the sky, but you cannot discern the signs of the times." By, "the signs of the times," He means the signs of His first and second coming. Those signs specific to His first coming, such as raising the dead and healing the sick, are meant to attract the people to Himself. Those specific to His second coming are the judgment and sentencing, and His coming in divine glory with the angels.

Several exegetes remark that, "You know how to discern the face of the sky," means, *You know the signs indicating clear weather or rain*, and, "But you cannot discern the signs of the times," means, *you cannot distinguish the signs of My coming. Understand what I need to do now, and what I will do at My second coming. You assume I do whatever is convenient; you might appear right in your earthly perceptions, but you are fatally ignorant in your religious judgment.*

---

[14] [Mark 8:12].

4 – In order to show that He knew their malicious thoughts in asking for a sign, He reproached them: "A wicked and adulterous generation seeks after a sign, and no sign shall be given to it except the sign of the prophet Jonah."[xiii] Next, the Gospel says the Savior "left them and departed," because they did not ask Him to elucidate His words, and because He only saw in them stubbornness, arrogance, and resistance to understand whatever contradicts their will and desire.

NINEVITES' FEAST THURSDAY
SALVATION THROUGH FAITH
(Faith in Christ the Master's Resurrection)

Linking the Readings:

All the readings of this day center on one theme: **Salvation through faith in the Resurrection of Christ the Master**

The Matins Gospel speaks of **His aid to those who believe in His ability to forgive their sins,** as He reminded the disciples (who had forgotten to take bread with them into the boat) of His aid to them on two previous occasions (symbolic of forgiving their sins); and the Liturgy Gospel speaks of **His authority to resurrect Himself from the dead,** as He verified this in telling the Jews[15], "Destroy this temple, and in three days I will raise it up," meaning the temple of His body.

The Pauline Epistle speaks of the **salvation of those who believe in His Resurrection,** as the Apostle states that whoever believes in His Resurrection will be saved; the Catholic Epistle speaks of their **salvation through baptism,** considering it symbolic of the Resurrection; and the Acts reading speaks of the **blessings of His Resurrection,** as Peter the apostle declared in his address to the Jews who were astonished at his healing of the crippled man.

PSALMS AND GOSPELS

Matins Psalm   Psalms 30:10–11

The second part of this psalm shows the gladness of sinners in God's forgiveness of their iniquities, which points to the Gospel reading. There,

---

[15] Those who requested a sign from Him to validate His authority to expel the merchants from the temple.

the Savior reminds His disciples of His aid to them on two previous occasions in which He satiated them with few loaves—symbolic of the forgiveness of sins. With the tongue of these sinners, the first part of the psalm confesses this Divine aid: "Hear, O Lord, and have mercy on me; Lord, be my helper! You have turned for me my mourning into dancing; You have put off my sackcloth and clothed me with gladness."

Matins Gospel   Mark 8:10–21

This passage speaks of the Savior's help to those who believe in His power to forgive sins, as He reminded the disciples that He had fed them twice from the bread (symbolic of [the Eucharistic bread] the means by which sins are forgiven): "Why do you reason because you have no bread? Do you not yet perceive nor understand?" (v. 17).

Liturgy Psalm   Psalms 118:5, 18

The psalm's beginning hints at the events concerning Jonah's prayer to God from the belly of the great fish who heard him and ordered it to vomit him out (through which Jonah was a type of Christ the Master who told the Jews in the Gospel passage, "Destroy this temple, and in three days I will raise it up" —meaning the temple of His body (John 2:19)). The psalm continues, indicating the trial Jonah underwent from which he was saved—again symbolic of Christ—and says, "I called on the Lord in distress; the Lord answered me and set me in a broad place. The Lord has chastened me severely, but He has not given me over to death."

Liturgy Gospel   John 2:12–25

This passage speaks of the Savior's authority to resurrect Himself, by Himself, as He told the Jews who requested a sign from Him to validate His authority to expel the merchants from the temple: "Destroy this temple, and in three days I will raise it up," meaning the temple of His body (v. 19).

EPISTLES

The Pauline Epistle   Romans 10:4–18

Salvation of those who believe in His Resurrection: The first part of this passage shows the difference between the righteousness of the law and the righteousness of faith in Christ the Master. Then, Paul charges the faithful to believe in the Savior's Resurrection from the dead by saying: "If you confess with your mouth the Lord Jesus and believe in your heart that God has raised Him from the dead, you will be saved." He further details that those who believe in Him will not be put to shame (whether Jews or Greeks) and that the Word will reach the Gentiles, who will accept it (v. 9).

The Catholic Epistle   1 Peter 3:17–22

Salvation through baptism (symbolic): The apostle shows believers that it is better if they suffer for doing good than to suffer for doing evil, giving them Christ the Master as an example, who, being just, suffered for the unjust: "There is also an antitype which now saves us—baptism (not the removal of the filth of the flesh, but the answer of a good conscience toward God), through the resurrection of Jesus Christ" (v. 21).

The Acts   Acts 3:22–26

Blessings of His Resurrection: As Peter the apostle addresses the Jews regarding the healed crippled man, he shows that faith in the name of Christ the Master is what strengthened this man, and that Moses preceded and foretold of the Savior, through whose name this man was healed. He further preached to them to believe in Jesus and His Resurrection, to receive His blessings, and to turn away from their iniquities: "To you first, God, having raised up His Servant Jesus, sent Him to bless you, in turning away every one of you from your iniquities" (v. 26).

Matins Gospel
The Pharisees Ask for a Sign
Mark 8:10–21
See Second Week Friday Matins Gospel of the Great Fast.

Liturgy Gospel
John 2:12–25
Expelling the Merchants from the Temple

EXPELLING THE MERCHANTS FROM THE TEMPLE

Overview

After His first miracle in the wedding of Cana in Galilee, where He turned the water into wine, Christ the Master went down to Capernaum with His mother and brothers. From there He went up to Jerusalem for the Passover, where He debated with the Jews about His authority to expel the merchants from the temple. This pericope talks about: Him cleansing the temple of merchants, the sign the Jews requested (to prove His authority to expel those merchants), His prediction of His resurrection, and finally the many who believed in Him after all the miracles they saw.

He Purifies the Temple

> 12 After this He went down to Capernaum, He, His mother, His brothers, and His disciples; and they did not stay there many days. 13 Now the Passover of the Jews was at hand, and Jesus went up to Jerusalem. 14 And He found in the temple those who sold oxen and sheep and doves, and the moneychangers doing business. 15 When He had made a whip of cords, He drove them all out of the temple, with the sheep and the oxen, and poured out the changers' money and overturned the tables. 16 And He said to those who sold doves, "Take these things away! Do not make My Father's house a house of merchandise!" 17 Then His disciples remembered that it was written, "Zeal for Your house has eaten Me up."

12 – Christ the Master decided to reside in Capernaum (instead of Nazareth) since it overlooks the Sea of Galilee and is considered a location for trade and travelers. Noting that it rests in a valley, the evangelist specified that Christ "went down" from Cana of Galilee with His mother, brothers, and disciples and stayed there for several days.

13 – Because the Passover[16] was approaching, the Savior went up to Jerusalem in obedience to the law—keeping the Jewish tradition, which He maintained out of respect throughout His life on earth.

14 – He found inside the temple those who sold oxen, sheep, and doves,[17] and the moneychangers sitting.

---

[16] Jewish Passover. The Lord ordered for the Jewish celebration to be an everlasting ordinance (Exodus 12:14) during the month of Abib—the month in which they left Egypt by night (Deuteronomy 16:1)—and for all the males to come before the Almighty in the place which He chooses three times each year: on Passover, on the Feast of Weeks, and on the Feast of Tabernacles (Deuteronomy 16:16).

[17] Temple merchants. The Lord ordered Israel of old to tithe every crop they planted, eating this tenth in the place the Lord chooses. If this place is too far, they could sell

15 – He made a whip from cords and, expelling everyone, He poured out the coins and overturned the tables of the moneychangers. This is the first time He sanctified the temple; this was at the beginning of His service, during the Passover after His baptism. Only John mentions this incident. As for the second time, it was four days before His crucifixion, and was mentioned by Matthew (21:12), Mark (11:15–17), and Luke (19:45–46); it was on the Monday following His Jerusalem Entry. Note that He started His ministry and ended it by purifying the temple—to show His authority over the Jews; He is the Messiah who has authority to reproach them for their sins and for desecrating the temple. By this, He is indicating that He is the One who cleanses the souls from their uncleanness, because through His blood is the forgiveness of sins.

The variation between the two times is that in the first time He made a whip from cords but not in the second time. Also, in the first time, He only reproached the Jews for commerce by saying, "Do not make My Father's house a house of merchandise," but in the second time, He reproached them for falsehood and stealing by saying, "You have made it a den of thieves." Finally, in the first time they answered Him saying, "What sign do You show to us, since You do these things?" but in the second time they were silent. His overturning the tables of the moneychangers and the seats of those who sold doves indicates they were selling fit-for-slaughter merchandise *inside* the temple for all who come from afar to purchase for sacrifice.

Expelling them from the temple was for the following reasons:
   1) The era of animal sacrifices ended by the sacrifice of His own body.
   2) His baptism cleansed all, making obsolete the cleansing by the blood of the animals.

---

part of it, and He said, "You shall spend that money for whatever your heart desires: for oxen or sheep, for wine or similar drink, for whatever your heart desires; you shall eat there before the Lord your God, and you shall rejoice, you and your household" (Deuteronomy 14:26).

3) He is the Lamb of God offered for all people.

4) To teach us that the sacrifice to God is in a purified intention and cleansed heart, not in shedding the blood of animals. (In Egypt, the Jewish people had worshipped idols and sacrificed animals to them. After the exodus from Egypt, God did not prohibit both things, but did allow the animal sacrifices; like youth who need patience to transcend from the earthly to the spiritual, they were forbidden from worshiping idols but were permitted to sacrifice animals).

5) To show His authority, power, and sovereignty over His Father's house.

6) To convey the destruction of the house, expose its people, and void its laws and practices.

7) To reveal that the priests collaborated with the merchants in doing wrong, as is clear from verse 16.

16 – After He ordered those who sold doves to remove their items, He scolded them saying, "Do not make My Father's house a house of merchandise," or, as in the second occasion, "A den of thieves." When an individual made a purchase from the merchants and carried it to the priest for offering, the priest would declare it unfit, asking the individual to sell it back and buy another, so the individual was forced to sell it at a loss and buy one for a higher cost—the priest and the merchant splitting the profit. Mark adds: "He would not allow anyone to carry wares through the temple,"[18] which indicates that the Jews were not satisfied with making the temple a marketplace, but also used it as a passageway, a shortcut from one side of the city to the other side. As for Him saying on the second occasion, "It is written, My house shall be called a house of prayer,"[19] He quoted the prophecies of Jeremiah, "Has this house, which is called by My name, become a den of thieves?" (Jeremiah 7:11), and of Isaiah, "My house shall be called a house of prayer for all nations" (Isaiah 65:7).

---

[18] [Mark 11:16].
[19] [Matthew 21:13].

17 – The disciples remembered that it was written, "Zeal for Your house has eaten Me up"; this phrase was written verbatim in Psalm 69:9.

Prophesying His own Resurrection

18 So the Jews answered and said to Him, "What sign do You show to us, since You do these things?" 19 Jesus answered and said to them, "Destroy this temple, and in three days I will raise it up." 20 Then the Jews said, "It has taken forty–six years to build this temple, and will You raise it up in three days?" 21 But He was speaking of the temple of His body. 22 Therefore, when He had risen from the dead, His disciples remembered that He had said this to them; and they believed the Scripture and the word which Jesus had said.

18 – Since the task of evicting the merchants and moneychangers from the temple was reserved for the priests and Levites only, the Jews asked the Savior, "What sign do You show to us, since You do these things?" *What miracle would You do for us, as Moses did in front of Pharaoh, to prove Your claim that You are a prophet, and to justify this authority by which You have acted?* Their question indicates they did not understand "My Father's house" to mean He is the Son of God; otherwise, they would not have posed this question.

19 – The Savior answered them promptly: "Destroy this temple, and in three days I will raise it up." He was not referring to the known temple, but rather the temple of His body. *You will kill My body but I will raise it up again on the third day, and if I rise, you should believe Me, but if I rise and you do not believe Me, then you have no excuse.* Calling His body a temple is only in simile, as when David called the manna, "angels' food" (Psalm 78:25), since there is little resemblance between them.

On this basis of resemblance, Paul the apostle said to the Corinthians, "Do you not know that you are the temple of God and that the Spirit of

God dwells in you? ...Or do you not know that your body is the temple of the Holy Spirit who is in you?" (1 Corinthians 3:16; 6:19). When he wanted to warn them against idol worship, he said, "What agreement has the temple of God with idols? For you are the temple of the living God. As God has said: 'I will dwell in them'" (2 Corinthians 6:16).

20 – When the Jews heard the Savior's answer, they mocked it because in their eyes it is impossible and invalid. *How can You, a poor Galilean do in three days what the rich powerful kings were unable to complete in 46 years?* —referring to Herod the Great's attempts at repairing the temple (as a way to strengthen his rule over the Jews) 16 years before the birth of Christ. At the time He gave this answer, the Savior was about 30 years old; 46 years had been spent in the repair and ornamentation of the temple.[20]

21 – The evangelist clarifies that the Savior was talking about the temple of His body. Chrysostom declares the Master did not reveal this to them because had He done so, they would have treated Him even worse, because they would have suspected His words.[xiv]

22 – The evangelist continues writing that the disciples remembered the Savior's words when He rose from the dead. This means they also did not comprehend what He was trying to say, yet kept it in their hearts and meditated on it, only understanding its full meaning at the fulfillment of the prophecy. "And they believed the Scripture," means their faith in everything written in the Old Testament concerning His death and resurrection was confirmed as the psalm says, "For You will not leave my soul in Sheol, nor will You allow Your Holy One to see

---

[20] The temple was built three times: 1) During the reign of Solomon which took seven years, yet was set ablaze and destroyed by the Chaldeans; 2) During the days of Zerubbabel, who rebuilt it after the return from captivity; and 3) During the days of Herod the Great, and this is what the Jews spoke of here. The renovations were not yet complete. According to Josephus the historian they continued until AD 64, only being completed during the days of Herod Agrippa the second.

corruption" (Psalms 16:10). Isaiah said of Him: "And they made His grave with the wicked—but with the rich at His death" (Isaiah 35:9). Believing "the word which Jesus had said," means seeing Him truly risen solidified their faith in Him.

Their Faith in Him

> 23 Now when He was in Jerusalem at the Passover, during the feast, many believed in His name when they saw the signs which He did. 24 But Jesus did not commit Himself to them, because He knew all men, 25 and had no need that anyone should testify of man, for He knew what was in man.

23 – Although the leaders and a multitude of the people hated Him, "many believed in His name" when He was at the feast of Passover, but their faith was not solid. They were astonished at "the signs which He did," believing the miracles were done by a supernatural power. The signs must have been many and widely proclaimed in order to carry the people to faith in Him.

24 – The Lord of Glory "did not commit Himself to them"; He did not consider them true disciples, knowing that faith was not firm in their hearts, and that they were unstable and could be easily deceived by the cunning of the scribes and Pharisees, and therefore would regress and leave Him at the first threat. He did not commit Himself to them "because He knew all men"; He is the searcher of hearts and knower of hidden things.

25 – Being the Creator of humanity, He "had no need that anyone should testify of man"; He was not in need of the means that humans use to figure out each other "for He knew what was in man." He knows what is in the heart and what a person aims to do, "for man looks at the outward appearance, but the Lord looks at the heart" (1 Samuel 16:7), because He "searches the minds and hearts" (Revelation 2:23).

UNIVERSAL THEME:
PREPARING TO FAST

LEAVE-TAKING SATURDAY
THE NEED TO REPENT

Linking the Readings:

All the readings of this day center on one theme: **The need to repent**

In the Vespers Gospel, the Savior exhorts believers on the need to **forgive those who sin against them**; in the Matins Gospel on **keeping vigil (watchfulness) against sin**; and in the Liturgy Gospel on **repentance**.

In the Pauline Epistle, Paul encourages them to sorrow—**sorrow leading to repentance**; in the Catholic Epistle to **rejoice over their salvation**; and in the Acts reading to **suffer for the sake of Christ**.

PSALMS AND GOSPELS

Vespers Psalm   Psalms 17:1–2

Speaking for believers who forgive those who sin against them (as instructed in the Gospel passage), the psalm beckons God to answer their prayers: "Hear a just cause, O Lord, attend to my cry; give ear to my prayer which is not from deceitful lips. Let my vindication come from Your presence; let Your eyes look on the things that are upright."

Vespers Gospel   Luke 17:3–6

In this passage, the Savior exhorts believers to forgive those who sin against them, saying: "And if he sins against you seven times in a day, and seven times in a day returns to you, saying, 'I repent', you shall forgive him" (v. 4).

Matins Psalm   Psalms 119:49, 52

Speaking for watchful believers who are cautious against sinning (as the Savior urges in the Gospel passage), this psalm seeks the Savior's promise to them, on which they have hope: "Remember the word to Your servant, upon which You have caused me to hope. I remembered Your judgments of old, O Lord, and have comforted myself."

Matins Gospel   Mark 13:33–37

In this passage, the Savior exhorts believers to keep vigil, to be watchful against sin, saying, "Watch therefore, for you do not know when the master of the house is coming" (v. 35).

Liturgy Psalm   Psalms 95:1–2

Speaking for believers who repented, and rejoiced in being rescued from the condemnation of non-penitents, this psalm praises God and encourages them to continue confessing their sins: "Oh come, let us sing to the Lord! Let us shout joyfully to the Rock of our salvation. Let us come before His presence with thanksgiving; let us shout joyfully to Him with psalms."

Liturgy Gospel   Luke 13:1–5

In this passage, the Savior exhorts believers to repent: "Unless you repent you will all likewise perish" (v. 5).

EPISTLES

The Pauline Epistle   2 Corinthians 6:14–7:16

Sorrow leading to repentance: The apostle charges believers to flee from the fellowship and defilement of idol worship (because their souls are temples of the living God), commanding them to cleanse themselves from the filthiness of the flesh and spirit. He expresses the extent of the great comfort he experienced in his tribulations when he learned from Titus about their desire, mourning, and zeal for himself. Although he saddened them with his letter, yet he says, "Now I rejoice, not that you were made sorry, but that your sorrow led to repentance... For godly sorrow produces repentance leading to salvation, not to be regretted; but the sorrow of the world produces death" (vv. 9–10).

The Catholic Epistle   1 Peter 1:1–12

Believers' joy over the salvation of their souls: The apostle blesses God for "an inheritance incorruptible and undefiled and that does not fade away, reserved in heaven," showing that, although they might be temporarily grieved now through various trials, they will rejoice with inexpressible joy and glory, "receiving the end of your faith—the salvation of your souls" (vv. 4, 9).

The Acts   Acts 21:1–14

Suffering for the sake of Christ: This passage shows how the disciples tried, in vain, to prevent Paul from going to Jerusalem and how Agabus prophesied, concerning Paul, by binding himself with Paul's belt. To this, Paul responded: "I am ready not only to be bound, but also to die at Jerusalem for the name of the Lord Jesus" (v. 13).

Vespers Gospel
Luke 17:3–6
Forgiveness of the Penitents
See Seventh Week Tuesday Matins Gospel of the Great Fast from verse three.

Matins Gospel
Mark 13:33–37
Watchfulness[xv]

WATCHFULNESS

Overview

On the last Tuesday of His life on earth, Christ the Master warned His disciples of two events: the destruction of Jerusalem and the end of the ages. In this Gospel chapter, the Lord of Glory first speaks of the hardships coming upon the Jews before the destruction of Jerusalem, the hardships faced by His disciples at that time, and the lessening of those days of their hardships. Second, He speaks of the signs of His second coming, of sending His angels to gather His chosen, and finally of His commandment to His disciples to keep watch anticipating this coming.

Keeping Watch to Meet Him

33 Take heed, watch and pray; for you do not know when the time is. 34 It is like a man going to a far country, who left his house and gave authority to his servants, and to each his work, and commanded the doorkeeper to watch. 35 Watch therefore, for you do not know when the master of the house

is coming—in the evening, at midnight, at the crowing of the rooster, or in the morning— 36 lest, coming suddenly, he find you sleeping. 37 And what I say to you, I say to all: Watch!

33 – Since His second coming will be sudden, and since concealing its timing keeps people in anticipation, He encouraged them to prepare for it by saying, "Keep watch and pray." By this, He wants to warn and alert them to continue fasting, praying, practicing virtues, and to be careful not to be blindsided.

34 – He gave them an example: "It is like a man going to a far country, who left his house and gave authority to his servants, and to each his work, and commanded the doorkeeper to watch." He meant Himself by the traveler; by ascending to heaven, He considers Himself traveling because He is not present before the eyes of the church, although He is her administrator, counselor, protector, and keeper, by His Spirit, and by His unseen presence. By "his servants," He means His apostles and their successors to whom He gave the authority to establish the church on earth. "To each his work" means there is no one in the church exempt from service. Talents are diverse, but the Spirit is the same, and every believer needs to be a living stone in the church. By "and commanded the doorkeeper to watch," He differentiates between the servants of the Divine word; just as every servant in the house has a specific duty, likewise every servant in the house of God needs to fulfill his own duty using the talents granted by God.

35 – The Savior repeated His commandment for them to keep watch by saying, "Watch therefore, for you do not know when the master of the house is coming—in the evening, at midnight, at the crowing of the rooster, or in the morning." He means to incite them to be alert, fearful of that hour, and always virtuous.

36 – "Lest, coming suddenly, he find you sleeping" just like a thief who comes at night.

37 – He concluded His commandment by saying, "what I say to you, I say to all: Watch!" Concerning this Paul the apostle says, "Therefore let us not sleep, as others do, but let us watch and be sober" (1 Thessalonians 5:6).

Liturgy Gospel
Luke 13:1–5
Destruction of those who Abandon Repentance
See Sixth week Monday Liturgy Gospel of the Great Fast.

LEAVE-TAKING SUNDAY
CORNERSTONES OF WORSHIP

Linking the Readings:

All the readings of this day center on one theme: **The cornerstones of worship**

In the Vespers Gospel, the Lord of Glory exhorts believers to **forgive those who wrong them**, so that they likewise are forgiven; in the Matins Gospel, on **their duty to worship Him**; in the Liturgy Gospel, on **observing the three cornerstones of worship**: charity (almsgiving), prayer, and fasting; and the Evening Gospel promises to **give them the Holy Spirit**, which He pours out on them in answer to their prayers.

In the Pauline Epistle, Paul calls their attention to the necessity of **caring for the service**, listing the internal and external hardships he suffered for the service; the Catholic Epistle speaks of **confirming their faith by good works**; and the Acts reading **warns them** to "keep themselves from things offered to idols, from blood, from things strangled, and from sexual immorality."

PSALMS AND GOSPELS

Vespers Psalm   Psalm 46:10

In the psalm, God exhorts believers to have faith in Him (as shown in the accompanying Gospel passage), showing them that He will be exalted in the nations by answering the requests of the steadfast in the faith: "Be still, and know that I am God; I will be exalted among the nations, I will be exalted in the earth!"

Vespers Gospel   Mark 11:22–26

In this passage, the Savior [tells believers to "have faith in God" and]

exhorts them to forgive those who wrong them (before standing up to pray), so that their heavenly Father would also forgive them: "And whenever you stand praying, if you have anything against anyone, forgive him, that your Father in heaven may also forgive you your trespasses" (v. 25).

Matins Psalm   Psalms 100:2–3

This psalm urges believers who forgive those who sin against them

(as shown in the accompanying Gospel passage) to serve God joyfully, not considering this forgiveness as a favor granted, but as their duty as sheep of His pasture: "Serve the Lord with gladness; come before His presence with singing. We are His people and the sheep of His pasture."

Matins Gospel   Luke 17:3–10

This passage speaks of believers' duty to worship God, as the Savior

commanded those who forgive others: "So likewise you, when you have done all those things which you are commanded, say, 'We are unprofitable servants. We have done what was our duty to do'" (v. 10).

Liturgy Psalm   Psalms 2:11, 10

This psalm shows that even people of high standing, like kings or

judges, need to fulfill the cornerstones of worship (those mentioned in the accompanying Gospel passage) with fear and trembling: "Serve the Lord with fear, and rejoice with trembling. Now therefore, be wise, O kings; be instructed, you judges of the earth."

Liturgy Gospel   Matthew 6:1–18

In this passage, the Savior encourages believers to observe the three

cornerstones of worship: charity (almsgiving), prayer, and fasting: "When you do a charitable deed, do not sound a trumpet before you ... when you pray, you shall not be like the hypocrites... when you fast, do not be like the hypocrites" (vv. 2, 5, 16).

Evening Psalm   Psalm 17:14

This psalm points to the believers who are filled with His Holy Spirit

and His gifts, who give of the overflow to their children (as He said In the accompanying Gospel that though they are wicked when compared with His Almighty Holiness they know how to give good gifts to their children): "And whose belly You fill with Your hidden treasure. They are satisfied with children [swine flesh], and leave the rest of their possession for their babes."

Evening Gospel   Luke 11:1–13

This passage speaks of the gift of the Holy Spirit that God pours out

on believers in answer to their prayers: "If you then, being evil, know how to give good gifts to your children, how much more will your heavenly Father give the Holy Spirit to those who ask Him!" (v. 13)

EPISTLES

The Pauline Epistle   2 Corinthians 11:16–28

Believers' concern for the service: The apostle reveals to the

Corinthians that, according to the law, he lags in nothing when compared with their esteemed false prophets. He shows that he endured much more than them in the service of Christ the Master; he endured various trials for the sake of this service. After listing these external hardships, he mentions the internal ones: "Besides the other things, what comes upon me daily: my deep concern for all the churches" (v. 28).

The Catholic Epistle   2 Peter 1:1–11

Confirming their faith through good works: The apostle establishes believers in the hope of God's abounding grace, charging them to add to their faith various good works (which he lists), concluding: "Therefore, brethren, be even more diligent to make your call and election sure [The Coptic text adds: "by good works"], for if you do these things you will never stumble" (v. 10).

The Acts   Acts 21:15–26

Some restrictions: This passage mentions Paul reaching Jerusalem and describing to the disciples all that God had done among the Gentiles through his ministry. Then comes James' decision regarding those who believe, instructing them to "keep themselves from things offered to idols, from blood, from things strangled, and from sexual immorality" (v. 25).

Vespers Gospel
Mark 11:22–26
Conditions for Answered Prayers[xvi]

CONDITIONS FOR ANSWERED PRAYERS

Overview

After Christ the Master cursed the fruitless fig tree on His last Monday on earth, His disciples (passing by on the following day with Him) found that it had withered, so Peter pointed this out to the Savior. Jesus' answer reveals the conditions for answered prayers. This pericope deals with these two conditions: faith and the importance of forgiving others in order to receive forgiveness.

Necessity of Faith

22 So Jesus answered and said to them, "Have faith in God. 23 For assuredly, I say to you, whoever says to this mountain, 'Be removed and be cast into the sea,' and does not doubt in his heart, but believes that those things he says will be done, he will have whatever he says. 24 Therefore I say to you, whatever things you ask when you pray, believe that you receive them, and you will have them."

22 – The Savior's disciples were amazed when they saw the rapid effect of His word on the fig tree that withered instantly once He cursed it. Peter, as usual, was the spokesperson expressing their amazement. The exegetes explained their amazement at this specific sign. *Although Jesus had done greater, more prestigious signs. The previous signs were for the benefit of others, but this one was the first sign related to destruction and annihilation.* Actually, it is the only sign in which He showed punishment, indicating that He decrees justice and judgment just as He decrees mercy. He taught the most amiable example of judgment in the kindest way by striking a tree, an emotionless body available for every passerby; He did not destroy any private property, but a tree fruitless and unprofitable to anyone.

Perhaps, by cursing the fig tree, He wanted to give another lesson. The foliaceous yet first-fruit lacking fig tree symbolizes hypocrites who appear in excessive piety, but do not live piously. This also points to the Jewish nation that claims monopoly to holiness on earth because she received the law, the temple, and all religious precepts, but was completely devoid of faith, love, holiness, humbleness, and readiness to accept Christ and follow His directions. They boasted of being the people of God, but refused His Son whom He sent. The astonishment of the disciples was a clear indication of their lacking faith; that is why the Savior spoke with them about the importance of faith by saying, "Have faith in God."

23 – He pointed to the importance of having a strong faith in order to do miracles: "Whoever says to this mountain, 'Be removed and be cast into the sea,' and does not doubt in his heart, but believes that those things he says will be done, he will have whatever he says." On another occasion, the Lord of Glory showed that the smallest amount of faith is sufficient: "If you have faith as a mustard seed, you will say to this mountain, 'Move from here to there,' and it will move; and nothing will be impossible for you"[xvii] *because the power of faith performs miracles in the material world, and removes obstacles in the spiritual world.* God's power is limitless and the disciples, their successors, and even the faithful could receive from it according to their faith. Those of strong faith are not prevented from doing miracles, on the condition, of course, that this is according to God's will and glorifies His holy name.

24 – The Savior assured His disciples that they are capable of more than moving a mountain, if they believe and couple their faith with prayer: "Whatever things you ask when you pray, believe that you receive them, and you will have them."[xviii] Or as Matthew wrote, "Whatever things you ask in prayer, believing, you will receive,"[21] on the condition that the request befits His majesty to grant; their requests should be in

---

[21] [Matthew 21:22].

accordance with His will. Concerning this the apostle wrote, "Now this is the confidence that we have in Him, that if we ask anything according to His will, He hears us" (1 John 5:14).

Obligation to Forgive

> 25 And whenever you stand praying, if you have anything against anyone, forgive him, that your Father in heaven may also forgive you your trespasses. 26 But if you do not forgive, neither will your Father in heaven forgive your trespasses.

25 – Since miracles must be through prayer, the Savior already mentioned that its first condition to be acceptable is faith. Here, He mentions the second condition: forgiveness. He says, "Whenever you stand praying... forgive... that your Father... may also forgive you." The wisdom behind the condition of forgiveness is that it is impossible that God would give the power of healing or other types of miracles to those who seek it for anger, vengeance, or schadenfreude.

26 – The Savior continues, showing that the heavenly Father will not forgive those who do not forgive the faults of others: "Judgment is without mercy to the one who has shown no mercy" (James 2:13). Therefore, the apostle exhorts us to "be kind to one another, tenderhearted, forgiving one another, even as God in Christ forgave you... bearing with one another, and forgiving one another, if anyone has a complaint against another; even as Christ forgave you, so you also must do" (Ephesians 4:32; Colossians 3:13).

Matins Gospel
Luke 17:3–10
The Disobedient Servant has no Credit
See Seventh Week Tuesday Matins Gospel of the Great Fast from verse three.

Liturgy Gospel
Matthew 6:1–18
Charity, Prayer, and Fasting

CHARITY, PRAYER, AND FASTING

Overview

Today, our church celebrates leave-taking Sunday, accordingly arranging for her children the Gospel reading about the cornerstones of worship as established by the Lord of Glory: charity, prayer, and fasting. In this pericope, the Savior revealed God the Father's public reward to those who practice them to perfection.

Reward for Charity

1 Take heed that you do not do your charitable deeds before men, to be seen by them. Otherwise you have no reward from your Father in heaven. 2 Therefore, when you do a charitable deed, do not sound a trumpet before you as the hypocrites do in the synagogues and in the streets, that they may have glory from men. Assuredly, I say to you, they have their reward. 3 But when you do a charitable deed, do not let your left hand know what your right hand is doing, 4 that your charitable deed may

be in secret; and your Father who sees in secret will Himself reward you openly.

1 – The Savior began speaking about charity, the first cornerstone of Christian worship: "Take heed that you do not do your charitable deeds before men." He means not to do them in front of people with the intention of receiving their praise, such that we lose our heavenly reward, but rather to do them in hope of pleasing God and fulfilling His will.

2 – He continues: "When you do a charitable deed, do not sound a trumpet before you as the hypocrites do," *who give charity in the synagogues and on street corners to receive praise from people, not to please God, and thus they have already received their reward.*

3 – Rather, when you give charity "do not let your left hand know what your right hand is doing." You should not aim for those who are near or those who are far away to be aware, but your goal should be to please God alone.

4 – If you do it "in secret," if you have no intention for people to see you giving (seeking praise), "your Father who sees in secret will Himself reward you openly." He will reveal it to the people and to the angels through whom you will earn praise. Note that the Lord of Glory said *reward* you, not *give* you, because He considers charity a dutiful loan to God. From the aforementioned, we learn that the Savior, by His commandment, did not mean we should not be charitable *before men*, but He prevented us from being so in front of them with the *intention* of seeking their praise, "for the letter kills, but the Spirit gives life" (2 Corinthians 3:6).

Prayer's Reward

> 5 And when you pray, you shall not be like the hypocrites. For they love to pray standing in the synagogues and on the corners of the streets, that they may be seen by men. Assuredly, I say to you, they have their reward. 6 But you, when you pray, go into your room, and when you have shut your door, pray to your Father who is in the secret place; and your Father who sees in secret will reward you openly. 7 And when you pray, do not use vain repetitions as the heathen do. For they think that they will be heard for their many words. 8 Therefore do not be like them. For your Father knows the things you have need of before you ask Him.

5 – The Savior moved on to talk about the second cornerstone of worship: prayer. He said, "When you pray, you shall not be like the hypocrites" *for they love to pray standing in the synagogues and on street corners for people to see and praise them. Thus, they will have fulfilled their desire and already received their wages.*

6 – "When you pray, go into your room, and when you have shut your door" —He does not mean the physical room (many people pray inside their rooms, to be unseen),[xix] the intended *room* is the mind, and the *door* is the thoughts. Based on this, the praying person withdraws into the conscience and purges the intentions through prayer. Naturally, the Savior's commandment does not mean to abstain from communal prayers at church. By saying, "Pray to your Father who is in the secret place," He does not want believers to seek people's praise (as previously mentioned about charity), so they may receive the far greater reward from heaven.

7 – The Savior resumes showing the conditions of answered prayers: "When you pray, do not use vain repetitions as the heathen do." He does not forbid much talking that is according to God's will or proper

long prayers, but forbids asking for authority, riches, leadership, vengeance, or longevity of life, and other earthly requests. He also forbids inquisitiveness that contradicts the conscience, like the heathen (who think the acceptance of their prayers depends on the length of their speech and the babbling of their tongue), as is clear from the prayer of the prophets of Baal in front of Elijah (1 King 18:26–28). The Jews were not exempt from resembling the dogma of the heathen; they placed many prayers and considered that the mere utterance of them should bring about answers. They placed a condition in the Talmud that whoever prays much will be answered.

8 – This is what led the Savior to advise His disciples: "Do not be like them."[xx] By saying, "Your Father knows the things you have need of before you ask Him," He does not mean to stop praying, but to refrain from the abovementioned vain petitions.

The Lord's Prayer

9 In this manner, therefore, pray: Our Father in heaven, Hallowed be Your name. 10 Your kingdom come. Your will be done on earth as it is in heaven. 11 Give us this day our daily bread. 12 And forgive us our debts, as we forgive our debtors. 13 And do not lead us into temptation, but deliver us from the evil one. For Yours is the kingdom and the power and the glory forever. Amen. 14 For if you forgive men their trespasses, your heavenly Father will also forgive you. 15 But if you do not forgive men their trespasses, neither will your Father forgive your trespasses.

9 to 13 – After revealing the necessary conditions for prayer, the Savior gave His disciples and the church the noblest example of prayer in the form of the Lord's Prayer. It is the source of great goodness to the whole world.[xxi]

14 – Emphasizing the condition of forgiving others included in the Lord's Prayer (if we want our prayers answered), the Lord of Glory said, "If you forgive men their trespasses, your heavenly Father will also forgive you."

15 – "But if you do not forgive men their trespasses, neither will your Father forgive your trespasses."

Reward for Fasting

16 Moreover, when you fast, do not be like the hypocrites, with a sad countenance. For they disfigure their faces that they may appear to men to be fasting. Assuredly, I say to you, they have their reward. 17 But you, when you fast, anoint your head and wash your face, 18 so that you do not appear to men to be fasting, but to your Father who is in the secret place; and your Father who sees in secret will reward you openly.

16 – The Savior moved onto the third and last cornerstone of worship—Fasting: "When you fast, do not be like the hypocrites, with a sad countenance." The fast He is referring to here is a private fast, which a person voluntarily undertakes for a specific purpose (not the public fasts arranged by the church for her children, since these by default are public knowledge). His commandment aims for the individual's fast not to be with the purpose of public display; otherwise, one becomes as one of the hypocrites, who frown so that other people know they are fasting—gaining praise while losing their heavenly reward.

17 – He continued: "You, when you fast, anoint your head and wash your face." By this, He means cleansing the intentions and clearing the conscience (not literally facial washing and anointing), otherwise, He is voiding the fasts of the monks and the other fasters. However, it appears He could also mean washing the face, not for the sake of the washing, but so that the effects of fasting do not appear on the face.

18 – Our Savior's intention becomes clear when He says, "So that you do not *appear* to men to be fasting, but to your Father who is in the secret place." The *intention* is not to conceal from people that this person is fasting, but that this concealment does not become the person's *focus*; at this point, the Father who sees what is in secret "will reward you openly."

Evening Gospel
Luke 11:1–13
Prayer[xxii]

PRAYER

Overview

When Christ the Master was approaching Jerusalem, on His way there for the last time, His disciples asked Him to teach them how to pray as John the Baptist had taught his disciples. The Lord of Glory answered their request. Of the four Gospels, Luke alone mentions this incident. In this pericope, the Savior rendered the words of the prayer He taught them, alerting them to the importance of persistence in prayer, and its guaranteed answer from the Father in heaven.

The Lord's Prayer

1 Now it came to pass, as He was praying in a certain place, when He ceased, that one of His disciples said to Him, "Lord, teach us to pray, as John also taught his disciples." 2 So He said to them, "When you pray, say: Our Father in heaven, Hallowed be Your name. Your kingdom come. Your will be done on earth

as it is in heaven. 3 Give us day by day our daily bread. 4 And forgive us our sins, for we also forgive everyone who is indebted to us. And do not lead us into temptation, but deliver us from the evil one."

1 – Our Savior was praying somewhere on the way to Jerusalem. His continuous prayer was not due to need, but to be a role model to His people. His prayer was fervent, contrary to the custom of the Pharisees who used to pray on street corners and the roads so the people would see them. His fervent prayer left a deep mark on one of His disciples, who was watching Him closely because he was eager to be fervent in his prayers like Him. Because he did not know how, he approached the Master saying, "Lord, teach us to pray." By saying, "teach *us*," he expressed the desire of his fellow disciples. Thus, he obtained for himself, for them, and for the whole church the most noble model prayer. Although this prayer, which the Master has set for them, uses brief phrases to keep the praying person from growing bored, He filled it with the greatest treasures at which the mind stands in awe, to the point it became a cause of great goodness for the whole universe.

Note, the Savior uttered this prayer on two separate occasions. The first during His Sermon on the Mount as mentioned by Matthew (6:9–13). The second on His way to Jerusalem as mentioned by Luke. Perhaps, by reciting it twice in an almost identical manner, He meant to alert the faithful to its solid goodness (Joseph likewise explained to Pharaoh that the reason for the repetition of his dream was to prove its solidity) and to direct attention to its sublime meanings and great benefits. No wonder, for God who of old wrote twice the Ten Commandments with His finger on the stone tablets (Deuteronomy 9:1–10:4) is the same who now taught this prayer by His pure mouth twice. We understand from the disciple's request for Jesus to teach them a prayer "as John also taught his disciples" that John, like the Jewish teachers, had taught his disciples to pray three times daily and to fast.

2 – When this request was presented to the Savior, He responded to the disciples saying, "When you pray, say: Our Father in heaven." By saying "Father," He wants to draw us to Him as our Father and Creator, making requests of Him as children do of their parents, not as servants do of their masters. He gave us "the Spirit of adoption by whom we cry out, 'Abba Father'" (Romans 8:15). He did not treat us as strangers who have no favor before Him, or as sinners who deserve punishment, but treated us as beloved children. For this reason, we approach Him with confidence as *His* children. We received this boldness during baptism, through which we became brethren to Christ and children to God (John 1:13).

By calling Him *Father*, we receive a weapon with which to fend off the devil from the start of prayer; this encourages us to adhere to God and obey His commandments, since He privileged the Christians (from among all the nations) with adoption. Furthermore, when we address Him in the first-person plural, calling Him *our* Father, we declare the church one body of equals: old and young, wise and foolish, thus removing from ourselves pride and envy. Let us not forget the meaning of *praying* for each other when saying "our Father." It encompasses our appeal to Him, as our Savior appealed to the Father in His prayer on the night of His passion, and it is the prayer in which He said, "O My Father, if it is possible, let this cup pass from Me" (Matthew 26:39). However, for this prayer to be genuine, it must stem from pure thoughts and upright consciences.

As for "in heaven," it does not mean God is limited to heaven—He is everywhere; its purpose is for us to ascend with our minds during prayer from the earthly to the heavenly. Following this introduction, the Savior continued to the phrases of the prayer. In the first half, He mentioned what concerns God—considering He is the focus of our worship. In the second half, He mentioned what concerns us. In the third and final half, He mentioned what concerns the great dangers awaiting us in this life.[22]

The first section includes three requests. First, saying, "Hallowed be Your name" does not mean we are asking for God to increase in holiness through our prayers (as He is complete in everything). We are expressing the extent of our longing to see His hallowed name, His divine attributes, and His amazing works acknowledged and glorified by people who walk uprightly with good works, according to His words to them: "Let your light so shine before men, that they may see your good works and glorify your Father in heaven" (Matthew 5:16).

By the second request: "Your kingdom come," we are expressing our longing to see the kingdom of Satan destroyed, and everyone submitting to God their true king. This is a reminder for the righteous to set their sights on the Kingdom awaiting them as if it is near. This helps them dispense with earthly things for the heavenly. Some say *kingdom* refers to the help of the Holy Spirit, through which we overcome hardships.

The third and final request is to have His "will be done on earth as it is in heaven." By this, we express our longing to see the believers who fulfill His will and pleasure increase in number until that joyful day comes when all the people will be sincere in worshiping God and serving Him, like all the pure angels in heaven.

---

[22] Some exegetes think the Lord's Prayer has ten phrases. Ten is a complete number and represents the Ten Commandments. The first five phrases concern the soul and the second five concern the body. Those in the first half precede those in the second half as the dignity of the soul precedes that of the body.

Other exegetes think this prayer includes seven requests, reminding us of the seven words the Savior uttered on the cross, and also reminding us of the seven incidents that occurred at the time of His passion and crucifixion (see *Al-Kharida Al-Nafissa* (1:573–574) [Arabic reference]).

3 – The second part of this prayer, which concerns the people, also includes three requests. The first concerns the body while the other two concern the soul. In the first request, we say "Give us day by day our daily bread,"[23] or as Matthew records it, "Give us this day our daily bread" (Matthew 6:11). *Day* refers to eternal life. *Bread* refers to the spiritual food—the words of the Savior and His body and blood—such that it does not contradict His words: "Therefore do not worry about tomorrow, for tomorrow will worry about its own things. Sufficient for the day is its own trouble... But seek first the kingdom of God and His righteousness, and all these things shall be added to you" (Matthew 6:34, 33), and, "I am the living bread which came down from heaven" (John 6:51). His apostle says, "For to be carnally minded is death, but to be spiritually minded is life and peace" (Romans 8:6). By this, we attain the heavenly manna.[24]

4 – In the second request of the second half of the prayer, we say "forgive us our sins." Thus, we confess our corruptness, admit our mistakes without giving ourselves excuses, submit before His majesty, take refuge in His mercies, and ask for forgiveness—not out of merit but relying on His compassion as a gentle Father.

---

[23] Our daily bread. In the Van Dyke, Jesuit, and London Versions, this phrase was translated "our needed bread." Thus, we request the needs: Food, drink, shelter, etc., only asking for the necessities and not more. In the case of those who have more than they need, then the request is for God to help them limit themselves to their needs and give the rest to those who are in need. This request does not mean there is no effort on our parts. It is necessary for us to put in effort to reach our desire, and in this effort, we need the power granted to us by God. By requesting sufficiency only, we admit that our life is in His hand alone, that without His Economy and Providence for us we could not survive for one second.

[24] Some exegetes see that the bread we ask for is not physical bread per se but also spiritual—His life-giving words, His body, His blood (see the *Al-Kharida Al-Nafissa* (59) [Arabic reference]).

In the third request, we make a sincere vow to abandon envy and retribution, to forgive those who wrong us by saying "we also forgive everyone who is indebted to us," until we are granted as we seek.

As for the third and last section of this prayer, it concerns the great dangers set before us—temptations and demons. For this reason and because of our weak nature, the Savior teaches us to ask first, "Do not lead us into temptation." This does not mean the Almighty is the source of temptations and evils, for the apostle said, "God cannot be tempted by evil, nor does He Himself tempt anyone. But each one is tempted when he is drawn away by his own desires and enticed" (James 1:13–14).

The goal is for us to beseech Him in whose hands are all our affairs, without whose orders nothing occurs; in His wisdom He has arranged this so that we are not tried above our ability. We entreat Him to save us from hardships, to grant us a passageway for survival, because He is faithful. As the apostle said, "God is faithful, who will not allow you to be tempted beyond what you are able, but with the temptation will also make the way of escape, that you may be able to bear it" (1 Corinthians 10:13).

The Savior meant to teach us by this request to persevere during temptations, to bear with them, and not to denounce the Truth due to the extent of the hardship. Thus, we pass through them victorious, as did Job, Abraham, and others. Needless to say, it is not fitting for us to throw ourselves into temptations and then cry out for rescue.

The Savior also teaches the second request: "But deliver us from the evil one," *the devil*. We ask for salvation from his fiery arrows, just as the Lord of Glory asked the Father to keep His disciples from him (John 17:15). The devil is the one who tempted Adam, tempted the Savior, and continually tempts us.

We need to point out here that after this final request, our fathers the apostles added: "Through Christ Jesus our Lord." Although the Savior did not personally add this, they derived it from His teachings, such as: "Whatever you ask in My name, that I will do" (John 14:13), and "Whatever you ask the Father in My name He will give you" (John 16:23).

Matthew alone mentions the conclusion to the Lord's Prayer: "For Yours is the kingdom and the power and the glory forever. Amen" (Matthew 6:13). By uttering this, we instantly *feel* we should not fear Satan, because he can do nothing without God's permission. This permission is granted either because of our sins, or to reveal our patience as was the case with Job. Standing before the throne, the angels chant this phrase, worshiping and praising Him who lives forever and ever (Revelations 7:12). The concluding word, "Amen," is a Hebrew word meaning, "So be it"; it differs from the Greek "Amen" which means "truly."

Persistence in Prayer

> 5 And He said to them, "Which of you shall have a friend, and go to him at midnight and say to him, 'Friend, lend me three loaves; 6 for a friend of mine has come to me on his journey, and I have nothing to set before him'; 7 and he will answer from within and say, 'Do not trouble me; the door is now shut, and my children are with me in bed; I cannot rise and give to you'? 8 I say to you, though he will not rise and give to him because he is his friend, yet because of his persistence he will rise and give him as many as he needs."

5 – Only Luke narrated the parable mentioned by the Savior about the necessity of persistence in prayer and its effect. This parable is about a

selfish lazy man who at first refused the request of his friend for three loaves because the request was at midnight, an inappropriate time.[25]

6 – The friend apologized for waking him up at such an hour by saying, "A friend of mine has come to me on his journey" and common courtesy dictates offering food to a traveler.

7 – Nonetheless, the man remained within his house. He would not even get up to open the door but answered from inside, "Do not trouble me; the door is now shut, and my children are with me in bed; I cannot rise and give to you." He implied by these excuses his rejection and that if he arose, he would trouble himself and disturb his household.

8 – It seems the borrower did not give up, but continued knocking, until his insistence forced the man to get up and answer his request. Here the Savior comments on the power of persistence: "Though he will not rise and give to him because he is his friend, yet because of his persistence he will rise and give him as many as he needs." Persistence was even stronger than friendship, the duty of hospitality, and personal and familial relationships. Did it not also force the unjust judge to avenge the widow justly (Luke 18:5)?

If this person, through his persistence, reached his goal in unfavorable conditions and from a prideful and lazy person, shall we not attain our goals by our unceasing appeals to God, His mercy, and His unending goodness—He who is generous, loves to give, calls us to ask of Him and promises to answer? To Him, it makes no difference if it is night or day. If He seems to delay in answering, this is not because He is weary but for our own good. Many times He tests our faith by this patience and many others He postpones answering because we are not ready

---

[25] Some exegetes see the three loaves of bread as referring to the grace of the Holy Trinity.

to receive the blessing, or because we do not feel our need for it, or because we ask without the proper humility and genuine intention.

Answering Prayers

> 9 So I say to you, ask, and it will be given to you; seek, and you will find; knock, and it will be opened to you. 10 For everyone who asks receives, and he who seeks finds, and to him who knocks it will be opened. 11 If a son asks for bread from any father among you, will he give him a stone? Or if he asks for a fish, will he give him a serpent instead of a fish? 12 Or if he asks for an egg, will he offer him a scorpion? 13 If you then, being evil, know how to give good gifts to your children, how much more will your heavenly Father give the Holy Spirit to those who ask Him!

9 – After the Savior showed the effectiveness of prayer and the benefit of persistence in it, He exhorted them to pray continually without boredom, awaiting patiently for its sure answer: "Ask, and it will be given to you; seek, and you will find; knock, and it will be opened to you."[26] Although He did not specify what to ask for, it becomes clear from His previous words, "Seek first the kingdom of God and His righteousness" (Matthew 6:33).

This means we should not assume that God, out of His goodness and grace, will grant us material goods, but should focus our hope towards receiving spiritual ones, such as teaching us His way, illuminating us, and granting us His Holy Spirit. We should not ask only for ourselves but for our loved ones, for our enemies, and for everyone.

10 – The Savior repeated this promise: "For everyone who asks receives, and he who seeks finds, and to him who knocks it will be opened."

---

[26] See Matthew 7:11.

However, not everyone who asks receives; there are conditions required in the praying person for the request to be answered. Primarily, prayer must be: with a sure faith (Mark 11:24), in the name of the Lord Jesus (John 16:23), with a contrite heart (Luke 18:9–14), with persistence (Luke 11:8, 18:1–5), with consistency (Luke 21:26), according to God's will (1 John 5:14), with fervency and fortitude (Colossians 4:2), with watchful listening (Matthew 15:8), and with hearts at peace with all (Mark 11:25). The most important reasons that may prevent the answer to a prayer are sin (Isaiah 59:1–2), disobeying the law (Proverbs 28:9), and not having mercy on the poor (Proverbs 21:13).

11 – To reveal God the Father's immeasurable love for His children and His magnificent gifts to them, the Savior said, "If a son asks for bread from any father among you, will he give him a stone? Or if he asks for a fish, will he give him a serpent instead of a fish?"

12 – "Or if he asks for an egg, will he offer him a scorpion?"

13 – Then He concluded, "If you then, being evil, know how to give good gifts to your children, how much more will your heavenly Father give the Holy Spirit to those who ask Him!" He called humans evil in comparison with the perfect divine nature and because humans are inclined towards evil, and to exhort them to watchfulness and prayer stemming from pure intentions.

Promising us the Holy Spirit is the greatest of His promises to us because the grace of the Holy Spirit is the most sublime grace. Gaining this signifies gaining hope, life, God's grace, the benefits of redemption, and eternal joy. Matthew adds here: "Therefore, whatever you want men to do to you, do also to them, for this is the Law and the Prophets" (Matthew 7:12). By this saying, He gathered all the virtues into one. The *Law* (the Torah and the prophets—everything since Moses until Christ) points to a sublime meaning which lies behind this brevity.

---

[i] See 1 Kings 10:1–13.

[ii] Commentary on this entire Gospel reading taken from the Second Sunday of Tobe Liturgy Gospel.

[iii] Commentary notes for this subsection are replicated in the Ninevites' Monday Liturgy Gospel verses 38–42.

[iv] See 1 Kings 10:1–13.

[v] The call of Jonah the prophet. The book of Jonah mentions: "And Jonah began to enter the city on the first day's walk. Then he cried out and said, 'Yet forty days, and Nineveh shall be overthrown!'" (Jonah 3:4–5). The 40 days reportedly represent the 40 years that passed between the crucifixion of Christ and the destruction of Jerusalem.

[vi] [These verses are also commented on by the Archdeacon in the First Week Sunday Liturgy Gospel of the Great Fast (Matthew 6:22–23)].

[vii] Commentary on this Gospel reading (except for the subsections from verses 25–27) taken from the Hathor 24 Vespers Gospel.

[viii] [Below the Archdeacon writes 70. The different numbers come from a variance in the Greek translations.]

[ix] Election and Rejection. Also known as predestination, it means God chose His servants from among the sinners who are perishing from before the ages to inherit Heavenly Jerusalem. There are two opinions on this subject:

The first opinion: Our church and all the apostolic churches observe this view. Its basis is that choosing or rejecting a person is based on "God's foreknowledge" before that person was created because the Almighty is able to see future events as if present or past. Proof:

1– Before I saw you in the womb, I knew you (Jeremiah 1:4).

2– Those whom He foreknew He chose (Romans 8:29). God begins our salvation by giving us the first grace: the grace of faith. He gives it to us freely, without having to deserve it. He then seals it by giving us the grace of confirmation. Between those two graces, we should put forth some effort. Complete free will requires grace from God and effort from humans. Incomplete grace is when God bestows His grace while the human contributes nothing.

The second opinion: Augustine and the Protestant churches claim that electing or rejecting the person is based solely on "God's pleasure" and His authoritative will for reasons unknown to humans. The goodness found in the chosen person is a result of being chosen and is not a result of his selection. Those appointed for life were picked by God for eternal glory through His grace and love only, without the person previously displaying faith or good works. All this is to glorify His grace (Ephesians 1:6). As for the rest of humanity, He allowed—for the glory of His absolute authority over His creation—disgrace and humiliation to befall them because of their sins and for them to praise His justice.

Those abiding by this second opinion rely on some biblical verses; the most popular one is when the Master said, "For so it seemed good in Your sight." This text does not reveal that the reason for the election or rejection is the joy of God and His will alone, but indicates that God allowed the arrogance of the scribes and the Pharisees to conceal the truth from their eyes.

They also rely on a verse in the book of Acts: "As many as had been appointed to eternal life believed" (Acts 13:47). In fact, this verse proves that when the Almighty saw, from the beginning, the insistence of those Jews (who resisted Paul and Barnabas) on their sins and their stubbornness, He left them disobedient because of what their souls desired. However, the Gentiles who rejoiced at His word and accepted it all believed; this mystery commended them for eternal life since infinity.

Evidence for the first opinion:

A) Many passages prove that God does not will for anyone to perish, the most well-known are: 1) 1 Timothy 2:3–4; 2) Titus 2:11; 3) Ezekiel 18:23; 4) John 3:16.

B) If election and rejection were based solely on the pleasure of God, the following consequences would take place:

1) God would be partial, since He would have mercy on one person, and not on another.

2) God would be unjust to punish a person whom He chose to reject.

3) This would contradict the principle of human free will and each one's responsibility for his actions.

4) This contradicts the Savior's order to His disciples to preach to *all* people (Matthew 28:19).

C) The second opinion could lead some people to carelessness and laziness and others to falling in despair. Between those two extremes, there is a great gulf ready to drown souls in eternal condemnation. The first opinion, however, combines feeling God's grace in electing us for salvation and feeling personal responsibility, which encourages the soul and directs it to God's will in the salvation of all and gives it the spirit of hope when its faith is tried.

[x] For feeding the 4,000, see also Mark 8:1–10.

[xi] See *Fifth Week Monday Liturgy Gospel of the Great Fast*.

[xii] For the Pharisees' request for a sign, see also Mark 8:11–12.

[xiii] This reproach was explained in the Ninevites Monday Liturgy Gospel (Luke 11:29–30).

[xiv] [John Chrysostom. In Nicene and Post-Nicene Fathers: First Series, Philip Schaff, ed. (1886-1889; repr. New York, NY: Christian Literature Publishing Co., 1886), Book 1, Homily 38, verse 18 (NPNF1 14:133) (henceforth cited as NPNF).

[xv] Commentary on this entire Gospel reading taken from the Fourth Sunday of Mesore Liturgy Gospel.

[xvi] For answered Prayers, see also Matthew 21:21–22.

[xvii] Moving the mountain. See *Second Week Thursday Liturgy Gospel of the Great Fast*.

---

xviii Power of faith. See *Second Week Thursday Liturgy Gospel of the Great Fast, verse 20.*

xix Raising the son of the Shunammite. Elisha entered where the dead child lay, "shut the door behind the two of them, and prayed to the Lord" (2 Kings 4:33).

xx Repetition in prayer. Protestants accuse the Coptic Church of repeating certain prayers more than once. For example, "Kyrie eleison," which means, "Lord, have mercy," is repeated 41 times after each of the hourly [Horologion] prayers, and is repeated hundreds of times on Great Friday. The Lord's Prayer and other prayers are also repeated, which they consider vain repetition forbidden by the Savior in the verse that said, "Do not use vain repetitions."

In rebuttal, the origin of this Greek word is *Battologeo,* which primarily means "mumblings, stuttering, or stammering in speech, or words of little benefit"; consequently, repeating such words is in vain and has no benefit. He forbids excessive, non-beneficial repetition—there is a big difference between the two. Repetition could be of value, and sometimes required, to show need and to stimulate response; in contrast, garrulousness has no value.

Furthermore, forbidding beneficial repetition in prayer contradicts the Savior's own words on the night of His Passion. He repeated the same words several times (Matthew 26:39–44). David likewise repeated, "Have mercy on me, O Lord," many times (Psalms 6:2, 9:13, 31:9, etc.). Moreover, asking forgiveness is not vain, but is good and profitable. It indicates humility, submission, and meekness of heart; it pleases God, and moves His Divine compassion. By it we receive grants and gifts—as did the two blind men (Matthew 9:27), the Canaanite woman (Matthew 15:22), and blind Bartimaeus (Mark 10:47)—all of whom cried out to Jesus saying, "Have mercy on us, Son of David." We only need to be cautious not to cry out to Him as they did, but with the confidence of children in the spirit of Zechariah. Whenever we ask for His mercy at the beginning and end of prayer (having left our sinful past behind and returned to Him, asking for His forgiveness and mercy), He will have compassion on us, opening His arms as a gentle Father, bestowing on us everything we ask, and enveloping us with His mercy as He did the people of Israel and the Ninevites (who repented and returned to obeying Him).

For all the above reasons, the church called for this principle from the early days, and there is no need to excuse abiding by it. It is worth mentioning here that asking for mercy is a duty, not only for ourselves but also for others (Numbers 6:25), and not only for the living, but also for the dead, as Paul asked for the soul of Onesiphorus (2 Timothy 1:18).

xxi See First Sunday of Paone Liturgy Gospel (Luke 11:1–4) [*See this day's Evening Gospel*].

xxii Commentary on this entire Gospel reading taken from the First Sunday of Paone Liturgy Gospel. For the Lord's Prayer, see also Matthew 6:9–13.

NINEVITES' FAST: SALVATION THROUGH FAITH IN CHRIST'S RESURRECTION

DAY	PROPHECY Jonah	PSALMS & GOSPELS Vespers	Matins	Liturgy	EPISTLES Pauline	Catholicon	Acts
MONDAY: THE CALL TO REPENTANCE	God calling sinners to repent	The Savior urges sinners to repent	The Savior mercy to sinners if they request forgiveness	He cautions penitents against relapsing to sin	Urging penitents to offer their bodies unto holiness	Destruction of the impenitent	Church expansion through repentance
TUESDAY: LISTENING TO THE GOSPEL	God listens to the repentance of sinners		God's patience with people's sins	He urges them to obey the Gospel	The importance of listening to the Gospel	Refraining from evil	The call to repentance
WEDNESDAY: FORGIVING THE PENITENTS	God accepts penitents		His compassion on the penitent	He forgives their sins	Saving the penitents by grace	Charging them not to love the world	Not overburdening the penitents
NINEVITES' FEAST: SALVATION THROUGH FAITH			The Savior's ability to forgive their sins	His authority to resurrect Himself	Saving those who believe in His Resurrection	Their salvation through baptism	The blessings of His Resurrection

LEAVE-TAKING DAYS: PREPARING TO FAST

DAY	PSALMS & GOSPELS Vespers	Matins	Liturgy	Evening	EPISTLES Pauline	Catholicon	Acts
SATURDAY: THE NEED TO REPENT	Believers need to forgive those who sin against them	Believers need to keep vigil (watchfulness) against sin	The Savior exhorts believers to repent		Sorrow leading to repentance	Joy over saving their souls	Suffering for the sake of Christ
SUNDAY: THE CORNERSTONES OF WORSHIP	Believers need to forgive those who wrong them	Believers have a duty to worship God	Observing the 3 cornerstones of worship: charity, prayer, and fasting	The Holy Spirit's gifts are poured out on believers in answer to their	Believers' concern for the service	Confirming their faith through good works	Some restrictions

PART I: FEATURES OF THE STRUGGLE

UNIVERSAL THEME:
Preparing for the Struggle

FIRST WEEK – MONDAY
FORSAKING EVIL

Linking the Readings:

All the readings of this day center on one theme: **Forsaking evil**

The first prophecy speaks of **God manifesting Himself to those who cry out to Him from sin**, as He appeared to Moses in the burning bush; and the second prophecy speaks of Him **admonishing His people to abandon sin**, as He admonished the Israelites on the mouth of His prophet Isaiah.

The Matins Gospel speaks of God's **wrath against sinners**, as was His wrath against the Pharisees for their blasphemy; and the Liturgy Gospel speaks of how **He gives life to those who forsake sin**.

The Pauline Epistle speaks of **the judgment of sinners**; the Catholic Epistle explains how **their condemnation will be without mercy**; and the Acts reading speaks of **opening the door of faith** to them, as God opened it to the Gentiles on the hands of Saints Paul and Barnabas.

PROPHECIES

First Prophecy   Exodus 2:23–3:5

God manifests Himself to those who cry out to Him from sin: This prophecy speaks of Israel's groaning and crying out to God over their slavery in Egypt—symbolic of slavery to sin. After mentioning God hearing them (remembering His covenant with Abraham, Isaac, and Jacob), it shows God manifesting Himself in the burning bush which burns with fire, but is not consumed. He calls out to Moses from within saying: "Take your sandals off your feet, for the place where you stand is holy ground"[27] (v. 5).

Old Testament Type: The bush is not consumed
New Testament Antitype:
1) Unity of the Divinity with the Humanity taken from Saint Mary without mixing, mingling, or change
2) The One Nature of Christ the Master
3) Saint Mary conceives and remains a virgin

Second Prophecy   Isaiah 1:2–18

Admonishing His people to abandon sin: In this passage, God laments the sins of the Israelites, announcing His rejection of their offerings, and His hatred of their New Moons and feasts, then He addresses them saying: "Your hands are full of blood. Wash yourselves, make yourselves clean; put away the evil of your doings from before My eyes. Cease to do evil" (vv. 15–16).

---

[27] The Burning Bush is located in the Monastery of Saint Catherine in Sinai. Behind the altar there is a small church consisting of one room named after Saint Mary. Reportedly, it has been erected on the spot of the burning bush from which God spoke to Moses. Every Saturday (except Bright Saturday), the monks pray in it barefoot, out of respect for the divine words spoken to Moses.

PSALMS AND GOSPELS

Matins Psalm   Psalms 6:1–2

Seeing God's anger toward the Pharisees for their evils (as comes in
the accompanying Gospel passage), the psalm speaks for the believers,
entreating God to heal them from the illness of sin: "O Lord, do not
rebuke me in Your anger, nor chasten me in Your hot displeasure. Have
mercy on me, O Lord, for I am weak; O Lord, heal me, for my bones
are troubled."

Matins Gospel   Matthew 12:24–34

This passage speaks of God's wrath upon sinners as shown by the
Savior's address to the Pharisees who accused Him of exorcizing the
demon by Beelzebub: "Brood of vipers! How can you, being evil, speak
good things?" (v. 34)

Sermon: Forsaking Sin
*In this sermon (read after the Matins Gospel), the author, Abba John, the
Patriarch of Antioch, instructs the believers to welcome the fast from its
beginning "with joyful faces, open bosoms, pure minds, clear consciences,
contrite hearts, and tearful eyes, accompanied by good works, generous
giving, plentiful prayers, perfect love, and sublime holiness." Then he
encourages them to abandon their trespasses, repent, and pursue what
is pleasing to God.*

Liturgy Psalm   Psalm 22:26

This psalm relates to three points made by the Savior in the
accompanying Gospel passage: extoling humility; His saying, "No one
who works a miracle in My name can soon afterward speak evil of Me"

(Mark 9:39); and to the eternal life awaiting those who forsake the causes of sin. "The poor shall eat and be satisfied; those who seek Him will praise the Lord. Let your heart live forever."

Liturgy Gospel   Mark 9:33–50

This passage speaks of the Savior giving life to those who forsake the causes of sin, as He said to His disciples, "If your hand causes you to sin, cut it off. It is better for you to enter into life maimed, rather than having two hands, to go to hell, into the fire that shall never be quenched" (v. 43).

EPISTLES

The Pauline Epistle   Romans 1:26–2:7

Judgment of sinners: In this epistle, Paul rebukes sinners, "Filled with all unrighteousness, sexual immorality, wickedness, covetousness, maliciousness; full of envy, murder, strife, deceit, evil-mindedness; they are whisperers... who, knowing the righteous judgment of God, that those who practice such things are deserving of death, not only do the same but also approve of those who practice them." Then he warns them: "And do you think this, O man, you who judge those practicing such things, and doing the same, that you will escape the judgment of God? Or do you despise the riches of His goodness, forbearance, and longsuffering... But in accordance with your hardness and your impenitent heart you are treasuring up for yourself wrath in the day of wrath and revelation of the righteous judgment of God" (vv. 1:29, 32; 2:3–5).

The Catholic Epistle   James 2:1–13

Their condemnation is without mercy: The apostle speaks of the sin of partiality, showing that one who is partial transgresses the law, and will be judged without mercy: "For judgment is without mercy to the one who has shown no mercy" (v. 13).

The Acts   Acts 14:19–28

Opening the door of faith to them: This passage speaks of Paul and Barnabas' successful mission, and "[Having] gathered the church together, they reported all that God had done with them, and that He had opened the door of faith to the Gentiles," which signifies that the door of faith is open to sinners (who are labeled as Gentiles) if they obey the voice of the Gospel (v. 27).

Matins Gospel
Matthew 12:24–34
Jesus Accused of Enlisting Beelzebub[i]

JESUS ACCUSED OF ENLISTING BEELZEBUB

Overview

During Christ the Master's second circuit of ministry in Galilee, they brought to Him a person who was blind, mute, and possessed; He healed him. This miracle amazed the crowd surrounding Him, but the Pharisees (whose chests boiled with envy against Him) blasphemed Him, accusing Him of using Beelzebub (the ruler of the demons) to exorcise the demon from that man. The pericope dealing with the issue of this blasphemy points first to the witchcraft of which the Pharisees accused the Lord of Glory, and then to the lethal excuses they used to support their accusations. His decree concerning this sin of blasphemy is that it is not forgivable and there is no avoiding its judgment on the last day.

Accusing Him of Witchcraft

> 24 Now when the Pharisees heard it they said, "This fellow does not cast out demons except by Beelzebub, the ruler of the demons."

24 – Envy blinded the Pharisees, His greatest detractors, from seeing the miracle in its truth. This is not strange, because the sin of envy—the first sin to enter the world (through it Satan was able to cause Adam to fall and to raise Cain up against his brother to kill him)—caused them to blaspheme against Him: "This fellow does not cast out demons except by Beelzebub, the ruler of the demons."[28] They accused Him of using witchcraft and magic in performing miracles.

Refuting Accusations

> 25 But Jesus knew their thoughts, and said to them: "Every kingdom divided against itself is brought to desolation, and every city or house divided against itself will not stand. 26 If Satan casts out Satan, he is divided against himself. How then will his kingdom stand? 27 And if I cast out demons by Beelzebub, by whom do your sons cast them out? Therefore they shall be your judges. 28 But if I cast out demons by the

---

[28] *Ba`al zebul* is the god of the flies. The Philistines worshiped it, convinced it protected them from harm and from the plague of the flies. Its statue looks like a fly. The Jews changed the final letter to a "B" out of disdain, nicknaming and ridiculing it (see *Elm-El-Lahoot* (1:146) [Arabic reference]).

Spirit of God, surely the kingdom of God has come upon you. 29 Or how can one enter a strong man's house and plunder his goods, unless he first binds the strong man? And then he will plunder his house. 30 He who is not with Me is against Me, and he who does not gather with Me scatters abroad."

25 – As for Jesus, the One "who searches the minds and hearts" (Revelations 2:23), who knows what is hidden within the heart (Psalm 44:21), of whom David said, "You know my sitting down and my rising up; you understand my thought afar off" (Psalm 139:2), He knew their thoughts—what went through their minds that they were afraid to admit. They *said* in the previous verse actually means they *thought*. Being merciful, He did not want to expose their inner thoughts, but as usual, He gave a gentle parable about a dispute that would disprove their arguments with powerful proofs that rebuked them: "Every kingdom divided against itself is brought to desolation." No wonder disputes and disagreements in homes, denominations, cities, and kingdoms lead to disaster and destruction!

26 – If the Savior enlisted the power of the ruler of the demons to exorcise his allies from people, as the Pharisees accused Him, then this would mean the kingdom of Satan has come to division and destruction. It is unthinkable that the Savior would sink to the level of using the power of the ruler who seeks after evil and despises repentance and goodness.[ii]

27 – The Savior continued, revealing His second proof that negates their accusation: "If I cast out demons by Beelzebub, by whom do your sons cast them out?" *If your accusation applies to me then it also applies to your own children*—His disciples who are also exorcising demons through His own strength. Since they were not also accused, "they shall be your judges"; they will testify to your false accusations against Me.

28 – *Since we have already established that I exorcise demons by the Spirit of God*—the might of the Holy Spirit— "surely the kingdom of God has come upon you." "The kingdom of God" means the awaited arrival of His first coming. *I have paved and prepared the way for its arrival.* Luke writes, "If I cast out demons with the finger of God"[29] — with the Spirit of God (Luke 11:20).

29 – The Savior continued giving evidence against their accusations: "Or how can one enter a strong man's house and plunder his goods, unless he first binds the strong man? And then he will plunder his house." The "strong man" refers to Beelzebub, his "house" are his friends, and "his goods" refer to those who obey Him. He cannot cast Beelzebub's soldiers out of people except after binding him (overcoming and destroying him). How is He casting them out through Beelzebub and by His own power simultaneously! In other words, the Savior cannot snatch the humans from Satan unless He first binds him through His cross. Once crucified, He has the right to bind him and plunder all his goods—human souls he has enslaved through sin. He snatched them from Satan at the moment of His death.

Luke writes, "When a strong man, fully armed, guards his own palace, his goods are in peace. But when a stronger person than he comes upon him and overcomes him, he takes from him all his armor in which he trusted and divides his spoils."[30] The "strong man" is Satan, and "his armor" is the body he dons as a weapon to overpower the souls and

---

[29] Our church teaches us to make the sign of the cross with one finger, not two or three, with the rest of the fingers wrapped into the palm of the hand, symbolizing the womb of the virgin where the divine incarnation occurred. When people sign themselves, they sign themselves with their thumb. Ebn-Al-Assaal's *Manners in the Church* [Arabic reference] dictates for the signing of the cross to be with the index finger. This is meant for when a person signs another with the sign of the cross to cast out demons, as our Savior said, "But if I cast out demons with the *finger* of God, surely the kingdom of God has come upon you" (Luke 11:20).
[30] [Luke 11:21–22].

cast them into sin. Jesus, who is stronger than he is, completely disarmed him of his trusted armor; Christ took a body that Satan assumed akin to all bodies, so Satan roused the Jews until they killed Him, but then the Lord demanded of him the price for His death and released those whom he had imprisoned through sin. He killed the body (which Satan enlisted to kill the souls) and divided the spoil, releasing those whom he imprisoned by sin. In this way, He taught us to mortify the body from its desires, to overcome Satan.

30 – The Savior concluded: "He who is not with Me is against Me, and he who does not gather with Me scatters abroad." *As long as I do what does not please Satan (teaching people to repent and bringing people from vice to virtue), he will always resist me.* Satan would not use anyone who is in such a condition to cast out demons. By this rebuke, He sealed His dialogue.

Sin of Blasphemers

31 Therefore I say to you, every sin and blasphemy will be forgiven men, but the blasphemy against the Spirit will not be forgiven men. 32 Anyone who speaks a word against the Son of Man, it will be forgiven him; but whoever speaks against the Holy Spirit, it will not be forgiven him, either in this age or in the age to come.

31 – To reveal the dangerous unforgivable nature of their sinful allegations, He said to them, "Every sin and blasphemy will be forgiven men, but the blasphemy against the Spirit will not be forgiven men." This verse declares two great principles in the church. The first is that there is no sin in this world that is unforgivable as long as it is followed by a genuine repentance and true confession coupled with a firm hope in the limitless merit of our Lord Jesus Christ. Second, the unforgivable sins are those that resist the Holy Spirit. The church fathers narrowed

this down to three: despair,[31] insistence on committing sin until death, and blasphemy against the Holy Spirit. Sin remains for someone who blasphemes and loses hope, one who does not listen to the warnings and rebukes of the Holy Spirit and despises the work of the Holy Spirit in the heart but rather pursues evil until death, and one who blasphemes against the Holy Spirit of God.

Attributing to Satan the miracles the Lord Jesus did by the might of His Holy Spirit, following the example of the Pharisees, is blasphemy against the Holy Spirit. Most often, those who fall into this sin are those who reached the highest [intellectual] knowledge of the truth. Since the one who brings the sinner to repentance is the Holy Spirit, the sin becomes unforgivable when the Spirit leaves the person who adamantly resists Him—the wretched soul will die in his sin. He will be like a traveler in a multi-routed desert without a map or direction; he is certain to perish. The one who does not seek the guidance of the Holy Spirit will not find the way of truth in life.[32]

In his epistle, John the apostle wrote about forgivable sins and other unforgivable sins: "If anyone sees his brother sinning a sin which does not lead to death, he will ask, and He will give him life for those who commit sin not leading to death. There is sin leading to death. I do not say that he should pray about that" (1 John 5:16).

---

[31] The church arranged not to pray over persons who commit suicide except if they repented, even if at the very last moment before death.
[32] Seeking the Holy Spirit. The church arranged for her children to pray morning and evening, saying with David the prophet, "Do not cast me away from Your presence, and do not take Your Holy Spirit from me" (Psalm 51:11). She also arranged in the Horologion for the person praying to say during the litany of the third hour: "Your Holy Spirit, O Lord whom You sent forth upon Your holy disciples and honored apostles in the third hour, do not take away from us, O Good One, but renew Him within us," and, "A right and life-giving spirit, a spirit of prophecy and chastity, a spirit of holiness, righteousness and authority," and also, "O heavenly King, the Comforter, the Spirit of truth... graciously come, and dwell in us and purify us from all defilement."

In his epistle to the Hebrews, Paul the apostle pointed to this deadly sin: "For it is impossible for those who were once enlightened, and have tasted the heavenly gift, and have become partakers of the Holy Spirit, and have tasted the good word of God and the powers of the age to come, if they fall away, to renew them again to repentance, since they crucify again for themselves the Son of God, and put Him to an open shame" (Hebrews 6:4–6). Paul also said, "For if we sin willfully after we have received the knowledge of the truth, there no longer remains a sacrifice for sins, but a certain fearful expectation of judgment, and fiery indignation which will devour the adversaries. Anyone who has rejected Moses' law dies without mercy on the testimony of two or three witnesses. Of how much worse punishment, do you suppose, will he be thought worthy who has trampled the Son of God underfoot, counted the blood of the covenant by which he was sanctified a common thing, and insulted the Spirit of grace?" (Hebrews 10:26–29).

32 – The Savior went on to reveal the gravity of the sin of blasphemy against the Holy Spirit: "Whoever speaks against the Holy Spirit, it will not be forgiven him, either in this age or in the age to come." This verse neither says the Holy Spirit is more honorable than the Son, nor denies the divinity of Christ the Master—as some atheists wrongfully object. In fact, the three Persons are equally divine. If someone blasphemed against the Son, out of genuine ignorance, while He was in human form, for example, calling Him a Samaritan, a deceiver, a winebibber and lover of tax collectors, this person is pardoned because the incarnate Savior's divinity was hidden from human eyes. These things are forgiven on the condition of repentance and asking forgiveness. As for the one who witnesses the miracles of Christ, which reveal His divinity, which can only be done by God, and blasphemes against Him, such as attributing them to Satan, his unforgivable sins are equal to the sin of blasphemy against the Holy Spirit.

The Lord of Glory wanted to tell the Pharisees that all their attacks against Him (calling Him crazy, a Samaritan, a lawbreaker), He will bear and forgive, just as He forgave Paul who said of himself, "Although I was formerly a blasphemer, a persecutor, and an insolent man; but I obtained mercy because I did it ignorantly in unbelief" (1 Timothy 1:13). Blasphemy against the Holy Spirit, however, is an unforgivable sin, in this world and in the one to come. This means there are two types of sins: one type is unforgivable both in this world and in the one to come; and the other forgivable in both the present life and in the one to come. Based on this, prayers for the souls of the good departed persons certainly benefit them and cover their unintentional sins.[iii]

Their Judgment

33 Either make the tree good and its fruit good, or else make the tree bad and its fruit bad; for a tree is known by its fruit. 34 Brood of vipers! How can you, being evil, speak good things? For out of the abundance of the heart the mouth speaks.

33 – The Savior took to showing them their self-contradiction. On one hand, they show amazement at His miracles and praise them, while on the other hand, they slander and insult Him for these very miracles. They neither expose them as rumors (which would require them to manifest the flaws in the miracles), nor do they praise Him for the miracles which are indeed praiseworthy. This is the significance of Him saying, "Either make the tree good and its fruit good, or else make the tree bad and its fruit bad." He is referring to Himself by the tree, and to His works by the fruit. In other words, He wants to tell them, *Your accusations that I exorcise demons by the power of Satan is a baseless accusation; exorcising demons is a good work. Since nothing good comes from Satan, either you are declaring that Satan does good, or that casting out demons is evil; neither one is acceptable logic. Therefore, your accusations against Me are vain. Since a tree is known by its fruit, then your accusations only reveal the evil intentions within your souls.*

34 – He clearly revealed to them with brutal honesty that it is no surprise that they accused Him, because out of the goodness of the heart the mouth speaks: "Brood of vipers! How can you, being evil, speak good things?" Thus, He broke their sharp pride in their ancestry.

Liturgy Gospel
Mark 9:33–50
Dispute among the Disciples

DISPUTE AMONG THE DISCIPLES

Overview[iv]

While our Master was in Capernaum (during His third circuit of ministry in Galilee), for the first time, a dispute occurred along the road between His disciples concerning who is the greatest. When they settled into the house, the Master began to show them (as the Gospel reveals) the danger of seeking after vainglory, and the benefits of humility as a remedy for this malady. He concludes, whoever puts forth effort, no matter how little, to destroy the kingdom of evil has his reward, even if he is not one of the disciples.

Offense of Vainglory[v]

33 Then He came to Capernaum. And when He was in the house He asked them, "What was it you disputed among yourselves on the road?" 34 But they kept silent, for on the road they had disputed among themselves who would be the greatest.

33 – The Savior asked His disciples the topic of their discussion while they were on the road to the house in Capernaum.

34 – They refrained from answering out of shame because they were discussing "who would be the greatest." It seems they thought the kingdom of Christ was earthly not heavenly, political not spiritual, and that they should be the prime administrators therein. With such a mindset, they disputed over authority and status.

Its Cure: Humility[33]

> 35 And He sat down, called the twelve, and said to them, "If anyone desires to be first, he shall be last of all and servant of all." 36 Then He took a little child and set him in the midst of them. And when He had taken him in His arms, He said to them, 37 "Whoever receives one of these little children in My name receives Me; and whoever receives Me, receives not Me but Him who sent Me."

35 [2] – When Jesus knew what was on their minds, as Luke mentions (Luke 9:47), and saw their hearts ill with the love of the ego and their chests heaving with envy and pride which led to dispute over authority, He did not answer them according to their question but according to their thoughts.

36 – He called to Himself "a little child"[34] and "set him in the midst of them," taking "him in His arms" (Mark 9:36). Making the boy stand in

---

[33] Commentary on these verses taken from the Second Sunday of Epep Liturgy Gospel (Matthew 18:2–5). The numbers in brackets refer to the verses in Matthew.

[34] It is said that this boy was Saint Ignatius Theophorus, Bishop of Antioch, who rejected and tore the order of Emperor Trajan in AD 98 (*Al-Kharida Al-Nafissa* (1:79, 105) [Arabic reference]). He is also the one who heard the angels chant the Trisagion, so he arranged its chanting in the church by decree of Peter the apostle. The church commemorates him on Koiahk 24 of each year.

their midst was to show them by practical action the attributes with which the true Christian should be adorned. The child has many virtues: he is humble, believes his father's words, is content with what is given to him, relies on his care, and obeys his orders. Likewise, the Christian should be meek, have faith in God, content with his share, dependent on Him, and obedient to His orders.

[3] – He told them, "Assuredly, I say to you, unless you are converted and become as little children, you will by no means enter the kingdom of heaven." By this, He does not mean for them to be indecisively ignorant, but to be like children: good intentioned, humble, loving to learn, truthful, and faithful. Paul the apostle likewise exhorts the faithful: "Brethren, do not be children in understanding; however, in malice be babes" (1 Corinthians 14:20). Peter clarifies the words even further: "Therefore, laying aside all malice, all deceit, hypocrisy, envy, and all evil speaking, as newborn babes, desire the pure milk of the word, that you may grow thereby, if indeed you have tasted that the Lord is gracious" (1 Peter 2:1–3).

37 [4] – The Savior led them to the true path of greatness—humility— by saying, "Therefore whoever humbles himself as this little child is the greatest in the kingdom of heaven." Serenity and humility (with knowledge, not with ignorance) are what lead to that greatness. Addressing the disciples, the Lord of Glory said, "Whoever desires to be first among you, let him be your slave" (Matthew 20:27). He also said, "Whoever exalts himself will be humbled, and he who humbles himself will be exalted" (Matthew 23:12).

Peter the apostle also commends humility: "Likewise you younger people, submit yourselves to your elders. Yes, all of you be submissive to one another, and be clothed with humility, for 'God resists the proud, but gives grace to the humble.' Therefore, humble yourselves under the mighty hand of God, that He may exalt you in due time, casting all your care upon Him, for He cares for you" (1 Peter 5:5–7).[vi] The Savior's response to His disciples shows that He wanted to cut off all thoughts of boasting, haughtiness, and egoism from their hearts. Had He wanted to appoint Peter as the head, He would have used this opportunity to reveal His will.[vii]

[5] – Jesus added: "Whoever receives one little child like this in My name receives Me." *Whoever accepts any person in this capacity and honors him for My sake (not for the sake of fame) with hospitality and goodness, has received and honored Me, and I will repay him accordingly.*

W age of the Workers[viii]

38 Now John answered Him, saying, "Teacher, we saw someone who does not follow us casting out demons in Your name, and we forbade Him because He does not follow us." 39 But Jesus said, "Do not forbid Him, for no one who works a miracle in My name can soon afterward speak evil of Me. 40 For He who is not against us is on our side. 41 For whoever gives you a cup of water to drink in My name, because you belong to Christ, assuredly, I say to you, He will by no means lose his reward.

38 – John and the disciples had seen a man exorcise demons in the name of Christ who was neither one of the 12 nor of the 70, but was *only* a believer (otherwise, he would not have been able to perform a miracle). They prevented him from doing so, not out of envy of him or of those whom he cured, but simply because he was not one of the followers of the Savior, as they said, "We forbade him because he does not follow us." Their motive was their love for their Master, and their assumption that no one deserves to gain praise in the name of Christ if he is not one of His followers, and that He gave the power to exorcise demons to them alone.

39 – When Jesus heard that he was prevented, realizing that the man was an obedient person (since he obeyed them once they told him), He told them, "Do not forbid him." He considered his work as good as the work done by His disciples in His name with the purpose of spreading His call. He told them that such a person cannot "soon afterward speak evil of Me." Whoever performs a miracle in the name of Christ cannot be a magician because God does not allow a magician to use the name of Christ as a means for deception. Since this person is such, then he is a believer—a believer cannot say evil of Christ. Paul the apostle says, "No one speaking by the Spirit of God calls Jesus accursed" (1 Corinthians 12:3). This reminds us of a similar incident in the Old Testament where Joshua the son of Nun asked Moses to stop Eldad and Medad from prophesying in the camp (Numbers 11:24–30).

40 – The Savior continued speaking to His disciples: "He who is not against us is on our side." *This man helps us exert effort to destroy the kingdom of Satan in action and heart; therefore, he is with us, not against us.*

41 – To assure John, who had denied the man's virtue, that this man's reward is great, He said, "For whoever gives you a cup of water to drink in My name, because you belong to Christ, assuredly, I say to you, he will by no means lose his reward." If the smallest service done in the name of Christ, such as a cup of water, has its reward, how much greater would be the reward of one who heals those who are overtaken with evil spirits. The apostle says, "God is not unjust to forget your work and labor of love which you have shown toward His name, in that you have ministered to the saints, and do minister" (Hebrews 6:10).[ix]

Punishment for Causing Offenses[35]

> 42 But whoever causes one of these little ones who believe in
> Me to stumble, it would be better for Him if a millstone were
> hung around his neck, and He were thrown into the sea.

42 [2] – The Savior shows the severity of the punishment awaiting those
who cause offense to the faithful: "It would be better for him if a
millstone were hung around his neck, and he were thrown into the sea."
*If given a choice between the punishment for causing offenses (eternal
fire) and drowning in the sea to be tortured for a time, he would surely
choose the latter option.* The gravest tragedies are *easier* than causing
offense to the believers—whom Jesus called "little ones," not because
they are little but because other people think they are little. The apostle
urges: "Give no offense, either to the Jews or to the Greeks or to the
church of God, just as I also please all men in all things, not seeking my
own profit, but the profit of many, that they may be saved" (1
Corinthians 10:32–33). He is reiterating what he said earlier: "We then
who are strong ought to bear with the scruples of the weak, and not to
please ourselves. Let each of us please his neighbor for his good,
leading to edification. For even Christ did not please Himself" (Romans
15:1–3).

Cutting off Offenses[36]

> 43 If your hand causes you to sin, cut it off. It is better for you
> to enter into life maimed, rather than having two hands, to go
> to hell, into the fire that shall never be quenched— 44 where
> "Their worm does not die and the fire is not quenched." 45 And

---

[35] Commentary on this verse taken from the Seventh Week Tuesday Matins Gospel
(Luke 17:2). The number in brackets refers to the verse in Luke.
[36] Commentary on these verses taken from the Second Sunday of Epep Liturgy Gospel
(Matthew 18:8–9). The numbers in brackets refer to the verses in Matthew.

if your foot causes you to sin, cut it off. It is better for you to enter life lame, rather than having two feet, to be cast into hell, into the fire that shall never be quenched— 46 where "Their worm does not die and the fire is not quenched." 47 And if your eye causes you to sin, pluck it out. It is better for you to enter the kingdom of God with one eye, rather than having two eyes, to be cast into hell fire— 48 where "Their worm does not die and the fire is not quenched."

43–44 [8] – Jesus decreed how we can avoid offenses: "If your hand or foot causes you to sin, cut it off and cast it from you."

45–48 [9] – "And if your eye causes you to sin, pluck it out and cast it from you." *If you have a relative or a friend, or a bad opinion that prevents you from the truth, turn and cast it away from you. For it is better for you to enter life crippled or blind than to be cast into the fire having two feet and two eyes. It is better for you to cling onto the Truth and unite with the Creator (avoiding these) than for these possessions to drag you away,* as the evangelist said of him [the rich young man], "He was sad at this word, and went away sorrowful, for he had great possessions" (Mark 10:22).

Duty of the Disciples

49 For everyone will be seasoned with fire, and every sacrifice will be seasoned with salt. 50 Salt is good, but if the salt loses its flavor, how will you season it? Have salt in yourselves, and have peace with one another.

49 – The Savior went on to say, "Everyone will be seasoned with fire." Just as all food is seasoned and tested by fire, to see if it is fit for food, likewise, everyone led to the Gospel, will be trained by the grace of the Holy Spirit. He said, "Seasoned with salt," because salt preserves the

humid body from decomposition, just as the Holy Spirit saves weak minds from the defilement of sin.

Some exegetes see "seasoned with fire" to mean that every mind trained by the grace of the Holy Spirit is enlightened by knowledge and piety. While some others see it to mean that in the age to come, everyone will be engulfed by fire—the saints will see themselves as being aflame, that is, being engulfed in light (being in a perpetual day because Christ will be their light), while the evil will truly be engulfed and aflame, being tormented by fire. By saying, "every sacrifice will be seasoned with salt,"ˣ He means the *sacrifice* of the human mind and actions, and the *salt* of the grace of the Holy Spirit, love, and mercy. No *unsalted* mind is fit for the kingdom of heaven.

Others see that the Savior wants to pair up the fire of Gehenna and its worms on one side, and the fire of faithfulness and the salt of wisdom on the other side; whoever seeks rescue from the first, seeks out the second. Still others see the intended meaning of the "fire" as the grace of the Holy Spirit, and "salt" as wisdom and prudence, as the apostle says: "According to the riches of His grace which He made to abound toward us in all wisdom and prudence" (Ephesians 1:7–8).

50 – By saying "have salt in yourselves," He means the grace of the Holy Spirit, which is the source of internal purity, deep longings, adoration, humility, disdaining the world, and self-denial. This is what preserves His disciples from corruption and prepares them to be "the salt of the earth" (Matthew 5:13). Paul the apostle reiterated this commandment by saying, "Let no corrupt word proceed out of your mouth, but what is good for necessary edification, that it may impart grace to the hearers" (Ephesians 4:29), and, "Let your speech always be with grace, seasoned with salt, that you may know how you ought to answer each one" (Colossians 4:6).

The Savior ends by commanding His disciples to "have peace with one another" to keep from quarreling among themselves about leadership positions, because love and peace are among the fruits of the Holy Spirit (Galatians 5:22). Resembling the Savior, Paul the apostle commended the believers, on more than one occasion, to have peace among themselves, saying, "If it is possible, as much as depends on you, live peaceably with all men" (Romans 12:18). He also said, "Therefore let us pursue the things which make for peace and the things by which one may edify another" (Romans 14:19), and again, "Live in peace; and the God of love and peace will be with you" (2 Corinthians 13:11).

FIRST WEEK – TUESDAY
CLINGING ONTO GOOD

Linking the Readings:

All the readings of this day center on one theme: **The believers' need to cling to good**

The first prophecy speaks of **guiding the Gentiles to God's law,** as Isaiah prophesied; and the second prophecy speaks of **God blessing them** as He blessed Judah and Israel.

The Matins Gospel **calls them to repent**, as the Lord Jesus frankly declares that He "did not come to call the righteous, but sinners, to repentance"; and the Liturgy Gospel speaks of the Savior's **mercy to penitent sinners** because of the forces opposing their repentance.

The Pauline Epistle speaks of **the riches of His glory** in calling sinners to become His people after having been Gentiles; the Catholic Epistle **exhorts them to do good;** and the Acts reading speaks of **enduring pain for Christ's sake**, as the Apostles endured from the Jews.

PROPHECIES

First Prophecy   Isaiah 1:19–2:3

Guiding the Gentiles to God's law: The evangelical prophet shows "how the faithful city has become a harlot" (meaning the house of Israel), how its silver has become dross, its wine mixed with water, and its princes rebellious (who love bribes and seek rewards), not defending the fatherless and ignoring the cause of the widow. He concludes that God will purify her dross: "Zion shall be redeemed with justice, and her penitents with righteousness." Then, he prophesies of the reign of Christ's kingdom and laws: "Now it shall come to pass in the latter days that the mountain of the Lord's house shall be established on the top of the mountains... and all nations shall flow to it... For out of Zion shall go forth the law, and the word of the Lord from Jerusalem" (vv. 1:21, 27; 2:1–3).

Second Prophecy   Zechariah 8:7–13

God blessing them: In this prophecy, the Lord of Hosts speaks on the tongue of His prophet Zechariah: "But now I will not treat the remnant of this people as in the former days... For the seed shall be prosperous, the vine shall give its fruit, the ground shall give her increase, and the heavens shall give their dew... Just as you were a curse among the nations, O house of Judah and house of Israel, so I will save you, and you shall be a blessing. Do not fear, let your hands be strong" (vv. 11–13).

PSALMS AND GOSPELS

Matins Psalm   Psalms 23:1, 3

The start of this psalm refers to the accompanying Gospel passage, which shows the coming of the Savior as His people's shepherd to call sinners to repentance, and then the psalm points to His response to John's disciples' question: "The Lord is my shepherd; I shall not want. He restores my soul; He leads me in the paths of righteousness."

Matins Gospel   Matthew 9:10–15

This passage speaks of the Savior's call for sinners to repent, as He told the Pharisees who derided Him for eating with tax collectors and sinners: "For I did not come to call the righteous, but sinners, to repentance" (v. 13).

Sermon: Good Deeds[xi]
In this sermon, written by Athanasius, the patriarch of Alexandria, he encourages the believers, during this fasting season, to lay aside "all deceit, all envy, all gossip, and all evil, to avoid drunkenness which can lead to defilement, and to stay away from the love of the corruptible and perishing riches." Then he explains that we are sojourners on this earth, therefore, we need to "persevere to prepare the food and store the supplies before traveling. This way we will be able to give alms to our needy brothers and sisters, comfort the widow, support the orphan, clothe the naked, quench the thirsty, relieve the sick, visit the prisoner, and strengthen the stranger." Thus, we will win the heavenly kingdom.

Liturgy Psalm   Psalms 25:16–17

This psalm points to the parable of the faithful steward that comes in the accompanying Gospel passage, and with the tongue of the penitents ([the faithful servant and the penitent sinner] who are exposed to resistance and sorrows for the sake of their repentance) the psalm begs for God's mercy, saying: "Turn Yourself to me, and have mercy on me, for I am desolate and afflicted. The troubles of my heart have enlarged."

Liturgy Gospel   Luke 12:41–50

This passage speaks of the Savior's mercy on penitent sinners against forces opposing them because of their repentance, saying: "I came to send fire on the earth, and how I wish it were already kindled," that is, as there is no salvation except through the fire of tribulations, I am eager to kindle it (v. 49).

EPISTLES

The Pauline Epistle   Romans 9:15–29

Calling Gentiles to repentance: The apostle reveals that God shows mercy to the merciful, and compassion on the compassionate, and in this there is absolutely no injustice: "What if God, wanting to show His wrath and to make His power known, endured with much longsuffering the vessels of wrath prepared for destruction, and that He might make known the riches of His glory on the vessels of mercy, which He had prepared beforehand for glory, even us whom He called, not of the Jews only, but also of the Gentiles? As He says also in Hosea: 'I will call them My people, who were not My people, and her beloved, who was not beloved.'" Next, the apostle witnesses to the honesty of His call, as Isaiah says of Israel: "Though the number of the children of Israel be as the sand of the sea, the remnant will be saved. For He will finish the work and cut it short in righteousness" (vv. 22–28).

The Catholic Epistle   1 Peter 4:3–11

Admonishing them to do good: If the Pauline Epistle discusses God calling the Gentiles to be His people, then this epistle advises them of the need to break off from evil and begin doing good. Here, the apostle urges them further: "For we have spent enough of our past lifetime in doing the will of the Gentiles—when we walked in lewdness, lusts, drunkenness, revelries, drinking parties, and abominable idolatries." He continues: "But the end of all things is at hand; therefore be serious and watchful in your prayers. And above all things have fervent love for one another, for love will cover a multitude of sins" (vv. 3, 7–8).

The Acts   Acts 5:34–42

Enduring pain for Christ's sake: This passage speaks of the faithful suffering pain for the sake of Christ, as shown by the following incident: being warned by Gamaliel not to harm the disciples, the Jews "agreed with him, and when they had called for the apostles and beaten them, they commanded that they should not speak in the name of Jesus, and let them go. So they departed from the presence of the council, rejoicing that they were counted worthy to suffer shame for His name" (vv. 40–41).

Matins Gospel
Matthew 9:10–15[37]
Leading Sinners to Repentance

LEADING SINNERS TO REPENTANCE

Overview

When the Lord Jesus began to preach in Galilee for the first time, He moved from Nazareth to Capernaum and called His first four disciples: Peter, Andrew, James, and John. He did some miracles, including healing the leper and the paralytic let down from the roof. After that, He called Matthew the tax collector who accepted the call and held a great banquet for the Savior in his house. This pericope discusses this banquet and speaks of Jesus' invitation to the sinners, their repentance and joy for His invitation, as well as their acceptance of His new law.

---

[37] Commentary on this entire reading taken from the Second Sunday of Mesore Liturgy Gospel (Luke 5:29–35). The numbers in brackets refer to the verses in Luke.

Inviting Sinners

> 10 Now it happened, as Jesus sat at the table in the house, that behold, many tax collectors and sinners came and sat down with Him and His disciples.

10 [29] – Wanting to ease some of his feeling of indebtedness to the Savior, Matthew held a grand banquet in his house and invited many of his fellow tax collectors and other sinners[38] (to boast in the honor of hosting the Savior) who were following Him (Mark 2:15), especially since many of them "drew near to Him to hear Him" (Luke 15:1).

Their Repentance

> 11 And when the Pharisees saw it, they said to His disciples, "Why does your Teacher eat with tax collectors and sinners?" 12 When Jesus heard that, He said to them, "Those who are well have no need of a physician, but those who are sick. 13 But go and learn what this means: 'I desire mercy and not sacrifice.' For I did not come to call the righteous, but sinners, to repentance."

11 [30] – Among the banqueters was a group of scribes and Pharisees who, as soon as they saw Jesus eat with the tax collectors and sinners, murmured against Him and His disciples: "Why do You eat and drink with tax collectors and sinners?" Perhaps they based their objection on the words of the psalm, "Blessed is the man who walks not in the counsel of the ungodly, nor stands in the path of sinners, nor sits in the seat of the scornful" (Psalm 1:1). This view was later supported by the Apostle Paul when he said, "But now I have written to you not to keep

---

[38] The *sinners* Luke describes as *others* in this verse are Gentiles, as evidenced by the apostle's words, "We who are Jews by nature, and not sinners of the Gentiles" (Galatians 2:15).

company with anyone named a brother, who is sexually immoral, or covetous, or an idolater, or a reviler, or a drunkard, or an extortioner—not even to eat with such a person" (1 Corinthians 5:11). Actually, their only intention was to stir up strife and conflict; had they seen Jesus doing something truly blameworthy, they would not have taken a stab at His disciples (as in the matter at hand), and had they seen His disciples doing what the law does not justify (such as picking wheat on Saturday), they would have challenged their behavior with their Master (Luke 6:2).

The Savior's intention in sitting to eat with tax collectors and sinners was to guide them to the truth and to repentance. Nevertheless, Paul's prohibition from mingling with sinners is focused on those who have entered the faith and remain persistent in doing evil deeds. As proof that their intention was not made in good faith and that if it indicates anything, it indicates that it is difficult to reform them, the Savior on another occasion said: "For John came neither eating nor drinking, and they say, 'He has a demon.' The Son of Man came eating and drinking, and they say, 'Look, a glutton and a winebibber, a friend of tax collectors and sinners!'" (Matthew 11:18–19).

12 [31] – When the Lord of Glory heard their complaint, He "answered and said to them, 'Those who are well have no need of a physician, but those who are sick.'" *Sinful patients need a shepherd to ferry them to virtue, and the duty of the shepherds and servants is to give them the greatest care.* Then He quoted from the Scriptures a verse that demonstrates their lack of understanding: "But go and learn what this means: 'I desire mercy and not sacrifice'" (Matthew 9:13).[39] The law does not only consist of the sacrifice; mercy, love, and guidance are required more than sacrifice.

---

[39] Many verses prove the superiority of mercy over sacrifice, most important of which are: Hosea 6:6; 1 Samuel 15:22; Psalm 51:16–17; Proverbs 21:3; Isaiah 1:10–17; Micah 6:6–8; Ecclesiastes 5:1.

13 [32] – He concluded: "I have not come to call the righteous, but sinners, to repentance." By "righteous," He means those who are good. Some exegetes see that He meant here the Pharisees, not as a means of honoring them but as a matter of mockery and disdain. God said of Adam: "Behold, the man has become like one of Us, to know good and evil" (Genesis 3:22). His coming to save sinners is corroborated by the words of the Apostle Paul: "This is a faithful saying and worthy of all acceptance, that Christ Jesus came into the world to save sinners, of whom I am chief" (1 Timothy 1:15). Let us be warned against counting ourselves righteous, lest we miss the opportunity to repent and accept Christ's call. When we accept His call, let us keep it to the last breath.

Their Joy over His Invitation

> 14 Then the disciples of John came to Him, saying, "Why do we and the Pharisees fast often, but Your disciples do not fast?" 15 And Jesus said to them, "Can the friends of the bridegroom mourn as long as the bridegroom is with them? But the days will come when the bridegroom will be taken away from them, and then they will fast.

14 [33] – Since John's disciples undertook fasts and prayers of their own accord that God had not imposed in the Torah, as did the Pharisees' disciples, the two groups—John's disciples and the Pharisees—approached the Savior. Moved by envy and a desire to find fault in Him, they asked, "Why do we fast while Your disciples eat and drink?"

15 [34] – To explain to them that fasting is a humbling of the soul and mourning, and that is why it does not suit the disciples who are joyful over the Savior's presence, the Lord of Glory said, "Can you make the friends of the bridegroom fast while the bridegroom is with them?" By the "bridegroom" He meant Himself, and by the "friends of the bridegroom," His disciples. *While I am with My disciples, they do not need [to humble] their souls. They cannot fast or grieve; it was not good*

for them. Likening Himself to the bridegroom must have resonated well with John's disciples because their teacher had referred to Him as such when he said, "He who has the bride is the bridegroom; but the friend of the bridegroom, who stands and hears him, rejoices greatly because of the bridegroom's voice. Therefore, this joy of mine is fulfilled" (John 3:29). In fact, the period of Christ's physical presence with His disciples was their opportunity for joy and happiness, not for humility and sadness. Had they fasted then, it would have been like people mourning during a wedding.

[35] – Then He said, "But the days will come when the bridegroom will be taken away from them; then they will fast in those days." He did not mean the days after His resurrection because people had not yet understood the resurrection; He was referring to the two days after the crucifixion during which all the disciples were sad and not eating. He said they would fast because they would encounter adversity after His departure. Thus He taught those who sin—a sin that would prevent them from partaking of His Body and Blood—to be sorrowfully fasting during their deprivation of communion, as His disciples were at the time of His crucifixion and burial.

"The days will come" could mean the days after His ascension; according to this divine statement, the apostles fasted after the ascension of the Lord as the book of Acts records (Acts 13:2–3).[xii]

Liturgy Gospel
Luke 12:41–50
Parable of the Faithful Steward

PARABLE OF THE FAITHFUL STEWARD
Overview[xiii]

When Christ the Master uttered the first round of woes against the scribes and Pharisees, while dining with one of them in Galilee, they were enraged against Him. They began to monitor, perhaps He would say a word they can use to bring charges against Him to the authorities. During this, many crowded around Him at the shore of the Sea of Galilee, to the point that they trampled each other. He warned His disciples against the leaven of the Pharisees, which is their hypocrisy. The pericope dealing with His commandments to the faithful speaks first of the need to consecrate the heart to God (not to earthly possessions); then of keeping vigil in preparation for His second coming; and finally, of His reward to those whom He comes and finds keeping watch.

Reward for the Watchful[xiv]

> 41 Then Peter said to Him, "Lord, do You speak this parable only to us, or to all people?" 42 And the Lord said, "Who then is that faithful and wise steward, whom his master will make ruler over his household, to give them their portion of food in due season? 43 Blessed is that servant whom his master will find so doing when he comes. 44 Truly, I say to you that he will make him ruler over all that he has.

41 – Peter was uncertain whether the Savior's words were addressed to himself, to the apostles, or to everyone, so he asked Him.

42 – Jesus answered with a parable that clarified that He was speaking to everyone: "Who then is that faithful and wise steward, whom his master will make ruler over his household, to give them their portion of food in due season?" The term "steward" applies to all Christians

because, being granted gifts, they will be held accountable. It applies specifically to servants of the religion because they are "servants of Christ and stewards of the mysteries of God" (1 Corinthians 4:1). The Savior describes the steward as *faithful* because he does not deceive and *wise* because he distributes appropriately. These are two indispensable characteristics. By *food*, He means nourishing the mind with divine knowledge, the spirit with personal grace, and the body with its fill of physical needs—at the appropriate time and in the proper amount.

43 – "When [his master] comes" —by *master*, He is referring to Himself; if his master will find him so doing, he will bless him.

44 – As his reward, "he will make him ruler over all that he has"; he will make him his equal, give him an inheritance, and bring him to himself, in accordance with His word: "If anyone serves Me, him *My* Father will honor" (John 12:26).[xv]

Penalty for the Negligent

45 But if that servant says in his heart, "My master is delaying his coming," and begins to beat the male and female servants, and to eat and drink and be drunk, 46 the master of that servant will come on a day when he is not looking for him, and at an hour when he is not aware, and will cut him in two and appoint him his portion with the unbelievers. 47 And that servant who knew his master's will, and did not prepare himself or do according to his will, shall be beaten with many stripes. 48 But he who did not know, yet committed things deserving of stripes, shall be beaten with few. For everyone to whom much is given, from him much will be required; and to whom much has been committed, of him they will ask the more.

45 – If that evil servant says in his heart, "My master is delaying his coming," he will think the master will delay his death and resurrection. He will begin to harm his friends and followers, either bodily (such as withholding food), or psychologically (such as hiding the truth from them), while he busies himself from obeying God by engaging in worldly affairs (such as eating, drinking, and drunkenness).

46 – Then his master "will come... at an hour when he is not aware," to keep him in fear and trembling, and he "will cut him in two." He will be forbidden from the heavenly gifts prepared for the righteous and will be consigned with the "hypocrites" (the unbelievers) to Hell. This decree from the Savior on the lazy deceptive servants is very stern and serious. If He shows His mercy with all gentleness and compassion on repentant sinners, He judges with strict punishment those who belittle the advice of God and refuse the good news of salvation.[40]

47 – The Savior went on to show the differing degrees in punishment between the careless servants based on their knowledge (or lack thereof) of the will of their master. He said of the one who knows: "That servant who knew his master's will, and did not prepare himself or do according to his will, shall be beaten with many stripes." The Savior placed a sublime religious foundation: the burden of responsibility falling on the individual will depend on his knowledge, his stature, and the means available to him. Thus, the higher ranks in the church should be avoided, rather than sought after. Those who long for them should understand that they are seeking that which will increase and magnify

---

[40] Five characteristics of the faithful servant: 1) Faithful to his master and in his work; 2) Wise in anticipating his master's arrival, always saying, "Behold, the Judge is standing at the door!" (James 5:9); 3) Patient for his master's eventual arrival; 4) Using his authority to benefit others; 5) Values his master's appreciation of him.
Five characteristics of the wicked servant: 1) He doubts his master's arrival, saying, "My master is delaying his coming"; 2) Uses his authority to harm others; 3) Indulges in bodily pleasures; 4) Lives with the worldly; 5) Suddenly receives fierce unending punishment.

their responsibility, and intensify their punishment if they are careless in doing their duties. Based on this, those who serve the Lord and perform His sacraments will have a greater reward if they are faithful, and a greater punishment if they are unfaithful.

"Shall be beaten with many stripes," means the one who hears Christ's words and is lazy, does not anticipate the coming of his master, does not keep watch to prepare what the master needs, and does not fulfill his duties, will likely receive a very harsh punishment in this world. In the age to come, he will receive eternal punishment because he failed despite his conscience and despite the words in the Divine Scriptures. In the Old Testament, this principle was mentioned: "But the person who does anything presumptuously, whether he is native-born or a stranger, that one brings reproach on the Lord, and he shall be cut off from among his people" (Numbers 15:30). The book of Deuteronomy shows the punishment: "If the wicked man deserves to be beaten, that the judge will cause him to lie down and be beaten in his presence, according to his guilt, with a certain number of blows" (Deuteronomy 25:2–3).

48 – Then He says about the one who neither knows nor is prepared: "But he who did not know, yet committed things deserving of stripes, shall be beaten with few." He does not mean one who is completely ignorant of the will of God, but rather one who is knowledgeable compared to his companion mentioned above, and so he will be deserving of less stripes. The reason for his punishment is not for disobeying the commandments unbeknownst to him, but rather for doing what deserves punishment, being contrary to the law of nature and the conscience. Considering this person guilty was also indicated in the old law: "If a person sins, and commits any of these things which are forbidden to be done by the commandments of the Lord, though he does not know it, yet he is guilty and shall bear his iniquity" (Leviticus 5:17). Paul said about himself in this regard: "Although I was formerly a

blasphemer, a persecutor, and an insolent man; but I obtained mercy because I did it ignorantly in unbelief" (1 Timothy 1:13).

The Master summarized all the above by saying, "Everyone to whom much is given, from him much will be required." This indicates that those who receive sublime gifts should use and trade with them more diligently, with great attention. The shepherd's duty in the church, for example, is more sublime than all jobs in the world, because he represents Christ on earth. Because he is entrusted with caring for souls, the highest commission, therefore his responsibility is great. To save himself and save others, he must fuel God's gift in himself, not neglecting it (1 Timothy 4:14), to be an example for the flock, to not be overtaken by life's cares, to focus on reading the Holy Bible and preaching the Word of God, and to be very concerned with his flock's external life (their physical comfort and success), as well as their spiritual well-being.

Persecution of the Watchful

> 49 I came to send fire on the earth, and how I wish it were already kindled! 50 But I have a baptism to be baptized with, and how distressed I am till it is accomplished!

49 – The Savior went on to reveal the primary reason He came to the world: "I came to send fire on the earth." The *fire* resembles war and resistance.[41] The spread of Christianity in this world—a world full of sin

---

[41] "Fire" is used in the Holy Bible symbolically to describe three conditions: 1) Purifying the faithful through the work of the Holy Spirit, as the Baptist told the Jews that the Savior would baptize with the Holy Spirit and fire (Matthew 3:11); 2) Anger and destruction, as the apostle described Christ's second coming as revealed "in flaming fire taking vengeance on those who do not know God" (2 Thessalonians 1:8) and, "For our God is a consuming fire" (Hebrews 12:29); 3) Wars and resistance, as the Psalmist said, "We went through fire and through water; but You brought us out to rich fulfillment" (Psalm 66:12), and as Peter the apostle says, "Beloved, do not think it strange concerning the fiery trial which is to try you" (1 Peter 4:12). The Savior intends this last meaning by saying, "I came to send fire on the earth."

and deception—has met and continues to be met with resistance from the enemies. The Master took upon Himself all the corrupt reactions of humanity, but the result was the elimination of deception and transgression in the same way that fire consumes hay. Until now, the preaching of the Gospel is a reason for the persecution of those who follow Christ, and it is a means to cleanse the world from transgression and deception. Speaking about this fire of wars and persecution, the Savior said, "How I wish it were already kindled." *Since there is no salvation or victory except by this fire, I want it aflame. I want to set the hearts aflame with this fire of God's love and worship, even though it will be met with great resistance.*

50 – In the Lord of Glory's desire to fulfill salvation, regardless of the extent of the pain He would suffer, He said, "I have a baptism to be baptized with, and how distressed I am till it is accomplished." He called His passion and death, an anointing, a baptism, because the baptized remains a little time in the water then comes out; likewise, the Savior remained in the tomb for a little time then arose and ascended. He expressed His desire to fulfill the redemption [of humanity] by being anointed by this type of baptism; this is what He meant by, "How distressed I am till it is accomplished."

FIRST WEEK – WEDNESDAY
LOVING OTHERS

Linking the Readings:

All the readings of this day center on one theme: **Loving others**

The first prophecy exhorts believers to **fear the Lord** in all their dealings, as Isaiah charged the house of Jacob; and the second prophecy speaks of **God's blessings to those who fear Him**, as Joel promised the people of God.

The Matins Gospel commissions believers to **love their enemies**, specifically, while the Liturgy Gospel speaks of **loving others**, generally, showing that their reward will be based on their deeds.

The Pauline Epistle speaks of **pleasing others**; the Catholic Epistle reveals that our **love for them must be practical**; and the Acts reading speaks of **loving the upright**, even if they are Gentiles, as Peter revealed to Cornelius.

PROPHECIES

First Prophecy   Isaiah 2:3–11

Believers fear the Lord in all their dealings: Isaiah shows that at the coming of Christ the Master's kingdom, many people will go to Zion—the source of the Law—and there the Lord will judge justly. Then, he charges the house of Jacob to fear God in all their dealings with others: "O house of Jacob, come and let us walk in the light of the Lord," showing that they were rejected because of their evil, that "the haughtiness of men shall be bowed down, and the Lord alone shall be exalted in that day" (vv. 5, 11).

Second Prophecy   Joel 2:12–27

God's blessings to those who fear Him: Joel the prophet charges God's people to return to Him, calling out to them: "Turn to Me with all your heart, with fasting, with weeping, and with mourning. So rend your heart, and not your garments." He mentions that the Lord is zealous for His land and pities His people: "Behold, I will send you grain and new wine and oil, and you will be satisfied by them; I will no longer make you a reproach among the nations." He then gladdens them by saying: "So I will restore to you the years that the swarming locust has eaten... You shall eat in plenty and be satisfied... My people shall never be put to shame" (vv. 12–13, 19, 25–27).

PSALMS AND GOSPELS

Matins Psalm   Psalms 25:6–7

Speaking for believers who have fulfilled the Savior's commandments mentioned in the accompanying Gospel (loving their enemies, doing good to those who hate them, and blessing those who curse them), the psalm supplicates God to forgive their sins, as they forgave others: "Remember, O Lord, Your tender mercies and Your loving-kindnesses, for they are from of old. Do not remember the sins of my youth, nor my transgressions."

Matins Gospel   Luke 6:24–34

This passage shows the Savior exhorting the believers to love their enemies: "Love your enemies, do good to those who hate you, bless those who curse you" (vv. 27–28).

Liturgy Psalm   Psalms 25:20, 16

Speaking for believers who have fulfilled the Savior's commandments

in the accompanying Gospel (loving others, doing good, and lending, in imitation of their heavenly Father), this psalm supplicates God to have mercy on them as they had mercy on others: "Keep my soul, and deliver me; let me not be ashamed, for I put my trust in You. Turn Yourself to me, and have mercy on me."

Liturgy Gospel   Luke 6:35–38

This passage shows that the Savior is just to those who love others,

rewarding them according to their works: "For with the same measure that you use, it will be measured back to you" (v. 38).

EPISTLES

The Pauline Epistle   Romans 14:19–15:7

Pleasing others: The apostle commands believers to pursue things

that make for peace and the things by which one may edify another. Then he says, "We then who are strong ought to bear with the scruples of the weak, and not to please ourselves. Let each of us please his neighbor for his good, leading to edification" (vv. 15:1–2).

The Catholic Epistle   2 Peter 1:4–11

Our love for them must be practical: The apostle commands

believers: "Add to your faith virtue, to virtue knowledge, to knowledge self-control, to self-control perseverance, to perseverance godliness, to godliness brotherly kindness, and to brotherly kindness love," revealing that love must be active: "Therefore, brethren, be even more diligent to make your call and election sure [the Coptic text adds "by good works"]" (vv. 5–7, 10).

The Acts   Acts 10:9–20

Loving the upright, even if they are Gentiles: This passage mentions Peter's vision, in which he saw a great sheet let down from heaven containing creeping things and birds of the air, and the first voice saying: "Rise, Peter; kill and eat," then the response based on his objection: "What God has cleansed you must not call common." Doubtless, this indicates the need to accept all the upright, even if they are Gentiles, as Peter revealed to Cornelius: "In every nation whoever fears Him and works righteousness is accepted by Him" (vv. 13, 15, 35).

Matins Gospel
Luke 6:24–34
Loving our Enemies[xvi]

LOVING OUR ENEMIES

Overview

Most exegetes agree that today's pericope is part of the Sermon on the Mount. The two evangelists who recorded it mentioned what agreed with their specific purpose in writing. Today's passage speaks about the manifestations of the love for enemies, its reward, and the nature of the just reward being the same in kind as the deed.

Jesus Pronounces Woes[42]

24 But woe to you who are rich, For you have received your consolation. 25 Woe to you who are full, For you shall hunger. Woe to you who laugh now, For you shall mourn and weep. 26 Woe to you when all men speak well of you, For so did their fathers to the false prophets.

Manifesting the Love of Enemies

27 But I say to you who hear: Love your enemies, do good to those who hate you, 28 bless those who curse you, and pray for those who spitefully use you. 29 To him who strikes you on the one cheek, offer the other also. And from him who takes away your cloak, do not withhold your tunic either. 30 Give to everyone who asks of you. And from him who takes away your goods do not ask them back. 31 And just as you want men to do to you, you also do to them likewise.

27 – Our Savior began to commend the love of enemies: "Love your enemies." This commandment is accompanied by a condition—hope in their goodness. Not every enemy is to be loved. Those devoid of goodness and inclined to evil are not to be loved, such as Satan, false prophets, heretics, skeptics, antichrists and the like. Peter destroyed Simon the magician, and Ananias with Sapphira his wife, while Paul struck the obstinate one with blindness, and cursed the high priest and Alexander the Coppersmith. We withhold love because their great corruption tips the balance in favor of seeking relief from them, rather than having compassion on them. In like manner, divorcing the adulteress outweighs living with her.

---

[42] The Archdeacon does not seem to have commented on these verses anywhere.

As for the wicked, for whom there is hope of goodness, even if we hate them for persisting in error, we should have mercy on them for the humanity we share with them and pray for God to restore them to the right path. Almighty God gives time and forgives, but on the wicked He will take vengeance and will punish on the day of judgment. He went on to say, "Do good to those who hate you." Similarly, Paul the apostle says, "If your enemy is hungry, feed him; If he is thirsty, give him a drink; for in so doing you will heap coals of fire on his head. Do not be overcome by evil, but overcome evil with good" (Romans 12:20–21).

28 – The Lord of Glory added, "Bless those who curse you." He was first to apply this commandment, as Peter said, "When He was reviled, did not revile in return; when He suffered, He did not threaten, but committed Himself to Him who judges righteously" (1 Peter 2:23). All His disciples did likewise, as evident from the words of Paul: "Being reviled, we bless; being persecuted, we endure" (1 Corinthians 4:12).

In addition, Paul advised the people of Rome: "Bless those who persecute you; bless and do not curse" (Romans 12:14). The Savior expounds: "Pray for those who spitefully use you." He applied this commandment when He prayed for His crucifiers saying, "Father, forgive them, for they do not know what they do" (Luke 23:34). Stephen the Proto-martyr followed in His footsteps; when the enemies began to stone him "he knelt down and cried out with a loud voice, 'Lord, do not charge them with this sin'" (Acts 7:60).

29 – Our Savior proceeded to list the characteristics of the love for enemies: "To him who strikes you on the one cheek, offer the other also," so that the aggressor may be ashamed, and the evil is not reciprocated by the blow being met with the same; fire is not extinguished by fire. He was our first role model in this, as Isaiah prophesied of Him: "I gave My back to those who struck Me, and My cheeks to those who plucked out the beard; I did not hide My face from shame and spitting" (Isaiah 50:6).

This does not mean we should not defend ourselves, such that the wicked take advantage of us and we become a prey to their injustice. Following the example of our Savior and Paul His apostle, we ought to defend ourselves, not by violence, but by the power of reason, the sword of endurance, and Christian wisdom. When the Lord Jesus was struck in front of the high priest, He replied to the servant who struck Him: "If I have spoken evil, bear witness of the evil; but if well, why do you strike Me?" (John 18:23). When Ananias, the high priest, ordered Paul to be struck on his mouth for saying in front of the Sanhedrin: "I have lived in all good conscience before God until this day," Paul replied, "You sit there to judge me according to the law, yet you yourself violate the law by commanding that I be struck!" (Acts 23:1, 3).

It is clear that whoever endures injustice (to honor Christ and for spiritual reasons) manifests true power, not cowardice and weakness, and the reward would be eternal honor. As for those who take revenge on their attackers, hasten to anger, tend to quarrel, and do not cease asking for their full rights, their spirit differs from Christ's; they are praised by the world, not by Jesus.

The Savior continued His teaching: "And from him who takes away your cloak, do not withhold your tunic either." This is to avoid the causes of evil. One might object that by doing so we become naked. Yet, if we comply with God's commandment, He of necessity will take care of us with His grace and goodness. Even if we were subject to nakedness for the sake of the truth, it would not be offensive because the offense is in not complying with God's commandments or obeying the truth. Perhaps, if the attacker sees us in this condition, he might return to God; this would be a blessing for both the oppressor and the oppressed. Some exegetes claim these orders were specific to the Savior's disciples, whom He sent among strange peoples who harmed them. Actually, if they were first given to them, they are conveyed to us through them.

30 – The Savior concluded the manifestations of the love of enemies by saying, "Give to everyone who asks of you. And from him who takes away your goods do not ask them back." It is clear the order to give is addressed to all, not just to the disciples; they had nothing to give! The implication is on what *may* be given away.

31 – The Lord Jesus summarized His lofty teachings in that golden verse: "Just as you want men to do to you, you also do to them likewise." It contains a principle unparalleled in all human books. In it the treasures of wisdom and philosophy are enclosed, and it is richer than all religious and worldly laws, as He delineated with His pure mouth: "This is the Law and the Prophets" (Matthew 7:12). There is no doubt, acting according to this divine principle eliminates absolute self-love, hatred, vengefulness, gossip, fraud, and embezzlement; it establishes unity and quality in human beings. It constrains each person to look for the benefit of others, cutting off rivalries and wars, transforming our miserable world into a paradise. Behaving according to this great verse does not deny people's instinctive love of the self, but makes it a measure of our love for others, and a servant of justice and charity.

Some exegetes distinguish between the types of reactions a person exhibits as follows: meeting the evil of others by a greater evil is a demonic act; treating them in kind is a heathen act; treating them as we would like to be treated is a Christian behavior; and treating them better than they treat us is a divine work.

Reward for Loving Enemies

32 But if you love those who love you, what credit is that to you? For even sinners love those who love them. 33 And if you do good to those who do good to you, what credit is that to you? For even sinners do the same. 34 And if you lend to those from whom you hope to receive back, what credit is that to you? For even sinners lend to sinners to receive as much back.

32 – The Lord of Glory transitioned from talking about the characteristics of loving the enemies to the reward for this love: "But if you love those who love you, what credit is that to you? For even sinners love those who love them."

33 – "And if you do good to those who do good to you, what credit is that to you? For even sinners do the same."

34 – "And if you lend to those from whom you hope to receive back, what credit is that to you? For even sinners lend to sinners to receive as much back."

Liturgy Gospel
Luke 6:35–38
Loving our Enemies[xvii]

LOVING OUR ENEMIES

Overview

Most exegetes agree that today's pericope is part of the Sermon on the Mount. The two evangelists who recorded it mentioned what agreed with their specific purpose in writing. Today's passage speaks about the manifestations of the love for enemies, its reward, and the nature of the just reward being the same in kind as the deed.

The Reward

35 But love your enemies, do good, and lend, hoping for nothing in return; and your reward will be great, and you will be sons of the Most High. For He is kind to the unthankful and evil.

35 – Then He commanded: "But love your enemies, do good, and lend, hoping for nothing in return." He demonstrated the reward by saying, "Your reward will be great, and you will be sons of the Most High."

Nature of the Reward

36 Therefore be merciful, just as your Father also is merciful. 37 "Judge not, and you shall not be judged. Condemn not, and you shall not be condemned. Forgive, and you will be forgiven. 38 Give, and it will be given to you: good measure, pressed down, shaken together, and running over will be put into your bosom. For with the same measure that you use, it will be measured back to you."

36 – After the Savior recommended mercy, resembling the Heavenly Father, He went on to show that the nature of the reward is of the same type as the work.

37 – "Judge not, that you be not judged." He neither means to overturn the sentence passed on the wrongdoers, nor means not to reprimand those who deserve reproach, or else we lose fairness and justice in the homes, in commerce, and in cities and kingdoms. This could not be His intention, since He is the One who said, "If your brother sins against you, go and tell him his fault between you and him alone. If he hears you, you have gained your brother. But if he will not hear, take with you one or two more, that by the mouth of two or three witnesses every

word may be established. And if he refuses to hear them, tell it to the church. But if he refuses even to hear the church, let him be to you like a heathen and a tax collector" (Matthew 18:15–17).

We see John the Baptist scolding the Jews: "Brood of vipers! Who warned you to flee from the wrath to come?" (Matthew 3:7). Paul the apostle also commands his disciple Timothy [*sic* Titus]: "Rebuke with all authority. Let no one despise you" (Titus 2:15). When the Master said, "Judge not," He meant *Do not judge (while you are a sinner) another sinner like you or one who is even less of a sinner than you*. Paul the apostle supports this by saying, "Therefore you are inexcusable, O man, whoever you are who judge, for in whatever you judge another you condemn yourself; for you who judge practice the same things... Who are you to judge another's servant? To his own master he stands or falls" (Romans 14:4; 2:1).

James the apostle also says, "Do not speak evil of one another, brethren. He who speaks evil of a brother and judges his brother, speaks evil of the law and judges the law. But if you judge the law, you are not a doer of the law but a judge. There is one Lawgiver, who can save or destroy. Who are you to judge another?" (James 4:11–12).

Additionally, the Savior's intention by "judge not," is for people to not grow accustomed to unjustly condemning others to satisfy a desire for revenge, and not to judge those who are more righteous than themselves, and not to judge with usurped authority. He also commanded saying, "Condemn not, and you shall not be condemned. Forgive, and you will be forgiven."

38 – He went on to say to the faithful, "Give, and it will be given to you." *People will treat you as you treat them. If you are miserly and judgmental, people will treat you in kind, and if you are generous and considerate, people will treat you in the same manner.* Saying: "Good measure, pressed down, shaken together, and running over" is

metaphorical from the process of measuring grain. This description of the measure in this manner points to the full reward to those who give to the poor and needy. Saying, "Will be put into your bosom," is taken from the custom in eastern countries where people wear long broad garments, binding them with a belt, where they can carry much grain in their bosoms. The Savior augments the aforementioned meaning: "For with the same measure that you use, it will be measured back to you." James illustrates this by saying: "For judgment is without mercy to the one who has shown no mercy" (James 2:13).

In summary, if a person shows kindness, love, and longsuffering in the treatment of others, he will never be harmed. Although some people might not be affected by this behavior, and the doer might even be harmed by them, in the end, he must see himself as having profited greatly, if not in this life, then in eternal life.

FIRST WEEK – THURSDAY
SPIRITUAL GROWTH

Linking the Readings:

All the readings of this day center on one theme: **Spiritual growth**, that is, the believers' growth in the grace of the Gospel

The first prophecy speaks of **the Gospel's superiority over idols**, as Isaiah prophesied of this at the coming of Christ's kingdom; and the second prophecy speaks of **all nations turning to Him**, as the Gentiles turned to Jerusalem seeking God's face when Jerusalem's glory was restored.

The Matins Gospel speaks of **His authority over nature**, as clearly seen in the Savior's authority over the wind and sea; and the Liturgy Gospel speaks of the **growth of those who seek and obey the Gospel**—spiritual growth by divine power, just as plants sprout and grow by God's power.

The Pauline Epistle addresses how **believers need to walk in the seriousness of the Gospel**, as Paul charged the Corinthians; the Catholic Epistle speaks of **steadfastness in the Gospel**, as John the apostle commanded; and the Acts reading speaks of the **signs that follow those who evangelize**, as was seen with Philip.

PROPHECIES

First Prophecy   Isaiah 2:11–19

The Gospel's superiority over idols: In this prophecy, Isaiah reveals what will happen when Christ's kingdom arises: "The lofty looks of man shall be humbled, the haughtiness of men shall be bowed down, and the Lord alone shall be exalted in that day... But the idols He shall utterly abolish," illustrating the superiority of the Gospel over idolatrous worship (vv. 11, 18).

Second Prophecy   Zechariah 8:18–23

All nations turn to Him: This prophecy shows that the mandated fasts will turn into joy, gladness, and cheerful feasts for the house of Judah. Then it clarifies that the Gentiles will turn to Jerusalem, seeking God's face when Jerusalem's glory is restored: "Many peoples and strong nations shall come to seek the Lord of hosts in Jerusalem, and to pray before the Lord... [Then] ten men from every language of the nations shall grasp the sleeve of a Jewish man, saying, 'Let us go with you, for we have heard that God is with you'" (vv. 22–23).

PSALMS AND GOSPELS

Matins Psalm   Psalms 24:1–2

This psalm alludes to the accompanying Gospel passage, where Christ the Master reveals His authority over nature: "The earth is the Lord's, and all its fullness, the world and those who dwell therein. For He has founded it upon the seas, and established it upon the waters."

Matins Gospel   Luke 8:22–25

In this passage, the Savior displays His authority over nature, as the disciples remarked when they saw Him still the wind and save the boat: "Who can this be? For He commands even the winds and water, and they obey Him" (v. 25).

Liturgy Psalm   Psalms 118:14, 18

Speaking for those who embrace the Gospel and obey it, this psalm confesses that God has enriched their spiritual growth and salvation (paralleling this spiritual growth with what comes in the accompanying

Gospel passage, which shows that God is the One who enriches crops—and not the farmer), and that Almighty God has allowed them to be chastened, yet has saved them: "The Lord is my strength and song, and He has become my salvation. The Lord has chastened me severely, but He has not given me over to death."

Liturgy Gospel   Mark 4:21–29

This passage shows that God provides spiritual growth for those who

receive and live by His Gospel—akin to the parable of the growth of the crop without the farmer's contribution. This is shown by the Savior's saying to His disciples: "For whoever has, to him more will be given; but whoever does not have, even what he has will be taken away from him," that is, whoever receives the word of life and lives by it grows spiritually in virtue, but the one who receives it and does not live by it forfeits its value (v. 25).

EPISTLES

The Pauline Epistle   1 Corinthians 4:16–5:9

Walking in the seriousness of the Gospel: In this epistle, Paul rebukes

the Corinthians for accepting the sexually immoral person, commanding them to deliver him "to Satan for the destruction of the flesh that his spirit may be saved." Then, he instructs them to purge out the old leaven to be a new lump, saying: "Therefore let us keep the feast, not with old leaven, nor with the leaven of malice and wickedness, but with the unleavened bread of sincerity and truth" (vv. 5:5, 8).

The Catholic Epistle   1 John 1:8–2:11

Steadfastness in the Gospel: Here, the apostle clarifies that whoever

claims to know Christ yet "does not keep His commandments, is a liar, and the truth is not in him." He continues: "He who says he abides in Him ought himself also to walk just as He walked," and gives an example: "He who loves his brother abides in the light, and there is no cause for stumbling in him" (vv. 2:4, 6, 10).

The Acts   Acts 8:3–13

Signs that follow those who evangelize: This passage catalogues the

great signs Philip had done, "For unclean spirits, crying with a loud voice, came out of many who were possessed; and many who were paralyzed and lame were healed." Then this passage shows that: "Simon himself also believed; and when he was baptized he continued with Philip, and was amazed, seeing the miracles and signs which were done" (vv. 7, 13).

Matins Gospel
Luke 8:22–25
Jesus Rebukes the Wind and the Water
See Fourth Week Wednesday Liturgy Gospel (Mark 4:35–41) of the Great Fast.

Liturgy Gospel
Mark 4:21–29
[Word of the Gospel]

[WORD OF THE GOSPEL]

Overview

During His second circuit of ministry in Galilee, when the Master told His disciples (and the multitude by the Sea of Galilee) the parable of the sower who went out to sow, the disciples came to ask Him its meaning privately. After He explained it to them, He proceeded (in today's pericope) to speak about the word of the Gospel, which is represented by the plant. First, He showed the need for spreading the Gospel to people, and then the spiritual growth of those who live by the Gospel. This growth will be by the power of God alone, for "neither he who plants is anything, nor he who waters, but God who gives the increase" (1 Corinthians 3:7).

Obligation to Spread the Gospel

> 21 Also He said to them, "Is a lamp brought to be put under a basket or under a bed? Is it not to be set on a lampstand? 22 For there is nothing hidden which will not be revealed, nor has anything been kept secret but that it should come to light. 23 If anyone has ears to hear, let him hear."

21 – The Savior emphasized to His disciples the importance of disseminating the teaching of the Gospel that they heard from Him to the people: "Is a lamp brought to be put under a basket or under a bed? Is it not to be set on a lampstand?" *Just as a lit lamp is not meant to be placed under a basket but on a lampstand to give light to those who are in the house, likewise, My Gospel must be uplifted to enlighten all and direct their paths.* Paul corroborated by advising for their behavior to be "without fault in the midst of a crooked and perverse generation, among whom you shine as lights in the world" (Philippians 2:15).

22 – Having explained the parable of the sower privately to the disciples (and not to the multitude), Jesus clarified that this condition is temporary "for nothing is secret that will not be revealed, nor anything hidden that will not be known and come to light" (Luke 8:17). Some exegetes explain that this signifies that the Christian teachings are available privately and publicly, unlike the pagan philosophy that appears to be for the multitude but is restricted to privileged individuals.

23 – After He showed them the importance of every word He had said, He directed their attention to how critical it is for them to open their hearts to understand and do accordingly: "If anyone has ears to hear, let him hear."

Their Spiritual Growth

24 Then He said to them, "Take heed what you hear. With the same measure you use, it will be measured to you; and to you who hear, more will be given. 25 For whoever has, to him more will be given; but whoever does not have, even what he has will be taken away from him."

24 – He proceeded to encourage them to benefit from His teachings by saying, "With the same measure you use, it will be measured to you." One who puts forth effort in teaching others will increase in knowledge.

25 – He revealed this mystery: "Whoever has, to him more will be given; but whoever does not have, even what he has will be taken away from him." *Whoever has good intentions and a clear mind, and accepts the word of God and lives by it, receives a full reward, inheriting God's kingdom and delight; whoever does not have good intentions, knows the law but does not live by it, whatever he has (his knowledge) will be taken away—he will gain nothing from it.* This relationship applies to the spiritual as it does to the physical, as Solomon the Sage says, "He who has a slack hand becomes poor, but the hand of the diligent makes

rich" (Proverbs 10:4). One who perseveres on the spiritual path will gradually advance on the ladder of virtue, and one who perseveres in teaching others increases in knowledge.

Their Divine Growth

26 And He said, "The kingdom of God is as if a man should scatter seed on the ground, 27 and should sleep by night and rise by day, and the seed should sprout and grow, he himself does not know how. 28 For the earth yields crops by itself: first the blade, then the head, after that the full grain in the head. 29 But when the grain ripens, immediately he puts in the sickle, because the harvest has come."

26 – After the Savior encouraged His disciples to spread the good news of the Gospel, indicating the spiritual growth of those who live by it, He went on to show that this growth will be by the power of God, giving this parable which was only mentioned in Mark's Gospel: "If a man should scatter seed on the ground." The intended man in the parable is not Christ, because it is unacceptable to say that the Lord of Glory does not know how spiritual growth occurs; the one intended is any farmer, any preacher. As a farmer plows the land, scatters the seeds, and waters it, and only Almighty God provides the growth, likewise, the servant of the Gospel needs to plant the word in the hearts of the hearers, and only God can cause the growth of the word until it bears fruit.

27 – As the farmer does not know how plants grow, is unable to understand the secret of the life of the plant, and can only see the result of this growth in the fruit, likewise, the servant of the word of God does not perceive the mode of spiritual growth, and only sees the outcome of this spiritual growth in repentance, faith, holiness, merciful acts, and prayer. We find the apostle saying, "I planted, Apollos watered, but God gave the increase" (1 Corinthians 3:6). This does not cancel the

individual's responsibility to take the necessary steps for spiritual growth, as one takes for physical growth; therefore, the apostle also says, "Work out your own salvation with fear and trembling" (Philippians 2:12). He encourages all the priests to teach the congregation the truth, neither forcing them to accept or live by the word, nor paying too much attention to the growth of what they planted in the hearts of the congregation, but to leave that to God who gives the increase, and to avoid falling into despair if they do not immediately see the fruits of their teachings.

28 – They will understand that, although the actual growth of the plant is invisible, even if its results are visible, likewise, spiritual growth is invisible, even if its results are visible.

29 – By saying, "But when the grain ripens, immediately he puts in the sickle, because the harvest has come," He means that at the end of time, Christ will send His angels to gather all the creation. John the Visionary supports this by writing, "Then I looked, and behold, a white cloud, and on the cloud sat One like the Son of Man, having on His head a golden crown, and in His hand a sharp sickle. And another angel came out of the temple, crying with a loud voice to Him who sat on the cloud, 'Thrust in Your sickle and reap, for the time has come for You to reap, for the harvest of the earth is ripe.' So, He who sat on the cloud thrust in His sickle on the earth, and the earth was reaped" (Revelation 14:14–16).

FIRST WEEK – FRIDAY
RELIANCE ON GOD

Linking the Readings:

All the readings of this day center on one theme: **Reliance on God**—the need of the believers to rely on Him

The first prophecy speaks of **God's blessings to those who rely on Him**, as He promised the children of Israel if they obey Him; while the second prophecy speaks of **the entire lack that the wicked** will endure, as Isaiah promised Jerusalem and Judah in consequence to their grave evils.

The Matins Gospel speaks of Him **healing those who take refuge in Him from the illness of sin**, as the Lord Jesus healed the leper; and the Liturgy Gospel speaks of **His goodness to all who ask of Him**, as He promised, "Ask, and it will be given to you; seek, and you will find; knock, and it will be opened to you."

The Pauline Epistle speaks of **serving others from what we have been granted**; the Catholic Epistle speaks of **welcoming strangers**, as John the apostle praised Gaius for his hospitality to strangers; and the Acts reading speaks of **serving from what we have**, as Peter, with the gift of healing that he was granted, healed the man crippled from his mother's womb.

PROPHECIES

First Prophecy   Deuteronomy 6:3–7:26

God's blessings to the obedient: This prophecy speaks of God's blessings to those who abide by His commandments [and rely on Him], as He said to Israel: "Because you listen to these judgments, and keep and do them, that the Lord your God will keep with you the covenant and the mercy which He swore to your fathers. And He will love you and bless you and multiply you; He will also bless the fruit of your womb and the fruit of your land, your grain and your new wine and your oil, the increase of your cattle and the offspring of your flock... there shall not be a male or female barren among you or among your livestock. And the Lord will take away from you all sickness" (vv. 7:12–15).

Second Prophecy   Isaiah 3:1–14

The entire lack of the wicked: This prophecy completes the previous meaning, showing that God plundered all from the wicked: "For behold, the Lord, the Lord of hosts, takes away from Jerusalem and from Judah the stock and the store, the whole supply of bread and the whole supply of water; the mighty man and the man of war, the judge and the prophet, and the diviner and the elder; the captain of fifty and the honorable man, the counselor and the skillful artisan, and the expert enchanter. I will give children to be their princes, and babes shall rule over them" (vv. 1–4).

PSALMS AND GOSPELS

Matins Psalm   Psalms 30:1–2

Speaking on behalf of the leper in the accompanying Gospel passage (symbolic of those leprous with sin), this psalm glorifies God for caring for and healing him: "I will extol You, O Lord, for You have lifted me up, and have not let my foes rejoice over me. O Lord my God, I cried out to You, and You healed me."

Matins Gospel   Luke 5:12–16

This passage shows that the Savior heals the sins of sick believers who take refuge in Him, as He answered the leper who entreated Him saying: "'Lord, if You are willing, You can make me clean'... 'I am willing; be cleansed.' Immediately the leprosy left him" (vv. 12–13).

Liturgy Psalm   Psalms 13:5–6

This psalm alludes to the Gospel passage which shows that God responds to the prayers of those who rely on Him, and so praises Him: "But I have trusted in Your mercy; my heart shall rejoice in Your salvation. I will sing to the Lord, because He has dealt bountifully with me."

Liturgy Gospel   Luke 11:1–10

This passage shows God's goodness to all who ask of Him, as He advised His disciples after giving them the example of borrowing three loaves: "So I say to you, ask, and it will be given to you; seek, and you will find; knock, and it will be opened to you" (v. 9).

EPISTLES

The Pauline Epistle   Romans 12:6–21

Serving others with their talents: In this passage, the apostle commands believers to serve each other with their various gifts, encouraging them to care for others: "Be kindly affectionate to one another with brotherly love... Do not set your mind on high things, but associate with the humble." He concludes his exhortation: "Do not be overcome by evil, but overcome evil with good" (vv. 10, 16, 21).

The Catholic Epistle   3 John 1:1–14[43]

Welcoming strangers: Here, the apostle praises the beloved Gaius for his kindly treatment of brethren and strangers: "We therefore ought to receive such, that we may become fellow workers for the truth." In blaming Diotrephes (who does not receive the brethren, but puts them out of the church), he addresses Gaius saying, "Do not imitate what is evil, but what is good. He who does good is of God, but he who does evil has not seen God" (vv. 8, 11).

The Acts   Acts 2:42–3:9

Serving from what they have: This passage starts by showing how "all who believed were together, and had all things in common." Then it speaks of Peter and John healing the man lame from his mother's womb, to whom Peter said: "Silver and gold I do not have, but what I do have I give you: In the name of Jesus Christ of Nazareth, rise up and walk" (vv. 2:44; 3:6).

Matins Gospel
Luke 5:12–16
Healing the Leper[44]

---

[43] This numbering differs in the Coptic text such that 1 John has 15 verses, while the English has only 14 verses; it is the same content of the entire epistle that is read here.
[44] Healing the leper was also mentioned in Matthew 8:1–4 and Mark 1:40–45.

HEALING THE LEPER

Overview

After the Savior called His first four disciples to follow Him (Peter, Andrew, James, and John—after performing His miracles in Capernaum), He started the first circuit of ministry in Galilee. While in one of the cities, a leper approached Him requesting to be cleansed. The pericope dealing with the issue of this sick man (sick with the leprosy of sin) speaks of seeking forgiveness (symbolized by the leper's request to be cleansed), of the Savior's compassion in granting the man's wish, and of broadcasting this miracle among the people.

Request for Cleansing

> 12 And it happened when He was in a certain city, that behold, a man who was full of leprosy saw Jesus; and he fell on his face and implored Him, saying, "Lord, if You are willing, You can make me clean."

12 – Christ the Master walked in the cities and towns preaching, and the multitude followed Him to listen to His teachings and see His miracles. Once, while He was in a certain city, a man full of leprosy saw Him and decided to touch Him in hopes of being cleansed from his disease. Perhaps hearing of His miracles and having confidence that he will attain his goal propelled the man to enter in among the crowd, despite the law's warning. The law prohibits a leper from interacting with the populace; this is to induce people to end their persistence in their desires that lead to this sickness, and to teach them that whatever is foreign to God's creation and human nature degrades humans from their status and makes them strangers. It shows the extent to which sins that defile a person can distance him from his Creator.

Someone might ask, "If his body was full of leprosy, how was he not prevented from entering among the crowd?" First and foremost, this was an act of mercy on him from God, and then secondly, his condition having become second nature to him [he was absentminded], and finally, for people to know that the nature of the leper is not in itself unclean but that the law sets the diseased person apart to be an example for others. This is evident in that when a leper is cleansed from the disease's spread throughout his body, he is restored to the community. Once this leper saw Christ, he came and bowed before Him saying, "Lord, if You are willing, You can make me clean." From the extent of his confidence and his sure belief that the Lord can cleanse him, he laid his case before Him—just as humans leave their problems before their Creator.

The Response

> 13 Then He put out His hand and touched him, saying, "I am willing; be cleansed." Immediately the leprosy left him. 14 And He charged him to tell no one, "But go and show yourself to the priest, and make an offering for your cleansing, as a testimony to them, just as Moses commanded."

13 – When Jesus heard the request of the leper, He had compassion on him, and, as Mark wrote, "stretched out His hand and touched him"[45] saying, "I am willing; be cleansed." Some exegetes ponder how the Savior of All, the keeper of the law, could place His hand on the head of a leper contrary to the law. Some answer that His actions were to declare that He is the Lord over the law. Others answer that He did not put His hand on a leprous body, rather, before He had stretched His hand, the area where He touched had become normal skin.

---

[45] [Mark 1:41].

A second group ponders why Christ did not just say a word so that the man would be cleansed, as He did with the daughter of the Canaanite woman and the daughter of Jairus, but rather put His hand on that man. They answer that He acted to show the Jews that He is not like Elijah who would not put out his hand for fear of breaking the law; He is the One who cleanses defilements by whatever method He desires.

A third group ponders why He accompanied: "I am willing; be cleansed" with laying His hand upon the man. They answer that He did this to reveal His divinity. As God, He can combine the word with the work, unlike the prophets and the apostles[xviii] who need to ask or receive power. The evangelist writes, "Immediately the leprosy left him," declaring that nature obeys its Creator.

14 – Before dismissing him, Jesus charged him to keep silent about the matter so that the priests do not antagonize him, claiming he is not completely cured, and forbid him from mingling with the crowd. This is incomparably extreme wisdom from the Lord of Glory and shows humility devoid of boasting.

At other times, the Master ordered the healed individual to go tell all that God did, so people do not become lax in offering thanks to the giver. To keep the priests from an opportunity to accuse the Savior, He ordered the leper to go show himself to the priests, so they do not declare him unclean. By adding, "Make an offering for your cleansing, as a testimony to them, just as Moses commanded," the Savior again intended to keep from giving the priests a chance of accusing him of not following the Mosaic law.[46] Note that before beginning His public

---

[46] The Offering of the leper. The cleansing ritual for lepers mentioned in Leviticus 14:1–32 may be summed up as follows: The one being cleansed takes two birds, cedar wood, scarlet, and hyssop. One of the birds is killed in a vessel over water, and the other bird and the wood are dipped in its blood and used to sprinkle the one being cleansed seven times, and then the bird is released. The person is to wash his clothes, shave his hair, enter the camp, and remain outside the house seven days. On the

ministry at the age of 30, the Master followed and kept all the Mosaic laws very meticulously, but during His public ministry, sometimes He kept the law to avoid the attack of the priests, and at others He dismissed the law because its time had ended by the unveiling of the new law. "As a testimony to them," meant for His action to be evidence against their accusations that He breaks the law.

Also note that the Savior did not send this leper to wash in the Pool of Siloam, as He did with the man born blind (John 9:7); this is to avoid the leper going through the market and being exposed to attack for mingling with people before his healing is declared.

The Report Spread

> 15 However, the report went around concerning Him all the more; and great multitudes came together to hear, and to be healed by Him of their infirmities. 16 So He Himself often withdrew into the wilderness and prayed.

15 – As for the man, "He went out and," as Mark writes, "began to proclaim it freely, and to spread the matter, so that Jesus could no longer openly enter the city, but was outside in deserted places; and they came to Him from every direction."[47] Christ's fame spreading was due to the many miracles He did, and due to the leper spreading the news everywhere.

16 – The evangelist saying, "He himself often withdrew into the wilderness and prayed" encourages the servants of the word not to

---

eighth day, he takes two lambs, one ewe lamb, and flour. He offers one of the lambs as a sin offering and offers the other as a burnt offering. If he is poor, he takes one lamb and two turtledoves or pigeons—one as a sin offering and the other as a burnt offering.
[47] [Mark 1:45].

exceed certain boundaries in dealing with the congregation in a way that demeans the dignity of their job, and shows them that their withdrawal at a certain time is one of their most important duties, because by doing so they will receive great benefits. If intermittent withdrawal and prayer were beneficial for the Lord of Glory—who is pure, free of any defects, without sin or any semblance of sin—how much more so for the servants and for us sinners.

Liturgy Gospel
Luke 11:1–10
Exhortation to Pray
See Leave–Taking Sunday Evening Gospel until verse ten.

FIRST WEEK – SATURDAY
WALKING IN PERFECTION

Linking the Readings:

All the readings of this day center on one theme: **Walking in perfection**

The Matins Gospel speaks of some of **the Savior's laws to believers who are walking in perfection**; and the Liturgy Gospel speaks of **encouraging them to imitate His perfection**.

The Pauline Epistle speaks of the **importance of doing good**; the Catholic Epistle speaks of **being patient during temptations**; and the Acts reading speaks of believers' **exposure to trials for the word's sake**, as Paul was subjected to by the Jews.

PSALMS AND GOSPELS

Matins Psalm   Psalms 119:57–58

This psalm alludes to the Savior's commandments to His people (that are mentioned in the accompanying Gospel passage), and speaking for them, it entreats Him, begging mercy, and saying: "You are my portion, O Lord; I have said that I would keep Your words. I entreated Your favor with my whole heart; be merciful to me according to Your word."

Matins Gospel   Matthew 5:25–37

This passage speaks of the Savior's commandments to His people:

"Agree with your adversary quickly, while you are on the way with him... But I say to you that whoever looks at a woman to lust for her has already committed adultery with her in his heart... But I say to you, do not swear at all... But let your 'Yes' be 'Yes,' and your 'No', 'No'" (vv. 25, 28, 34, 37).

Liturgy Psalm   Psalms 5:1–2

Speaking for believers, this psalm confesses God's royalty and divinity (indicating His befitting perfection that is mentioned in the accompanying Gospel) and pleads with Him to answer their requests: "Give ear to my words, O Lord, consider my meditation. Give heed to the voice of my cry, my King and my God."

Liturgy Gospel   Matthew 5:38–48

This passage shows how the Savior encourages believers to imitate His perfection: "Therefore you shall be perfect, just as your Father in heaven is perfect" (v. 48).

EPISTLES

The Pauline Epistle   Romans 12:1–21

The importance of doing good: In this epistle, Paul commissions believers not to imitate this world, then he says: "But be transformed by the renewing of your mind, that you may prove what is that good and acceptable and perfect will of God." Then, he urges them to "abhor what is evil. Cling to what is good... [and]... Have regard for good things in the sight of all men" (vv. 2, 9, 17).

The Catholic Epistle   James 1:1–12

Being patient during temptations: Here, James encourages believers to be patient and endure when they fall into various trials, and then reveals the reward for those who endure: "Blessed is the man who endures temptation; for when he has been approved, he will receive the crown of life which the Lord has promised to those who love Him" (v. 12).

The Acts   Acts 21:27–39

Exposure to trials for the word's sake: This passage speaks of Paul being tried before the commander after the whole city became unsettled: "And all the city was disturbed; and the people ran together, seized Paul, and dragged him out of the temple; and immediately the doors were shut." They sought to kill him, but news of him reached the commander, who inquired into his case (v. 30).

Matins Gospel
Matthew 5:25–37
Some of the Savior's Commandments

SOME OF THE SAVIOR'S COMMANDMENTS

Overview[xix]

After Christ selected His 12 disciples (during the second of His three circuits of ministry in Galilee), He began to present His new law—the Law of Christian goodness and perfection—for the first time from atop the mountain. This Law, known as the Sermon on the Mount, occupies three full chapters in Matthew's Gospel. This pericope, dealing with one aspect of this ageless sermon—the characteristics of Christian perfection—is arranged in the following order: avoiding swearing in conversations with people [the subject of the Matins Gospel], peacefulness with all, and the love of enemies—to imitate the perfect and holy God.

Danger of neglecting the opportunity of life[48]

25 Agree with your adversary quickly, while you are on the way with him, lest your adversary deliver you to the judge, the judge hand you over to the officer, and you be thrown into prison. 26 Assuredly, I say to you, you will by no means get out of there till you have paid the last penny.[49]

25 [58] – After the Savior reproached the sinners in the previous verses for insisting on their stubbornness and wasting the opportunity given during the age of grace, without taking advantage of it to complete their repentance, here, He started to show them the resulting great danger. He portrayed the sinner as a man taken by his adversary to the court for judgment. Then He explained how [the accused] should interact with him while they are still on the way: "When you go with your adversary to the magistrate, make every effort along the way to settle with him." Our great strong *adversary* who is ready to present his case against us in great detail is God's just law that demands all His dues. The *magistrate* is the just judge who sits to judge on the day of judgment. The *way* is life, the lifetime opportunity. *Settling* with the adversary is reconciling with him before reaching the place of judgment. All this would mean that we should ask for remission and forgiveness from God before we leave this earth to the eternal world.

---

[48] Commentary on these verses taken from the Third Week Tuesday Matins Gospel (Luke 12:58–59). The numbers in brackets refer to the verses in Luke.
[49] See the Sermon on the Mount (Matthew 5:25–26). There, they urge people to seek peace and to forgive others' sins, while the intent here is to seek forgiveness from God and to reconcile with Him.

Matthew says, "Agree with your adversary quickly, while you are on the way with him," *before death overtakes you and you miss the opportunity to meet your accomplishments because the wise person takes advantage of every opportunity before losing it and uses all the means in their due time.* Similarly, the Sage said, "Do not go hastily to court; for what will you do in the end, when your neighbor has put you to shame" (Proverbs 25:8). In the same spirit Isaiah said, "Seek the Lord while He may be found, call upon Him while He is near" (Isaiah 55:6). The psalmist said, "For this cause everyone who is godly shall pray to You in a time when You may be found" (Psalm 32:6). In the same manner, the Savior addressed the Jews who refused to believe in Him: "You will seek Me and not find Me" (John 7:34).

After the previous command, Jesus warned them against irreconcilability: "Lest he drag you to the judge, the judge deliver you to the officer, and the officer throw you into prison." Matthew writes, "Lest your *adversary*[50] deliver you to the judge, the judge hand you over to the officer, and you be thrown into prison." The *judge* is the Just Judge. The *officer* refers to His angels. The *prison* is Hades. All of this means that if we continue in our stubbornness—in our sins—not asking for forgiveness before death, we will be sentenced to eternal imprisonment—Hades.

26 [59] – The Lord of Glory summed this up: "I tell you, you shall not depart from there till you have paid the very last mite,"[xx] *[answered for] the slightest sin [oversight].* Thus, He concluded His reproach to the multitude for their inability to discern the time of His coming while emphasizing the importance of reconciling with God through repentance and faith before it is too late.

---

[50] Some exegetes think the *adversary* refers to the lusts, others think it refers to Satan, while Chrysostom thinks it refers to whoever is owed something from a compatriot [1.16.13 (NPNF1 10:111)].

Cutting off Offenses[51]

> 27 You have heard that it was said, "You shall not commit adultery"; 28 but I say to you that everyone who looks at a woman with lust for her has already committed adultery with her in his heart. 29 If your right eye makes you stumble, tear it out and throw it from you; for it is better for you to lose one of the parts of your body, than for your whole body to be thrown into hell. 30 If your right hand makes you stumble, cut it off and throw it from you; for it is better for you to lose one of the parts of your body, than for your whole body to go into hell.

27–30 [8][xxi] – Jesus decreed how we can avoid offenses: "If your hand or foot causes you to sin, cut it off and cast it from you."

[9] – "And if your eye causes you to sin, pluck it out and cast it from you." *If you have a relative or a friend, or a bad opinion that prevents you from the truth, turn and cast it away from you. For it is better for you to enter life crippled or blind than to be cast into the fire having two feet and two eyes. It is better for you to cling onto the Truth and unite with the Creator (avoiding these) than for these possessions to drag you away,* as the evangelist said of him [the rich young man], "He was sad at this word, and went away sorrowful, for he had great possessions" (Mark 10:22).

---

[51] Commentary on these verses taken from the Second Sunday of Epep Liturgy Gospel (Matthew 18:8–9). The numbers in brackets refer to the verses in Matthew 18.

[On Divorce][52]

> 31 Furthermore it has been said, "Whoever divorces his wife, let him give her a certificate of divorce." 32 But I say to you that whoever divorces his wife for any reason except sexual immorality causes her to commit adultery; and whoever marries a woman who is divorced commits adultery. 33 Again you have heard that it was said to those of old, "You shall not swear falsely, but shall perform your oaths to the Lord."

31–33 [9] Although the Savior forbade divorce because it is detrimental, He decided the marriage should not continue in the case where the wife commits sexual immorality; He permitted divorce for this reason only. He stated that whoever divorces his wife for any reason except sexual immorality causes her to commit adultery (Matthew 5:31) because she marries another man while her husband is still alive, as Paul the apostle writes, "So then if, while her husband lives, she marries another man, she will be called an adulteress" (Romans 7:3). Then, the Lord of Glory said that whoever divorces his wife for any reason except sexual immorality and marries another woman becomes an adulterer, and likewise, whoever marries a divorced woman becomes an adulterer.

Avoid Swearing

> 34 But I say to you, do not swear at all: neither by heaven, for it is God's throne; 35 nor by the earth, for it is His footstool; nor by Jerusalem, for it is the city of the great King. 36 Nor shall you swear by your head, because you cannot make one hair white or black. 37 But let your "Yes" be "Yes," and your "No," "No." For whatever is more than these is from the evil one.

---

[52] Commentary on these verses taken from the Fifth Week Wednesday Matins Gospel (Mark 10:9). The number in brackets refers to the verse in Mark.

34 – Our Savior began His words on the first characteristic of Christian perfection in the Gospel passage—avoiding swearing. He cross-referenced to the words in the law of Moses by saying: "Again you have heard that it was said to those of old, 'You shall not swear falsely, but shall perform your oaths to the Lord.'" Here, He is referring to the third commandment: "You shall not take the name of the Lord your God in vain, for the Lord will not hold him guiltless who takes His name in vain" (Exodus 20:7), and to God's words: "And you shall not swear by My name falsely, nor shall you profane the name of your God: I am the Lord" (Leviticus 19:12).

The Savior wanted to draw the attention of His hearers to the fact that the Law of Justice requires people to have genuine faith, but the Law of Virtue and Perfection (whose foundation He began to lay on the Mount) requires otherwise: "But I say to you, do not swear at all"; the person is neither to confirm nor to lie. The Israelites used to swear by idols. Since they could not be dissuaded from swearing altogether, the first law allowed them to take honest oaths, and Christ came and forbade swearing altogether. By saying, "Do not swear at all," He wanted to destroy the two views held by Jewish scholars: the first of which is that God forbids only false oaths; and the second is that swearing by the creation (such as heaven or earth) is not a sin in the first place.

The Savior's words, "Do not swear at all," should not be understood as an absolute ban on oaths. There are two types of oath; one forbidden while the other permitted. The forbidden oath is uttered to support falsehood, is used in ordinary unnecessary speech, or is useless—it causes contempt for God.

The Savior's intention to forbid oaths that issue from normal discussions is evident in His words: "But let your 'Yes' be 'Yes,' and your 'No,' 'No.'" As for permissible oaths, they are the legal oaths; they are the only way to show the truth and end every dispute when evidence is lacking. Moses allowed this for the children of Israel, by the commandment of God: "If a man delivers to his neighbor a donkey, an ox, a sheep, or any animal to keep, and it dies, is hurt, or driven away, no one seeing it, then an oath of the Lord shall be between them both, that he has not put his hand into his neighbor's goods; and the owner of it shall accept that, and he shall not make it good" (Exodus 22:10, 11). Concerning this decisive oath, Paul the apostle said, "For men indeed swear by the greater, and an oath for confirmation is for them an end of all dispute" (Hebrews 6:16).

Evidence that legal oaths are permissible are the oath God personally took on Himself, of Christ on the night of His crucifixion, of the angels, the prophets, and the apostles.[xxii] The following conditions must be met for an oath to be legal: swearing truthfully (swearing falsely desecrates the name of God), swearing by something decent and possible (not on something despicable or impermissible, such as joking, jesting, or harming), and swearing for a valid reason or of extreme necessity. Whoever takes swearing lightly insults the name of God. Bearing these conditions in mind, a Christian, when legally ordered to take an oath, must swear reverently, not as a means to be forced to speak truthfully, but to convince others of his honesty.

This is concerning swearing by God Almighty. Oaths by His righteous ones and all His creatures have been forbidden by some as a pagan custom because they imply that those created are sinless, while some allowed them under the pretext that swearing by those created applies the oath to their Creator. Honoring or despising them applies to their Master.

After the Savior had finished forbidding swearing in general, He more specifically said, "Do not swear at all: neither by heaven, for it is God's throne..."

35 – "...nor by the earth, for it is His footstool; nor by Jerusalem, for it is the city of the great King." The Israelites had sworn by these things in the past, but He forbade this. They had believed that God was a body (they described Him as a body); in fact, He is Spirit and has no throne or footstool. As for the prohibition from swearing by heaven or earth, it is to keep people from worshiping them under the illusion that these are great in and of themselves.

36 – Regarding His words: "Nor shall you swear by your head," its purpose (as many scholars surmise) is to protect the head from damage if one commits perjury. Whoever swears by his head for any reason is as if he is asking God to preserve his head if he is telling the truth, or destroy him if his oath is false.

37 – "But let your 'Yes' be 'Yes,' and your 'No,' 'No.' For whatever is more than these is from the evil one." The phrase "For whatever is more than these" means either a negative oath or a lie, both of which are the work of Satan. If a person were truthful in saying yes or no, the oath would be unnecessary.

Liturgy Gospel
Matthew 5:38–48
Christian Perfection[xxiii]

CHRISTIAN PERFECTION

Overview

After Christ selected His 12 disciples (during the second of His three circuits of ministry in Galilee), He began to present His new law—the Law of Christian goodness and perfection—for the first time from atop the mountain. This Law, known as the Sermon on the Mount, occupies three full chapters in Matthew's Gospel. This pericope, dealing with one aspect of this ageless sermon—the characteristics of Christian perfection—is arranged in the following order: avoiding swearing in conversations with people, peacefulness with all, and the love of enemies—to imitate the perfect and holy God.

Peace with All

> 38 You have heard that it was said, "An eye for an eye and a tooth for a tooth." 39 But I tell you not to resist an evil person. But whoever slaps you on your right cheek, turn the other to him also. 40 If anyone wants to sue you and take away your tunic, let him have your cloak also. 41 And whoever compels you to go one mile, go with him two. 42 Give to him who asks you, and from him who wants to borrow from you do not turn away.

38 – After the Savior finished speaking about swearing and the importance of avoiding it, He touched on the second characteristic of Christian perfection: peace with all. He said, "You have heard that it was said, 'An eye for an eye and a tooth for a tooth.'" He is referring to the legal decree of making the punishment of the same nature as the deed, to keep people from committing evils out of fear that they will be punished in kind.

39 – "But I tell you not to resist an evil person." *I command you to endure harm,* or as Paul the apostle said, "Beloved, do not avenge yourselves, but rather give place to wrath; for it is written, 'Vengeance is Mine, I will repay,' says the Lord" (Romans 12:19). Peter the apostle supported this by saying, "Not returning evil for evil or reviling for reviling, but on the contrary blessing, knowing that you were called to this, that you may inherit a blessing" (1 Peter 3:9).

Since the primitive nature of the Israelites had not yet been trained to doing good—to deserve the law of perfection—they had been indoctrinated with the law of justice. There is no contradiction between the two laws, for the former completes the latter. The law of perfection pervades all creation (because it was impossible for the minds to conjure up this law), and the Gentiles accepted it with confidence in its Author, whose sincere desire for the salvation of Israel they witnessed. After saying not to "resist an evil person," He further commented, "But whoever slaps you on your right cheek, turn the other to him also."

40 [29][53] – Our Savior proceeded to list the characteristics of the love for enemies: "To him who strikes you on the one cheek, offer the other also," so that the aggressor may be ashamed, and the evil is not reciprocated by the blow being met with the same; fire is not extinguished by fire. He was our first role model in this, as Isaiah prophesied of Him: "I gave My back to those who struck Me, and My cheeks to those who plucked out the beard; I did not hide My face from shame and spitting" (Isaiah 50:6).

---

[53] Commentary on this verse taken from the First Week Wednesday Matins Gospel (Luke 6:29). The number in brackets refers to the verse in Luke.

This does not mean we should not defend ourselves, such that the wicked take advantage of us and we become a prey to their injustice. Following the example of our Savior and Paul His apostle, we ought to defend ourselves, not by violence, but by the power of reason, the sword of endurance, and Christian wisdom. When the Lord Jesus was struck in front of the high priest, He replied to the servant who struck Him: "If I have spoken evil, bear witness of the evil; but if well, why do you strike Me?" (John 18:23). When Ananias, the high priest, ordered Paul to be struck on his mouth for saying in front of the Sanhedrin: "I have lived in all good conscience before God until this day," Paul replied, "You sit there to judge me according to the law, yet you yourself violate the law by commanding that I be struck!" (Acts 23:1, 3).

It is clear that whoever endures injustice (to honor Christ and for spiritual reasons) manifests true power, not cowardice and weakness, and the reward would be eternal honor. As for those who take revenge on their attackers, hasten to anger, tend to quarrel, and do not cease asking for their full rights, their spirit differs from Christ's; they are praised by the world, not by Jesus.

The Savior continued His teaching: "And from him who takes away your cloak, do not withhold your tunic either." This is to avoid the causes of evil. One might object that by doing so we become naked. Yet, if we comply with God's commandment, He of necessity will take care of us with His grace and goodness. Even if we were subject to nakedness for the sake of the truth, it would not be offensive because the offense is in not complying with God's commandments or obeying the truth. Perhaps, if the attacker sees us in this condition, he might return to God; this would be a blessing for both the oppressor and the oppressed. Some exegetes claim these orders were specific to the Savior's disciples, whom He sent among strange peoples who harmed them. Actually, if they were first given to them, they are conveyed to us through them.

41 – Then He said, "And whoever compels you to go one mile, go with him two" *to ensure the permanence of the love-and-peace relationship between people.*[54]

42 – He concluded this section about maintaining peace with everyone by saying, "Give to him who asks you, and from him who wants to borrow from you do not turn away."[55] Obviously, the command to give is directed to everyone, not specifically to the disciples, as they had nothing to give. It is implicitly understood that this command focuses on what it is necessary to give. As for the loan He intends, it is the one that is not in usury, but as a gift or for a period (if the loan has a return date).

In Luke, He says, "Give to everyone who asks of you. And from him who takes away your goods do not ask them back" (Luke 6:30). He also says, "But love your enemies, do good, and lend, hoping for nothing in return; and your reward will be great" (Luke 6:35). Although lending to others is a kind of charity, it is the duty of the borrower legally and customarily to repay the loan on time. Although the Savior said, "lend, hoping for nothing in return," He did not mean to follow this principle literally, but rather to show compassion and persistence in love, even if this leads to renouncing debts, if we are financially capable and not in need of it.

---

[54] The Jews compelled Simon of Cyrene to carry the cross for Jesus, and he complied without opposition (Mk 15:21). [Note: The Romans, not the Jews, compelled Simon to carry the cross].

[55] Lending. God's words say, in the book of Deuteronomy, "If there is among you a poor man of your brethren... you shall not harden your heart nor shut your hand from your poor brother, but you shall open your hand wide to him and willingly lend him sufficient for his need... You shall surely give to him, and your heart should not be grieved when you give to him, because for this thing the Lord your God will bless you in all your works and in all to which you put your hand" (Deuteronomy 15:7–8, 10).

Love for Enemies

43 "You have heard that it was said, "You shall love your neighbor and hate your enemy." 44 But I say to you, love your enemies, bless those who curse you, do good to those who hate you, and pray for those who spitefully use you and persecute you, 45 that you may be sons of your Father in heaven; for He makes His sun rise on the evil and on the good, and sends rain on the just and on the unjust. 46 For if you love those who love you, what reward have you? Do not even the tax collectors do the same? 47 And if you greet your brethren only, what do you do more than others? Do not even the tax collectors do so? 48 Therefore you shall be perfect, just as your Father in heaven is perfect.

43 – Our Savior went on to speak of the third characteristic of Christian perfection—love for enemies: "You have heard that it was said, 'You shall love your neighbor and hate your enemy.'" He referred to what is stated in the law about loving one's neighbor: "You shall not take vengeance, nor bear any grudge against the children of your people, but you shall love your neighbor as yourself: I am the Lord" (Leviticus 19:18). He also referred to what was written about hating the enemy (written about the Ammonites and the Moabites because they did not meet the children of Israel with bread and water on the way when they left the land of Egypt): "You shall not seek their peace nor their prosperity all your days forever" (Deuteronomy 23:6), and David's words about his enemies, "But You, O Lord, be merciful to me, and raise me up, that I may repay them" (Psalm 41:10).

44 [27][56] – Our Savior began to commend the love of enemies: "Love your enemies." This commandment is accompanied by a condition— hope in their goodness. Not every enemy is to be loved. Those devoid of goodness and inclined to evil are not to be loved, such as Satan, false prophets, heretics, skeptics, antichrists and the like. Peter destroyed Simon the magician, and Ananias with Sapphira his wife, while Paul struck the obstinate one with blindness, and cursed the high priest and Alexander the Coppersmith. We withhold love because their great corruption tips the balance in favor of seeking relief from them, rather than having compassion on them. In like manner, divorcing the adulteress outweighs living with her.

As for the wicked, for whom there is hope of goodness, even if we hate them for persisting in error, we should have mercy on them for the humanity we share with them and pray for God to restore them to the right path. Almighty God gives time and forgives, but on the wicked He will take vengeance and will punish on the day of judgment. He went on to say, "Do good to those who hate you." Similarly, Paul the apostle says, "If your enemy is hungry, feed him; If he is thirsty, give him a drink; for in so doing you will heap coals of fire on his head. Do not be overcome by evil, but overcome evil with good" (Romans 12:20–21).

[28] – In addition, Paul advised the people of Rome: "Bless those who persecute you; bless and do not curse" (Romans 12:14). The Savior expounds: "Pray for those who spitefully use you." He applied this commandment when He prayed for His crucifiers saying, "Father, forgive them, for they do not know what they do" (Luke 23:34). Stephen the Proto-martyr followed in His footsteps; when the enemies began to stone him "he knelt down and cried out with a loud voice, 'Lord, do not charge them with this sin'" (Acts 7:60).

---

[56] Commentary on this verse (until the reference of Acts 7:60) taken from the First Week Wednesday Matins Gospel (Luke 6:27–28). The numbers in brackets refer to the verses in Luke.

One who contemplates the Savior's commandments sees that He gradually led us to the highest ranks of virtue. First, He recommended that we should not avenge ourselves by taking an eye for an eye and a tooth for a tooth—rewarding evil in kind. Second, to give of ourselves more than people seek, "turn the other to him also." Third, to do more for them than they ask (perhaps those who would curse us might benefit). Fourth, to love our enemies. Fifth, to pray for those who cursed us. And sixth, we should do good to those who hate us and pray for those who offend us.

If we gauge the types of love, we will find: to love those who love us is human justice; to love those who do not like us is angelic love; to love those who hate us is divine love. But, to hate those who love us is a demonic act.

45 – The Savior went on to encourage His hearers to follow these commandments, "that you may be sons of your Father in heaven." He made the reward not food, or drink, or earthly inheritance, but elevation to the rank of sonship to God and imitation of Him, "for He makes His sun rise on the evil and on the good, and sends rain on the just and on the unjust." There is no doubt that the duty of children requires them to imitate Him. In seeing the Holy Father flooding rivers of blessings on multitudes of humans despite their disobedience, disbelief, and lack of thanksgiving, His children should not cease doing good deeds and showing love to all, despite the lack of gratitude of many.

46 – The Savior went on to demonstrate the validity of His teachings by saying "if you love those who love you..."

47 – "... And if you greet your brethren only, what do you do more than others? Do not even the tax collectors do so?" He wants believers not to imitate the scribes who reward evil with evil, but to imitate all who reward evil with good.

48 – He explained what He meant explicitly: "Therefore you shall be perfect, just as your Father in heaven is perfect." No doubt this gracious desire by God—who is perfect and holy—was for His creation from the beginning of the world until its end. He is the One who said to Abraham: "I am Almighty God; walk before Me and be blameless. And I will make My covenant between Me and you, and will multiply you exceedingly" (Genesis 17:1–2). And the One who said to the sons of Israel: "For I am the Lord your God. You shall therefore consecrate yourselves, and you shall be holy; for I am holy" (Leviticus 11:44). Peter the apostle repeats this wish when he commends holiness: "But as He who called you is holy, you also be holy in all your conduct, because it is written, "Be holy, for I am holy" (1 Peter 1:15–16).

FIRST WEEK – SUNDAY[57]
LEADING TO GOD'S KINGDOM

Linking the Readings:

All the readings of this day center on one theme: **Leading to God's Kingdom**—the Savior leading the believers to this kingdom

The Vespers Gospel speaks of the Savior **exhorting believers to pray;** the Matins Gospel speaks of Him **confirming those who keep His sayings;** the Liturgy Gospel speaks of the Savior **guiding them to His kingdom;** and the Evening Gospel speaks of **His commandments to them.**

The Pauline Epistle speaks of the need for the believers to **walk properly;** the Catholic Epistle speaks of them **accepting the word with meekness;** and the Acts reading speaks of them **calling on the Name of the Lord,** as Ananias also encouraged Paul to do.

PSALMS AND GOSPELS

Vespers Psalm   Psalms 17:1–2

This psalm alludes to the accompanying Gospel passage in which the Lord said "ask, and it will be given to you; seek and you will find," and speaking for faithful believers (who walk in perfection), it cries out to Him and says: "Hear a just cause, O Lord, attend to my cry; give ear to my prayer which is not from deceitful lips. Let my vindication come from Your presence; let Your eyes look on the things that are upright."

---

[57] Since the readings of this preceding week (the weeks here culminate on Sunday) center on preparing for the struggle, it has been called "Preparation Week" since the time of Pope Demetrius the Vinedresser in the fourth century.

Vespers Gospel   Matthew 6:34–7:12

This passage exhorts believers to pray, as the Savior directed His disciples: "Ask, and it will be given to you; seek, and you will find; knock, and it will be opened to you" (v. 7).

Matins Psalm   Psalms 18:1–2

This psalm alludes to the accompanying Gospel passage in which the Savior likened those who hear His sayings and keep them to one who built his house on the rock, and speaking for the believers who rely on Him: "I will love You, O Lord, my strength. The Lord is my rock and my fortress and my deliverer; my God, my strength, in whom I will trust."

Matins Gospel   Matthew 7:22–29

In this passage, the Savior confirms those who keep His sayings: "Therefore whoever hears these sayings of Mine, and does them, I will liken him to a wise man who built his house on the rock" (v. 24).

Liturgy Psalm   Psalms 25:1–2, 4–5

This psalm alludes to the accompanying Gospel passage in which the Lord of Glory directs the believers' attention to seek first the kingdom of God and His righteousness, and to rely on Him: "To You, O Lord, I lift up my soul. O my God, I trust in You; let me not be ashamed; show me Your ways, O Lord; teach me Your paths. Lead me in Your truth."

Liturgy Gospel   Matthew 6:19–33

This passage speaks of the Savior leading believers to the kingdom of God and His righteousness as He said to them: "But seek first the kingdom of God and His righteousness, and all these things shall be added to you" (v. 33).

Evening Psalm   Psalms 48:10–11

This psalm alludes to the accompanying Gospel passage in which the Savior establishes commandments for believers to follow, exhorting them to rejoice in them: "Your right hand is full of righteousness. Let Mount Zion rejoice, let the daughters of Judah be glad, because of Your judgments."

Evening Gospel   Luke 6:27–38

In this passage, the Savior commands believers to love their enemies: "But love your enemies, do good, and lend, hoping for nothing in return" (v. 35).

EPISTLES

The Pauline Epistle   Romans 13:1–14

Needing to walk properly: In this epistle, Paul charges believers to be subject to authorities, to love one another, and to walk properly as in the day. Summing up this behavior, he says, "But put on the Lord Jesus Christ, and make no provision for the flesh, to fulfill its lusts" (v. 14).

The Catholic Epistle   James 1:13–21

Accepting the word with meekness: Here, James shows that a person is tempted when drawn away by desires, and that when desire conceives, it gives birth to sin. Then he commands believers: "Therefore lay aside all filthiness and overflow of wickedness, and receive with meekness the implanted word, which is able to save your souls" (v. 21).

The Acts   Acts 21:40–22:16

Calling on the Name of the Lord: This passage shows Paul's defense before the commander in which he retells how he was called [to the faith], and what Ananias said to him after he regained his sight: "The God of our fathers has chosen you that you should know His will, and see the Just One, and hear the voice of His mouth. For you will be His witness to all men of what you have seen and heard. And now why are you waiting? Arise and be baptized, and wash away your sins, calling on the name of the Lord" (vv. 22:14–16).

Vespers Gospel
Matthew 6:43–7:12
Exhortation to Pray

EXHORTATION TO PRAY

Overview

After Christ the Master chose His 12 disciples, He began to introduce His new law for the first time from atop the mountain during His second circuit of ministry in Galilee. This law occupies three complete chapters in Matthew's Gospel. In this Vespers Gospel, which is part of the Sermon on the Mount, the Savior exhorts the faithful neither to be concerned about tomorrow, nor to judge others, nor to throw what is holy to the dogs, but to be always occupied with prayer.

Let Tomorrow Be

34 Therefore do not worry about tomorrow, for tomorrow will worry about its own things. Sufficient for the day is its own trouble.

34 – The Lord of Glory noticed that the faithful were excessively concerned with worldly possessions and with collecting them, although all they really need is the bare minimum of food and clothing. Desiring to alert them to the mistake of excessive concern with what will happen tomorrow, He said, "Do not worry about tomorrow, for tomorrow will worry about its own things." If they survive until tomorrow, then they can be concerned with tomorrow's concerns, but for now, "sufficient for the day is its own trouble." *For the current moment, today's toils suffice; there is no need to think about tomorrow or reach forward.*

Avoid Judgment

1 Judge not, that you be not judged. 2 For with what judgment you judge, you will be judged; and with the measure you use, it will be measured back to you. 3 And why do you look at the speck in your brother's eye, but do not consider the plank in your own eye? 4 Or how can you say to your brother, "Let me remove the speck from your eye"; and look, a plank is in your own eye? 5 Hypocrite! First remove the plank from your own eye, and then you will see clearly to remove the speck from your brother's eye.

1 – The Master directed their attention to the mistake of judging others: "Judge not, that you be not judged." He neither means to overturn the sentence passed on the wrongdoers, nor means not to reprimand those who deserve reproach, or else we lose fairness and justice in the homes, in commerce, and in cities and kingdoms. This could not be His

intention, since He is the One who said, "If your brother sins against you, go and tell him his fault between you and him alone. If he hears you, you have gained your brother. But if he will not hear, take with you one or two more, that by the mouth of two or three witnesses every word may be established. And if he refuses to hear them, tell it to the church. But if he refuses even to hear the church, let him be to you like a heathen and a tax collector" (Matthew 18:15–17).

We see John the Baptist scolding the Jews: "Brood of vipers! Who warned you to flee from the wrath to come?" (Matthew 3:7). Paul the apostle also commands his disciple Timothy [sic Titus]: "Rebuke with all authority. Let no one despise you" (Titus 2:15). When the Master said, "Judge not," He meant *Do not judge (while you are a sinner) another sinner like you or one who is even less of a sinner than you.* Paul the apostle supports this by saying, "Therefore you are inexcusable, O man, whoever you are who judge, for in whatever you judge another you condemn yourself; for you who judge practice the same things... Who are you to judge another's servant? To his own master he stands or falls" (Romans 14:4; 2:1).

James the apostle also says, "Do not speak evil of one another, brethren. He who speaks evil of a brother and judges his brother, speaks evil of the law and judges the law. But if you judge the law, you are not a doer of the law but a judge. There is one Lawgiver, who can save or destroy. Who are you to judge another?" (James 4:11–12).

Additionally, the Savior's intention by "judge not," is for people to not grow accustomed to unjustly condemning others to satisfy a desire for revenge, and not to judge those who are more righteous than themselves, and not to judge with usurped authority.

2 – If they judge others, they would be judged accordingly.[xxiv] By saying, "With the measure you use, it will be measured back to you," He does

not want us to be harsh when we judge others, because we will be judged in like manner.

3 – He marveled at those who look at the speck in their brother's eye without realizing the plank in their own eyes. By speck, the Savior is referring to a small sin, while the plank represents a great sin, such as apostasy, murder, or injustice.

4 – He further wondered how a person could possibly demand the removal of the speck from his brother's eye while the plank remains in his own eye.

5 – He reproached this individual's hypocrisy, for pretending to be just while being internally corrupt: "Hypocrite! First remove the plank from your own eye, and then you will see clearly to remove the speck from your brother's eye." He does not thus overrule rebuke, or call for those who reproach their brethren to be free from sin (if this were the case then all teaching and preaching would have been eliminated from the world), as "There is none righteous, no, not one" (Romans 3:10). This would result in the ungodly remaining wicked without anyone reproaching them, which contradicts the teaching of the Holy Bible.

The Savior's intention was to clarify to the guides and teachers the importance of behaving honorably and not contradicting with their lives and deeds what they preach with their mouths, like the scribes and Pharisees of whom He warned the people: "The scribes and the Pharisees sit in Moses' seat. Therefore whatever they tell you to observe, that observe and do, but do not do according to their works; for they say, and do not do" (Matthew 23:2–3). The teacher, regardless of the honorable job, prestigious position, abundance in knowledge, or correct convictions, cannot have any influence in the souls of his listeners if they see him corrupt, worldly, or controlled by his desires—his deeds contradict his speech.

We see Paul the apostle strongly reproach saying, "You, therefore, who teach another, do you not teach yourself? You who preach that a man should not steal, do you steal? You who say, 'Do not commit adultery,' do you commit adultery? You who abhor idols, do you rob temples? You who make your boast in the law, do you dishonor God through breaking the law? For 'the name of God is blasphemed among the Gentiles because of you,' as it is written" (Romans 2:21–24). This admonition is not directed only to the church servants but to all the people, and to all those who object to teaching and instruction.

Accordingly, we see Paul the apostle command his disciple Timothy: "Take heed to yourself and to the doctrine. Continue in them" (1 Timothy 4:16). He likewise instructs the bishops: "Take heed to yourselves and to all the flock, among which the Holy Spirit has made you overseers, to shepherd the church of God which He purchased with His own blood" (Acts 20:28). Peter the apostle likewise advises them to be examples to the flock: "Shepherd the flock of God which is among you, serving as overseers, not by compulsion but willingly, not for dishonest gain but eagerly; nor as being lords over those entrusted to you, but being examples to the flock" (1 Peter 5:2–3).

The Holies are not for the Dogs

> 6 Do not give what is holy to the dogs; nor cast your pearls before swine, lest they trample them under their feet, and turn and tear you in pieces.

6 – The Lord of Glory continued giving His commandments: "Do not give what is holy to the dogs." Some exegetes think the Lord is referring to His *holy* body and blood, and by "dogs" and "swine," He is referring to those who partake of them without a clear conscience. Since they will not benefit any thereof, they should not partake of them.

Others believe "holy" and "pearls" refer to His commandments (the true teachings), while "dogs" and "swine" refer to liars who have unclean minds on which the truth and His commandments cannot be imprinted. Such persons should not be in communion with us lest they only come for conflict, and because of their small-mindedness, distorted understanding, and impure conscience they disdain it like the swine and dogs who trample over jewels. They trample them not because they are beautiful, but because of their own ignorance. In olden days, Solomon the Sage said, "Do not speak in the hearing of a fool, for he will despise the wisdom of your words" (Proverbs 23:9).

A third group of exegetes ponder how our Savior would forbid giving the *holy* to the *dogs* (the ignorant) while elsewhere He says, "What you hear in the ear, preach on the housetops" (Matthew 10:27). They respond that He meant preaching, not to those who will reject, but to those who will accept.

Exhortation to Pray

7 Ask, and it will be given to you; seek, and you will find; knock, and it will be opened to you. 8 For everyone who asks receives, and he who seeks finds, and to him who knocks it will be opened. 9 Or what man is there among you who, if his son asks for bread, will give him a stone? 10 Or if he asks for a fish, will he give him a serpent? 11 If you then, being evil, know how to give good gifts to your children, how much more will your Father who is in heaven give good things to those who ask Him! 12 Therefore, whatever you want men to do to you, do also to them, for this is the Law and the Prophets.

7 – After speaking about prayer, the Savior began exhorting His audience to pray: "Ask, and it will be given to you; seek, and you will find; knock, and it will be opened to you." Although He did not outline the appropriate request, this can be inferred from His previous words:

"Seek first the kingdom of God and His righteousness" (Matthew 6:33). We should not set our expectation on God's goodness and generosity to provide us with temporal things, but with spiritual (such as teaching us His ways, giving us enlightenment, and giving us His Holy Spirit). We should not ask for ourselves only but also for our loved ones, our enemies, and for everyone.

8 – He repeated His promise of answering our prayers: "For everyone who asks receives, and he who seeks finds, and to him who knocks it will be opened." This promise has certain necessary requirements (for the praying person), for God to grant the request. The primary requirements for prayer are: it must be with firm faith, in the name of the Lord Jesus, with a contrite heart, persistence, consistency, according to God's will, with fervor and steadfastness, with open ears and attention, and with a heart reconciled with all.[xxv]

9 – To indicate the immense love of God the Father for His children, and His great gifts to them, Jesus said, "What man is there among you who, if his son asks for bread, will give him a stone?"

10 – "Or if he asks for a fish, will he give him a serpent?"

11 – He summed up by saying, "If you then, being evil, know how to give good gifts to your children, how much more will your Father who is in heaven give good things to those who ask Him!" In comparison to the perfect divine nature of God, He called human nature evil because humans tend towards evil. It was also to motivate them to watchfulness and prayer with a pure conscience.[xxvi]

12 – By saying, "Whatever you want men to do to you, do also to them," He gathered all the virtues into one. If I want my friend to forgive me, for example, I should likewise forgive him. Accordingly, we should do no hurt to others, so that we do not suffer hurt; we should benefit others, so that we can benefit as well. This divine principle decreed by

the Lord of Glory has no comparison in any other books, because it encompasses all treasures of wisdom and philosophy, and is more valuable than all the religious and secular laws. He proves this by saying, "For this is the Law and the Prophets." By the "law," He means the Torah. The "prophets" are those from the time of Moses until His coming.

There is no doubt that living by this divine principle eliminates egoism, hatred, revenge, gossip, deception, and fraud. Rather, it emphasizes unity and equality among people, and forces each of them to seek the good of the other, thus ending disputes and wars, and converting our troubled world into a paradise. Although behaving according to this great verse will not entirely eliminate our instinctual egoism, it will turn it into a gauge to measure our love of others, and an instrument for justice and goodness.

Some exegetes ranked a person's reaction to the action of another: they said meeting an evil act with a greater evil act is a demonic work; responding in kind is the reaction of an idolater; treating others as we want to be treated is Christian; but treating others better than they treat us is a divine work.[xxvii]

Matins Gospel
Matthew 7:22–29
Building on a Rock

BUILDING ON A ROCK

Overview[xxviii]

After Christ the Master chose His 12 apostles (during His second circuit of ministry in Galilee), He delivered His famous Sermon on the

Mount. In this pericope, which is part of that sermon, the church wants to underscore that the sinners, even if they are believers, are destined to be distant from the Savior on the day of judgment, while the righteous will stand firm as a mountain.

Distancing the Wicked[xxix]

22 Many will say to Me in that day, "Lord, Lord, have we not prophesied in Your name, cast out demons in Your name, and done many wonders in Your name?" 23 And then I will declare to them, "I never knew you; depart from Me, you who practice lawlessness!"

22 – All of the Lord of Glory's teachings aim at guiding the people to the kingdom of heaven. They show that the way is not simply through faith only, but by faith and good works. He says, "Not everyone who says to Me, 'Lord, Lord,' shall enter the kingdom of heaven, but he who does the will of My Father in heaven" (Matthew 7:21).

Supporting this sublime principle, He described the difference between the two. The one whose religion was limited to listening and proclaiming, whose evil actions contradicted his faith, is destined on the day of judgment to the loss of the kingdom: "Many will say to Me in that day, 'Lord, Lord, have we not prophesied in Your name, cast out demons in Your name, and done many wonders in Your name.'" Those *many* who asked Him this question, are the ones who knew the truth, taught it, did miracles by it, but did not live by it. Perhaps such are those who simply tried to use these words to draw close to Him, or those who were originally in good standing, and did miracles, but then reneged, such as Arius. In this case, they are recalling their original condition. Some exegetes say those *many* are those whose insides were evil while their outside seemed good, and the miracles they did were for the sake of others. Others see them as the magicians; they achieve their desire through magic, and then claim that it is in the name of Christ for it to be accepted.

23 – He answers them, "I never knew you," *neither when you did what you say, nor now. I do not know you the knowledge coupled with love. I have heard that you try to appear as My disciples, but I do not know you as My own, because you did not truly know Me. You deceived people, but you will not deceive Me. I send you away from me; you have no connection to Me and will not be allowed into My kingdom.*

This reveals that the basis of salvation is faith and works together, not faith alone. One who only has one of them does not have a share in the kingdom of heaven. Proof of this is that the foolish virgins, when they had all the virtues, but had no mercy, lost the kingdom, as was told them, "Assuredly, I say to you, I do not know you" (Matthew 25:12).ˣˣˣ

S tability of the Doers⁵⁸

24 Therefore whoever hears these sayings of Mine, and does them, I will liken him to a wise man who built his house on the rock: 25 and the rain descended, the floods came, and the winds blew and beat on that house; and it did not fall, for it was founded on the rock. 26 But everyone who hears these sayings of Mine, and does not do them, will be like a foolish man who built his house on the sand: 27 and the rain descended, the floods came, and the winds blew and beat on that house; and it fell. And great was its fall.

24 [47] – Then He started to reveal the destiny of those who are doers, likening them to...

---

⁵⁸ Commentary on these verses taken from the Second Week Friday Liturgy Gospel (Luke 6:47–49). The numbers in brackets refer to the verses in Luke.

[48] – "...a man building a house, who dug deep and laid the foundation on the rock." Every Christian knows that doing what is pleasing to the Lord is not an easy task; rather, it is full of difficulties, hard work, and continual strenuous warfare. This requires labor, seriousness, and struggle, just like the person who builds his house on the rock needs self-denial, steering away from pride, being adorned with humility, crucifying the will and desires, clinging to the mind that is in Christ, and considering everything as nothing and rubbish for His sake. A person whose religion is as such has true faith that is solid as a house built on the rock.

25 – He symbolized His law with a rock for its stability and solid stand against evil opinions, stubbornness, or resistance. The Savior continues, "The flood arose, the stream beat vehemently against that house, and could not shake it, for it was founded on the rock." *If a flood of disasters or the shock of persecutory quakes struck that religion, it would not be shaken or destroyed, but rather will resemble a protective fortified fortress.* This is the religion where upright faith and good works meet.[59]

26 [49] – Finally, the Lord of Glory spoke about those who listen and do not do, likening them to a person "who built a house on the earth without a foundation." This house might appear good and stable, akin to a person who listens to the Gospel and appears to be good and truthful. People who see him would not be able to differentiate between him and one who hears and does (both of them attending the same church and carrying out the religious rituals in the same manner), just as there appears to be no difference between the house built on the rock and that built on the earth without foundation.

---

[59] The Protestant declaration that salvation is by faith only (not by faith and works as the apostolic churches believe) is a vain opinion. If their principal is applied, it produces a harmful result: the equality between those who respect the law and those who disdain it. This contradicts the words of the Savior that those who listen and do are likened to those who build the house on the rock, but those who listen and do not do are likened to those who build the house on the sand.

First Week

27 – However, when the winds of misfortune and hardships hit the house with no foundation, its decorated walls that appeared strong during the gentle times come crumbling down and its flawed foundationless structure is revealed. Such is anyone whose religion suffices with listening, researching, and knowing, without pairing it with good works; this leads to failure. Instead of turning a profit or benefit, it leads him to the most insurmountable loss. Is there a greater loss than the loss of the soul? This loss is the one the Savior is pointing to: "The ruin of that house was great," leading to hell.

His Teaching Authority[60]

> 28 And so it was, when Jesus had ended these sayings, that the people were astonished at His teaching, 29 for He taught them as one having authority, and not as the scribes.

28–29 [22] – The crowds were astonished at the beauty of His sublime teachings, and His authority in establishing His teachings. He personally gives the orders, explains what contradicts the law, and completes it as He sees fit, unlike Moses, the prophets, and the scribes who only interpreted what they said about God Almighty. In much of His words, He said the law says such and such, but I say to you to do such and such; this is proof of His authority in teaching.

Liturgy Gospel
Matthew 6:19–33
Guidance to the Heavenly Kingdom[xxxi]

---

[60] Commentary taken from Hathor 27 Vespers Gospel (Mk 1:22). The number in brackets refers to the verse in Mark.

GUIDANCE TO THE HEAVENLY KINGDOM

Overview

After choosing the 12 apostles, during His second circuit of ministry in Galilee, Christ the Master started delivering His new commandment for the first time from atop the mountain. This took up three complete chapters in Matthew's Gospel. In today's Gospel reading (which is part of this sermon), the Savior urges the believers not to store their treasures on earth but in heaven. He directs their attention to the difficulty of combining both service to God and to money. He exhorts them not to be overly worried about the needs of this life, but to make their first goal seeking the kingdom of God and His righteousness.

Treasure in Heavens

> 19 Do not lay up for yourselves treasures on earth, where moth and rust destroy and where thieves break in and steal; 20 but lay up for yourselves treasures in heaven, where neither moth nor rust destroys and where thieves do not break in and steal. 21 For where your treasure is, there your heart will be also. 22 The lamp of the body is the eye. If therefore your eye is good, your whole body will be full of light. 23 But if your eye is bad, your whole body will be full of darkness. If therefore the light that is in you is darkness, how great is that darkness!

19 – Our Savior commanded the faithful not to prioritize gathering and amassing money: "Do not lay up for yourselves treasures on earth." *Such treasures are subject to spoil by moth and rust (gradual loss) or to theft (losing them all at once).* Solomon the Sage said of old, "Do not overwork to be rich" (Proverbs 23:4). Paul the apostle was even more candid: "Having food and clothing, with these we shall be content. But those who desire to be rich fall into temptation and a snare, and into

many foolish and harmful lusts which drown men in destruction and perdition. For the love of money is a root of all kinds of evil, for which some have strayed from the faith in their greediness, and pierced themselves through with many sorrows" (1 Timothy 6:8–10).

Paul continues, showing that God does not forsake those who are satisfied with what they have: "Let your conduct be without covetousness; be content with such things as you have. For He Himself has said, 'I will never leave you nor forsake you'" (Hebrews 13:5). James the apostle explains the destiny of those who hoard money: "Come now, you rich, weep and howl for your miseries that are coming upon you! Your riches are corrupted, and your garments are moth-eaten. Your gold and silver are corroded, and their corrosion will be a witness against you and will eat your flesh like fire. You have heaped up treasure in the last days" (James 5:1–3).

20 – The Master continued: "But lay up for yourselves treasures in heaven" *by giving to the poor and assisting the needy.* His advice to the rich young man later confirms this: "If you want to be perfect, go, sell what you have and give to the poor, and you will have treasure in heaven; and come, follow Me" (Matthew 19:21). The Savior explains that the treasures in heaven do not fail, as He later commands His disciples, "Sell what you have and give alms; provide yourselves money bags which do not grow old, a treasure in the heavens that does not fail, where no thief approaches nor moth destroys" (Luke 12:33).

Paul the apostle reveals the reward for the rich who store their treasures in heaven by saying to his disciple Timothy: "Command those who are rich in this present age not to be haughty, nor to trust in uncertain riches but in the living God, who gives us richly all things to enjoy. Let them do good, that they be rich in good works, ready to give, willing to share, storing up for themselves a good foundation for the time to come, that they may lay hold on eternal life" (1 Timothy 6:17–19).

21 – The Savior explained His commandment: "For where your treasure is, there your heart will be also." *If the treasures are on earth, the heart would cling to earthly matters; if the treasures are in heaven, the heart would be occupied with heavenly matters.*

22 – The Master continues further: "The lamp of the body is the eye." *If the eye is good, then the whole body will be enlightened.* Since the heart is to the soul as the eye is to the body, He means, if the soul is free from the authority of desires, arrogance, and error, then it will see the light of His teachings and will be illumined.

23 – "But if your eye is bad," *if the heart is darkened by wicked opinions, the soul will be darkened.* This will inevitably affect all of a person's characteristics, attributes, and behaviors, making one tense, unstable, self-contradictory, and indecisive. By saying, "If therefore the light that is in you is darkness, how great is that darkness!" He means, if your mind is darkened, your darkness will be great on the last day.

Some exegetes see that by light, He means righteousness and charity. Building on this, He wants to say that if one person's charity to another human being is darkened, then how dark can his condition be! The error in charity is that either one gives haughtily, or instead of giving, one actually asks to take despite being able to give. In both cases, the fault is on the giver, not the receiver.[61]

---

[61] Some exegetes believe the *light* refers to the disciples and scholars. The words would thus mean if the ones who know and teach are described by wicked characteristics, how wicked will be their students.

Serving God not Mammon

> 24 No one can serve two masters; for either he will hate the one and love the other, or else he will be loyal to the one and despise the other. You cannot serve God and mammon.

24 – Then the Lord of Glory began to warn of the difficulty of combining two contradictions: worshiping God and collecting money. He said, "No one can serve two masters." This obviously applies if the two are contradictory; if their wills agree, then this is possible. Some exegetes ponder why possessions are contrary to God. They answer that those who hoard possessions worship them as they would worship a God; God is worshipped in truth, while these items are worshipped mentally. Their worship is in the person craving them, hoarding them from every cause, and never spending them for right causes.

If a person objects, saying that Abraham, Isaac, Jacob, Job, and others who were rich worshipped God, the response is that they were not enslaved by their possessions, but spent them to please God. James the apostle explains that the love of money is enmity to God: "Do you not know that friendship with the world is enmity with God? Whoever therefore wants to be a friend of the world makes himself an enemy of God" (James 4:4). John the apostle explains this more vividly: "Do not love the world or the things in the world. If anyone loves the world, the love of the Father is not in him. For all that is in the world—the lust of the flesh, the lust of the eyes, and the pride of life—is not of the Father but is of the world. And the world is passing away, and the lust of it; but he who does the will of God abides forever" (1 John 2:15–17).

Not Worrying about Life

> 25 Therefore I say to you, do not worry about your life, what you will eat or what you will drink; nor about your body, what

you will put on. Is not life more than food and the body more than clothing? 26 Look at the birds of the air, for they neither sow nor reap nor gather into barns; yet your heavenly Father feeds them. Are you not of more value than they? 27 Which of you by worrying can add one cubit to his stature? 28 So why do you worry about clothing? Consider the lilies of the field, how they grow: they neither toil nor spin; 29 and yet I say to you that even Solomon in all his glory was not arrayed like one of these. 30 Now if God so clothes the grass of the field, which today is, and tomorrow is thrown into the oven, will He not much more clothe you, O you of little faith? 31 Therefore do not worry, saying, "What shall we eat?" or "What shall we drink?" or "What shall we wear?" 32 For after all these things the Gentiles seek. For your heavenly Father knows that you need all these things.

25 – The Master of All went on to advise the faithful: "I say to you, do not worry about your life, what you will eat or what you will drink; nor about your body, what you will put on." David stressed this by saying, "Cast your burden on the Lord, and He shall sustain you; He shall never permit the righteous to be moved" (Psalm 55:22). Likewise, Peter the apostle says, "Therefore humble yourselves under the mighty hand of God, that He may exalt you in due time, casting all your care upon Him, for He cares for you" (1 Peter 5:7).

Our Savior enumerates the reasons for His commandment: "Is not life more than food and the body more than clothing?" He means if God gave us a soul and a body, which are more honorable than food and clothing, He will also give us these things. Skeptics try to found their cynicism on the Savior basing the food for the *soul*, which does not eat. The truth is that He spoke in a manner the people were accustomed to think, as indicated in the Bible: "A satisfied soul loathes the honeycomb, but to a hungry soul every bitter thing is sweet" (Proverbs 27:7). Perhaps He is indicating the body where the soul resides.

26 – The Savior gave us one example about food from the birds of heaven and another about clothing from the lilies of the field, to support His words. He said about food: "Look at the birds of the air, for they neither sow nor reap nor gather into barns; yet your heavenly Father feeds them." Job says concerning this, "Who provides food for the raven, when its hatchlings cry to God, and wander about for lack of food?" (Job 38:41). David also says, "He gives to the beast its food, and to the young ravens that cry" (Psalm 147:9).

Jesus gave the parable of birds (not of people or animals) because they are considered trivial. If God does not ignore the birds, but rather takes care of them, how much more would He care for the humans whom He created in His image and likeness? This is the meaning of "are you not of more value than they?"

Luke writes, "Consider the ravens,"[62] instead of "the birds of the air." Some exegetical manuscripts explained that Jesus specifically selected the raven because when a raven's eggs hatch, it leaves its hatchlings without food. Therefore, God sends mosquitos into their mouths for nourishment, until their plumage develops, and their parents return to feed them. This example alerts us to forsake the world and seek only sufficient food, to not be preoccupied with possessions, but rather with what is beneficial—caring for God's will as Moses did on the mountain, and Elijah and John did in the wilderness.

We should not understand this commandment to mean we ought to avoid work altogether, but only avoid excessive preoccupation and hoarding. Diligence for necessary food would not affect the virtues. Similarly, birds search for their food and God feeds them, because He gave them strength to forage for their nourishment.

---

[62] [Luke 12:24].

27 – By saying, "Which of you by worrying can add one cubit to his stature?" He wants to clarify that God is the One who can do this, and He is the One who will also feed us. Some exegetes ponder why the Savior did not give a parable about the soul, to show His care for it, as He did with the body. They answer that this is not appropriate because the food of the soul is knowledge and wisdom; these should be cared for to the highest degree, because the soul is dependent on them, and because the body is visible—that is why the Savior gave this parable.

28 – Next, He gave them a second parable about clothing: "Consider the lilies of the field, how they grow: they neither toil nor spin."

29 – "And yet I say to you that even Solomon in all his glory was not arrayed like one of these." *The Creator's work, a manufacturer cannot replicate.* He said this parable in this way, not to honor the plants, but to show the extent of His care for them (of the beauty of their colors), to bring people to be less concerned with worldly things.

30 – He reproached the weakness of their faith, showing that if such was God's attention to the grass of the field (which exists today and is thrown into the fire tomorrow), how much more will He take care of those whom He created for His glory and to dwell in His abode forever.

31 – He concluded: "Therefore do not worry, saying, 'What shall we eat?' or 'What shall we drink?' or 'What shall we wear?'"

32 – He clarified the wisdom of His commandment: "For after all these things the Gentiles seek." Because of the extent of their stupidity and deep ignorance, they think their life is about money. His intention was to shame them, because by their behavior they have made themselves equivalent to the faithless Gentiles; as He cares about the Gentiles, He

also cares about them, especially since He knows[63] all their needs. Since He is Omniscient and knows all our needs let our minds rest and our hearts be at peace in His sympathy and compassion on us.

Seeking the Kingdom of God

> 33 But seek first the kingdom of God and His righteousness, and all these things shall be added to you.

33 – The Savior concluded: "But seek first the kingdom of God and His righteousness." He is referring to the heavenly blessings to come (which cannot be gained except by godliness), as the apostle told his disciple Timothy: "Exercise yourself toward godliness. For bodily exercise profits a little, but godliness is profitable for all things, having promise of the life that now is and of that which is to come" (1 Timothy 4:8). As for the phrase, "And all these things shall be added to you," it does not refer to food and clothing or worldly concerns, but points to the age to come.

Many times, God also grants us temporary things in addition to the spiritual blessings. This is clear in the story of Solomon the Sage when he sat on the throne after his father David while he was still young. He asked God for an understanding heart to govern the concerns of the people. God answered him: "Because you have asked this thing, and have not asked long life for yourself, nor have asked riches for yourself, nor have asked the life of your enemies, but have asked for yourself understanding to discern justice, behold, I have done according to your words; see, I have given you a wise and understanding heart, so that there has not been anyone like you before you, nor shall any like you arise after you. And I have also given you what you have not asked:

---

[63] God's Omniscience encompasses everything, great and small, lowly and exalted. Concerning this the apostle says, "And there is no creature hidden from His sight, but all things are naked and open to the eyes of Him to whom we must give account" (Hebrews 4:13).

both riches and honor, so that there shall not be anyone like you among the kings all your days" (1 Kings 3:11–13).

Evening Gospel
Luke 6:27–38
Loving the Enemy
See First Week Wednesday Matins and Liturgy Gospel of the Great Fast.

---

[i] Commentary on this entire reading taken from the Third Sunday of Paone Liturgy Gospel.

[ii] Miracles of Jesus. Atheists and those who deny the divinity of Jesus Christ doubt the authenticity of His miracles. They claim these were optical illusions, natural occurrences, or using the power of Satan. In truth, these miracles are authentically solid; they are to prove His divine authority. If they were optical illusions, those who received them would not have felt them in their souls, such as the blind who saw, the sick who were healed, and the dead who were raised; His enemies would not have ceased revealing their fraud and deception.

Were they by natural means, they would not have occurred, because nature can never restore a person to life or create something out of nothing. Natural powers use means suitable for their own purposes, while the Savior often used means contrary to their natural purposes; He used mud, which distorts vision, to smear the eyes of the man born blind so that he saw. Furthermore, works occur naturally over time, while Jesus performed miracles in a moment of time, either by touch, word, or will. He touched the leper and said, "I am willing; be cleansed" (Matthew 8:3). Oftentimes, He performed miracles remotely while in a place distant from the location of the miracle; we see Him heal the ill son of the woman in Capernaum, and likewise in the case of the daughter of the Canaanite woman (Matthew 15:28).

His miracles could not be through the power of Satan. This is for two reasons: the first concerns the action itself and the second concerns its goal. Although Satan is able to move in space, use natural means, and deceive the senses, it is impossible for him to give life to a dead person, sight to the blind, speech to the mute. As for His goal, Jesus did not do miracles to lighten the burdens of people and draw them to Himself per se, but also to destroy the power of Satan. It is illogical to enlist the help of Satan for the destruction of the kingdom of Satan, as the scribes and Pharisees had accused Him; otherwise, a kingdom divided against itself falls apart.

Some might argue that the prophets and apostles did many miracles and no one considered this proof of their divinity. The response is that the Savior's miracles surpass those miracles in quantity and magnitude. In quantity, Jesus' miracles far surpassed the miracles of all the prophets and apostles combined. The Evangelist said, "And there are also many other things that Jesus did, which if they were written one by one, I suppose that even the world itself could not contain the books that would be written" (John 21:25). In magnitude, Jesus performed miracles in *His* name, *His* authority, by *His* command, and by *His* personal might, being Almighty God. The prophets did miracles in the name and by the authority of another, after offering many requests and petitions. Peter told the crippled man, "In the name of Jesus Christ of Nazareth, rise up and walk" (Acts 3:6), while Jesus said to the leper, "I am willing; be cleansed." This is what made the first human, and the second divine. (See *Elm-El-Lahoot* (1:59–72) [Arabic reference]).

iii Prayer over the departed. This is one of the issues of difference between the apostolic churches and the Protestant churches. Our church has much strong biblical and traditional evidence to support the benefits of praying over the souls of the righteous who have departed, some of which follow:

Biblical evidence:

1) The Savior's words that blasphemy against the Holy Spirit will not be forgiven "either in this age or in the age to come" (Matthew 12:32); this attests that in the age to come there is forgiveness.

2) The words of Paul the apostle about Onesiphorus, who had departed from this world at that time: "The Lord grant to him that he may find mercy from the Lord in that Day" (2 Timothy 1:18). If one objects that Onesiphorus was alive at the time, the response would be that if he were alive, he would have received the same greeting as the rest of his household; moreover, Paul would have greeted him first since he was the head of the household and was very gracious to the church. Had Paul not known the benefit of prayer over the departed, he would not have prayed to the Lord for their sake.

3) The words of John the apostle: "If anyone sees his brother sinning a sin which does not lead to death, he will ask, and He will give him life for those who commit sin not leading to death" (1 John 5:16). Yes, this saying applies to the sinners who are alive, yet it is more specifically meant for the sinners who have departed, because for the apostle to specify prayers only (without the other means of forgiveness like offering guidance and preaching) indicates that those for whom the prayers are requested have departed–these prayers are the only available means for their forgiveness.

4) In the book of Maccabees (one of the books removed by the Protestants but accepted by the Orthodox and the Catholic churches), Judas the warrior, collecting alms, sent to Jerusalem 12,000 silver dirhams to be offered for the sins of the departed, because he was meditating on those who accepted death piously, for

whom a great new grace is reserved (Maccabees 22:42). Furthermore, until this day, Jews continue to offer prayers for the sake of the dead.

Traditional evidence:

1) The Didascalia says, "Gather diligently in the church, read the Holy Scriptures, and sing over the reposed person... then offer the liturgy of thanksgiving."

2) Prayers are recited daily during the Divine Liturgy for the departed; the liturgy was placed from the time of the apostles.

3) Petrolianos says, "The bloodless sacrifice is offered for the living and the dead." Dionysius says that through the prayers of the priest, the inadvertently neglected sins of the departed person are forgiven. John Chrysostom says we need to aid the dead with our prayers. There are also other sayings by fathers of the eastern and western church.

4) The witness of the Protestant themselves: The protestant priest Benjamin Thyander writes in his book *Scent of the Soul* that the prayer for the sake of the dead began in the early ages of the Christian religion (*Elm-El-Lahoot* (2:503–511) [Arabic reference]).

[iv] Overview taken from Meshir 2 Liturgy Gospel.

[v] Commentary on these verses taken from Meshir 2 Liturgy Gospel.

[vi] Humility. See also Psalm 131: "Lord, my heart is not haughty, nor my eyes lofty."

[vii] The Heresy of Peters primacy. See the discussion in Thoout 16 liturgy [*See Sixth Week Tuesday Liturgy Gospel of the Great Fast*].

[viii] Commentary on these verses taken from Meshir 2 Liturgy Gospel.

[ix] See Matthew 10:42 for further explanation.

[x] "Every sacrifice will be seasoned with salt" is further explained in the Seventh Week Matins Gospel of the Great Fast (Luke 14:34).

[xi] The Sermon was removed in the new Katameros published in 1952.

[xii] Apostles' Fast. Following the command of our Lord Jesus Christ, the apostles fasted after His ascension: "As they ministered to the Lord and fasted, the Holy Spirit said, 'Now separate to Me Barnabas and Saul for the work to which I have called them.' Then, having fasted and prayed, and laid hands on them, they sent them away" (Acts 13:2–3). See also Acts 14:23. Similarly, "Now when much time had been spent, and sailing was now dangerous because the Fast was already over" (Acts 27:9). Also, "But after long abstinence from food, then Paul stood in the midst of them" (Acts 27:21). The Apostles' Fast, which is arranged in all apostolic churches, is an apostolic tradition. It was decreed in support of the words of the apostles: "After you celebrate the Pentecost ...fast, for it is obligatory to rejoice and delight in the gifts given to us by God, and to fast after our joy" (*Al-Magmoo Al-Soofy* (174) [Arabic reference]). In their time, it was called the Fast of Pentecost, but the fathers at the Council of Nicaea named it after the apostles, in their honor. The duration of this fast increases or decreases, as the total number of its days, plus the days of the Holy Fifty Days must

be 81 days, according to the Epact calculation issued by Pope Demetrius the Vinedresser.

[xiii] Overview taken from Tobe 22 Liturgy Gospel.

[xiv] Commentary on this section taken from Tobe 22 Liturgy Gospel.

[xv] Application. All these promises apply to Saint Anthony and his children the monks: He was faithful and wise over all his gifts; he distributed all his possessions to the poor; his heart was not attached to anything earthly, but rather the heavenly; righteousness was the core of his composition; and faithfulness girt his loins. He insisted on monasticism (instead of marriage), left his relatives, possessions, and worldly desires, preferring to live in the desert, wear wool, and gird his waist like John the Baptist, declining meat and delicacies, and subsisting on the base necessities. His vigil-lamp remained lit while he spent his whole life in fasting, praying, and reading books. He and his children the monks imitated the Master and His disciples in their whole demeanor. As such, they all became earthly-angels/heavenly-humans and stars that shone in the wilderness of this dark world.

The church, by celebrating him, wants her children to imitate him in his watchfulness, according to the words of the apostle, "For you yourselves know perfectly that the day of the Lord so comes as a thief in the night. For when they say, 'Peace and safety!' then sudden destruction comes upon them, as labor pains upon a pregnant woman. And they shall not escape. But you, brethren, are not in darkness, so that this Day should overtake you as a thief. You are all sons of light and sons of the day. We are not of the night nor of darkness. Therefore, let us not sleep, as others do, but let us watch and be sober. For those who sleep, sleep at night, and those who get drunk are drunk at night. But let us who are of the day be sober, putting on the breastplate of faith and love, and as a helmet the hope of salvation" (1 Thessalonians 5:2–8).

Applying this, the church arranged for the person praying the first service of the midnight watch [of the Horologion] to say, "Behold, the Bridegroom is coming at midnight, blessed is the servant whom He finds watching. But he whom He finds sleeping is unworthy of going with Him. Therefore, take heed, O my soul, that you may not fall into deep sleep, and them be cast out of the kingdom," and also, "O my soul, be mindful of that awesome day, and wake up and light your lamp with the oil of joy, for you do not know when the voice will call upon you, saying, 'Behold, the Bridegroom is coming.' So, take heed, my soul, not to fall asleep, lest you stand outside knocking like the five foolish virgins."

[xvi] Commentary on this entire reading taken from the Fourth Sunday of Paone Liturgy Gospel.

[xvii] Commentary on this entire reading taken from the Fourth Sunday of Paone Liturgy Gospel.

[xviii] Miracles of Jesus. See footnote on the cure of the leper in the Third Sunday of Paone Liturgy Gospel [*First Week Monday Matins Gospel of the Great Fast*].

xix Commentary on this reading taken from the Fourth Sunday of Paone Vespers Gospel.

xx Catholics see that this verse justifies the dogma of Purgatory, but we refuted their opinion in the Matins Gospel for the 28th of Mesore in the footnote on (Matthew 25:46) *[See Fourth Week Saturday Matins Gospel of the Great Fast]*.

xxi [The Archdeacon does not seem to comment specifically on verses 27–28 anywhere].

xxii Permitted Oaths. God took oaths in special circumstances. He swore to Abraham: "Blessing I will bless you, and multiplying I will multiply your descendants as the stars of the heaven and as the sand which is on the seashore; and your descendants shall possess the gate of their enemies" (Genesis 22:17). He swore to David as the psalm says, "The Lord has sworn in truth to David; He will not turn from it: 'I will set upon your throne the fruit of your body'" (Psalm 132:11). He also swore to His Son, as Paul says: "For they have become priests without an oath, but He with an oath by Him who said to Him: 'The Lord has sworn and will not relent, "You are a priest forever according to the order of Melchizedek"'" (Hebrews 7:21). He not only swore an oath to confirm His words to the hearers, but also ordered an oath, as we have seen in Exodus 22:10–11.

Our Lord, God and Savior Jesus Christ Himself proved that taking an oath before judges is permissible in what is true and venerable. When the high priest put our Lord under oath by saying: "I put You under oath by the living God: Tell us if You are the Christ, the Son of God" (Matthew 26:63), He did not refuse to answer, but said, "It is as you said," meaning, what you said is true.

The angels swore as witnessed in the Book of Revelation: "The angel whom I saw standing on the sea and on the land raised up his hand to heaven and swore by Him who lives forever and ever" (Revelation 10:5,6).

The prophets swore: Elijah said, "As the Lord God of Israel lives, before whom I stand, there shall not be dew nor rain these years, except at my word" (1 Kings 17:1).

Paul the apostle swore more than once. To the Romans he said, "For God is my witness, whom I serve with my spirit in the gospel of His Son, that without ceasing I make mention of you always in my prayers," (Romans 1:9). To the people of Galatia he said, "Now concerning the things which I write to you, indeed, before God, I do not lie" (Galatians 1:20). To the people of Philippi he said, "For God is my witness, how greatly I long for you all with the affection of Jesus Christ" (Philippians 1:8). See also 2 Corinthians 1:23.

xxiii Commentary on this reading taken from the Fourth Sunday of Paone Vespers Gospel.

xxiv See Fourth Sunday of Paone Liturgy Gospel (Luke 6:37) *[First Week Wednesday Liturgy Gospel of the Great Fast]*.

xxv Conditions for prayer were discussed in detail in Leave-taking Sunday Liturgy Gospel.

---

xxvi For Encouragement to pray see Leave-taking Sunday Evening Gospel (Luke 11:9–12).

xxvii See First Week Wednesday Matins Gospel of the Great Fast (Luke 6:31).

xxviii Overview taken from the Mesore 3 Vespers Gospel.

xxix Commentary on these verses taken from the Mesore 3 Vespers Gospel.

xxx Standing ranks. Saint Gregory the Great says that in the general resurrection, humans will be divided into four ranks.

1. The rank of those who judge and are not judged: These are the great saints, such as the apostles, of whom the Savior said, "When the Son of Man sits on the throne of His glory, you who have followed Me will also sit on twelve thrones, judging the twelve tribes of Israel" (Matthew 19:28).

2. Those who are judged and are saved: Those are the ones who wash their sins with the blood of repentance and correct the corruption of their works by good work, and so gain the mercy of the Judge (Matthew 24:31).

3. Those who are judged and perish: Those are the sinful believers who claimed to know God, but their evil works contradict their words. They are the ones the Master referred to in saying, "Many will say to Me in that day, 'Lord, Lord, have we not prophesied in Your name, cast out demons in Your name, and done many wonders in Your name?' And then I will declare to them, 'I never knew you; depart from Me, you who practice lawlessness!" (Matthew 7:22–23).

4. Those who are not judged and perish: The ones who do not believe (such as the heathen), who, although they do not have a written law, yet have God's unwritten law written on their consciences, by which they can determine what is lawful and what is unlawful. They were to live guided by this, yet they rejected it and perished. They do not need to be judged, because their condemnation is determined by their lack of faith. These are the ones to whom Paul pointed when he said, "For as many as have sinned without law will also perish without law" (Romans 2:12).

xxxi Guidance to the heavenly kingdom. See Luke 12:22–31.

WEEK 1: PREPARING FOR THE STRUGGLE

DAY	PROPHECIES		PSALMS & GOSPELS Matins	PSALMS & GOSPELS Liturgy	EPISTLES Pauline	EPISTLES Catholicon	EPISTLES Acts
MONDAY: FORSAKING EVIL	*1 Ex: God is manifest to those crying out to Him from sin*	*2 Is: God admonishes His people to leave sin*	God's wrath against sinners	God gives life to those who forsake sin	*Judgment of sinners*	*Their judgment is without mercy*	*Opening the door of faith to them*
TUESDAY: CLINGING ONTO GOOD	*1 Is: Guiding the Gentiles to God's law*	*2 Zech: His blessings to them*	Calling them to repentance	The Savior's mercy to penitent sinners	*The richness of His glory in calling Gentiles to repentance*	*Admonishing them to do good*	*Enduring pain for Christ's sake*
WEDNESDAY: LOVING OTHERS	*1 Is: Believers fear the Lord in all their dealings*	*2 Joel: God's blessings to those who fear Him*	Believers are commissioned to love their enemies, specifically	Loving others, for the reward will be based on their deeds	*Pleasing others*	*Our love for them must be practical*	*Loving the upright, even if they are Gentiles*
THURSDAY: SPIRITUAL GROWTH	*1 Is: The Gospel's superiority over idols*	*2 Zech: All nations turn to Him*	His authority over nature	Spiritual growth of those who seek and obey Him	*Walking in the seriousness of the Gospel*	*Steadfastness in living the Gospel*	*Signs of those who evangelize*
FRIDAY: RELIANCE ON GOD	*1 Deut: His blessings to the obedient*	*2 Is: The lack (want) of the wicked in everything*	Healing those who take refuge in Him from the illness of sin	His goodness to those who ask of Him	*Serving others with our gifts*	*Welcoming strangers*	*Serving from our possessions*
SATURDAY: WALKING IN PERFECTION			The Savior's commandments to His people	He encourages believers to imitate His perfection	*The importance of doing good*	*Being patient in temptations*	*Exposure to trials for the word's sake*
SUNDAY: LEADING BELIEVERS TO GOD'S	**Vespers Gospel** He exhorts believers to pray	**Matins Gospel** He confirms those who keep His sayings	**Liturgy Gospel** Leading believers to the kingdom of God	**Evening Gospel** Commanding believers to love their enemies	*Needing to walk properly*	*Accepting the word with meekness*	*Calling on His Name*

UNIVERSAL THEME:
NATURE OF THE STRUGGLE

SECOND WEEK – MONDAY
STRUGGLING TO PRAY
(Prayer as one cornerstone of struggle)

Linking the Readings:

All the readings of this day center on one theme: **The need to pray—as a cornerstone of the struggle**

The first prophecy speaks of **God answering the prayers of those who fear Him**, as He answered the cries of the Israelites in Egypt; and the second prophecy speaks of **Him rejecting the prayers of the wicked**, as He commanded the clouds not to rain on His vineyard, Israel, which produced wild grapes.

The Matins Gospel speaks of **God's mercy on those who pray to Him with faith**, as the Savior did for the father of the demon-possessed boy; and the Liturgy Gospel speaks of **offering prayers persistently, until they are answered**, as the widow did with the unjust judge.

The Pauline Epistle speaks of **God's wrath on those who forsake prayer**; the Catholic Epistle speaks of **their condemnation as a warning or an example to others**; and the Acts reading speaks of the **retribution on those who offer prayer unfaithfully**, as occurred with Ananias and Sapphira.

PROPHECIES

First Prophecy   Exodus 3:6–14

God answers the prayers of those who fear Him: This passage speaks of God calling out to Moses from the burning bush: "I have surely seen the oppression of My people who are in Egypt, and have heard their cry because of their taskmasters, for I know their sorrows. So I have come down to deliver them... Come now, therefore, and I will send you to Pharaoh that you may bring My people, the children of Israel, out of Egypt." Doubtless, this incident represents the believers' enslavement to Satan and sin, their cry to God for liberation, and His answer to them by sending His Son for their salvation (vv. 7–8, 10).

Second Prophecy   Isaiah 4:2–5:7

Rejecting the prayers of the wicked: Isaiah the prophet opens by indicating the coming of Christ the Master's kingdom (when the children of Israel's wickedness reaches its climax), then continues, revealing their pending punishment and God's rejection of their prayers, because He expected His vineyard (His people) "to bring forth good grapes, but it brought forth wild grapes." So, He says, "And now, please let Me tell you what I will do to My vineyard: I will take away its hedge, and it shall be burned; and break down its wall, and it shall be trampled down. I will lay it waste; it shall not be pruned or dug, but there shall come up briers and thorns. I will also command the clouds that they rain no rain on it" (vv. 5:2, 5–6).

PSALMS AND GOSPELS

Matins Psalm   Psalm 40:11

Speaking for the father of the demon-possessed boy from whom the disciples were unable to exorcise the demon (mentioned in the accompanying Gospel passage), the psalm successfully entreats God's mercy: "Do not withhold Your tender mercies from me, O Lord; let Your lovingkindness and Your truth continually preserve me."

Matins Gospel   Mark 9:25–29

This passage speaks of the Savior's mercy on those who entreat Him with faith, asking for salvation from captivity to Satan, as did the demon-possessed boy's father. The Master's words to His disciples, after He exorcised the demon, confirm: "This kind can come out by nothing but prayer and fasting" (v. 29).

Liturgy Psalm   Psalms 29:1–2

This psalm urges believers to present God with the holy offertory unceasingly, and the sacrifices of praise (prayers) —unrelenting until they are answered—just as the widow did with the unjust judge in the accompanying Gospel passage: "Bring to the Lord, ye sons of God, bring to the Lord young rams; bring to the Lord glory and honor. Bring to the Lord glory, due to his name."[64]

Liturgy Gospel   Luke 18:1–8

In this passage, the Savior urges believers to lift up their prayers to God persistently until they are answered, as the widow did with the

---

[64] Here the LXX version was used for accuracy.

unjust judge, and He says: "And shall God not avenge His own elect who cry out day and night to Him, though He bears long with them?" (v.7)

EPISTLES

The Pauline Epistle   Romans 1:18–25

God's wrath on those who forsake prayer: The apostle opens this passage by saying: "For the wrath of God is revealed from heaven against all ungodliness and unrighteousness of men," revealing the reason: "Because, although they knew God, they did not glorify Him as God, nor were thankful, but became futile in their thoughts, and their foolish hearts were darkened." He finishes by revealing what will become of them: "Therefore God also gave them up to uncleanness, in the lusts of their hearts, to dishonor their bodies among themselves" (vv. 18, 21, 24).

The Catholic Epistle   Jude 1:1–8

Their condemnation is a warning: In this passage, Jude commands believers to "contend earnestly for the faith which was once for all delivered to the saints. For certain men have crept in unnoticed, who long ago were marked out for this condemnation, ungodly men, who turn the grace of our God into lewdness and deny the only Lord God and our Lord Jesus Christ." He proceeds to reveal that even "the angels who did not keep their proper domain... He has reserved in everlasting chains under darkness for the judgment of the great day," and, "Sodom and Gomorrah... are set forth as an example, suffering the vengeance of eternal fire" (vv. 3–4, 6, 7).

The Acts   Acts 4:36–5:11

Retribution for unfaithfulness in prayer: This passage shows the story of Ananias and Sapphira (his wife). When the devil filled their hearts, they sold the land and kept back part of the price, giving the rest to the apostles. Peter told them that they had not lied to men but to God, and as a result they speedily received their just recompense, falling dead, one after the other, and "great fear came upon all the church" (v. 11).

Matins Gospel
Mark 9:25–29
Exorcizing the Deaf-Mute Spirit
See Fifth Week Thursday Matins Gospel (Matthew 17:18–21) of the Great Fast.

Liturgy Gospel
Luke 18:1–8
The Unjust Judge

THE UNJUST JUDGE

Overview

Coming to Ephraim (on His way to Jerusalem for the last time), Christ the Master healed ten men from leprosy in one of the villages of Samaria. After telling His disciples how the kingdom of God will come, He exhorted them to the importance of persevering in prayer, giving them the parable of the unjust judge and the widow. In the pericope dealing with this subject, the Savior depicts the condition of the believer who lifts up prayers to God, stressing the need for persistence in this prayer, and God's answer in His due time.

Prayer of Faith

> 1 Then He spoke a parable to them, that men always ought to pray and not lose heart, 2 saying: "There was in a certain city a judge who did not fear God nor regard man. 3 Now there was a widow in that city; and she came to him, saying, 'Get justice for me from my adversary.'"

1 – Christ the Master sought to explain to His disciples the importance of always raising prayers to God without boredom, until He answers their requests. He gave them the parable of the unjust judge. The evangelist mentions that He instructed them to pray *always*; one should pray at the church-appointed times, whenever initiating an important venture, and at times of happiness, sadness, temptation, doubt, and persecution.

Just as the Lord of Glory continued in prayer, His disciples also continued in prayer regularly and also encouraged others to pray: "These all continued with one accord in prayer and supplication, with the women and Mary the mother of Jesus, and with His brothers" (Acts 1:14). Paul commanded: "Continue earnestly in prayer, being vigilant in it with thanksgiving" (Colossians 4:2). Our Savior also said, "Watch therefore, and pray always that you may be counted worthy to escape all these things that will come to pass" (Luke 21:36).

2 – In the parable Jesus narrated, He said, "There was in a certain city a judge who did not fear God nor regard man." Literally, this means the unjust judge hated people, and they hated him in return. He judged between them unfairly with tyranny, loved evil, and hated good. Spiritually, this refers to all the physical desires and evil thoughts implanted in us from outside or those born from our own carnal

inclinations. These are truly like an unjust judge that leads us to sin, like a judge that does not fear God nor regard man and who takes us away from God. They expel the fear of God from the heart of whomever they control and drive modesty away from people.

3 – The Savior continues: "There was a widow in that city." Literally, a widow is one who has lost her husband and support and become a universally easy target for oppression by greedy enemies. Since she is easily beguiled and lacks defenders, she became the subject of God's care, who ordered the judges to "rebuke the oppressor; defend the fatherless, plead for the *widow*" (Isaiah 1:17). Jeremiah also says, "Thus says the Lord: 'Execute judgment and righteousness, and deliver the plundered out of the hand of the oppressor. Do no wrong and do no violence to the stranger, the fatherless, or the widow, nor shed innocent blood in this place'" (Jeremiah 22:3). Spiritually, the city represents our body, and the widow represents our humanity. This humanity has no helper from the claws of this body's desires to which all humanity is subject (it has to overcome them personally), just as the widow has no one to support her.

This widow would go to the judge saying, "Get justice for me from my adversary." Her going to him is symbolic of the unceasing prayer believers raise up to God asking Him to protect them from the desires that distract them from Him. (In contrast, instead of seeking salvation for their souls from their desires, the wicked, in their prayers seek strength to fulfill their physical pleasures.) The adversary she is seeking justice from is the annoying desires at enmity with her, of which Paul the apostle said, "But I see another law in my members, warring against the law of my mind, and bringing me into captivity to the law of sin which is in my members" (Romans 7:23). He frankly reveals the cause by saying, "For the good that I will to do, I do not do; but the evil I will not to do, that I practice" (Romans 7:19). The justice the widow seeks from her adversary is to save her soul from those desires because God is the One who knows her inner secrets.

Persistence in Prayer

> 4 And he would not for a while; but afterward he said within himself, "Though I do not fear God nor regard man, 5 yet because this widow troubles me I will avenge her, lest by her continual coming she weary me."

4 – The Savior continued talking about that judge and his stance against avenging the widow at first, saying that he "would not for a while." For a long time, the judge neither had pity on her nor answered her request. Thereafter, he said to himself "though I do not fear God nor regard man..."

5 – "...Yet because this widow troubles me I will avenge her, lest by her continual coming she weary me."[65] Here the judge is exaggerating, to show the extent of his irritation by her persistence. This is similar to our Savior's parable about the person who lent his friend three loaves of bread: "I say to you, though he will not rise and give to him because he is his friend, yet because of his persistence he will rise and give him as many as he needs" (Luke 11:8).

Answered Prayers

> 6 Then the Lord said, Hear what the unjust judge said. 7 And shall God not avenge His own elect who cry out day and night to Him, though He bears long with them? 8 I tell you that He will avenge them speedily. Nevertheless, when the Son of Man comes, will He really find faith on the earth?

---

[65] In the Van Dyke Arabic translation of the Bible (AVD) the word used means "To beat with a piece of wood on the head to humiliate and insult" that person.

6 – The Lord directed His listeners to the words of this unjust judge. Although he does not fear God nor regard man, he avenged the widow just to find relief from her nagging.

7 – He said, "Shall God not avenge His own elect who cry out day and night to Him?" If this is the verdict from the people-hating unjust judge, who is in turn hated, who judges unjustly and loves evil, how much more will God avenge His chosen ones who cry out to Him from the devil's snares? The Almighty, unlike the unjust judge, loves people, judges fairly, and loves goodness. The Savior reveals that God's delay in answering the prayers of His chosen is because He "bears long with them."

The apostle says, "The Lord is not slack concerning His promise, as some count slackness, but is longsuffering toward us, not willing that any should perish but that all should come to repentance" (2 Peter 3:9). Therefore, he commands to "consider that the longsuffering of our Lord is salvation" (2 Peter 3:15). The apostle gives the example of the spirits to whom the Savior preached in the prison "who formerly were disobedient, when once the Divine longsuffering waited in the days of Noah, while the ark was being prepared" (1 Peter 3:20).

Another example of His longsuffering is in withholding His mercy from Jerusalem, until the angel petitioned Him: "O Lord of hosts, how long will You not have mercy on Jerusalem and on the cities of Judah, against which You were angry these seventy years?" (Zechariah 1:12). Likewise, is His patience to avenge the children of Bethlehem who were killed by Herod (who assumed Christ was among them), and their cry to Him saying, "How long, O Lord, holy and true, until You judge and avenge our blood on those who dwell on the earth?" (Revelation 6:10). Thus, one can understand that even if God were slow to answer the petitions of those who cry out to Him for a time, He will eventually answer their pleas and save them.

8 – The Savior confirmed this by saying, "I tell you that He will avenge them speedily." *He will avenge them at the right time; the Christian will not suffer in the crucible of scourging more than is needed to examine him.* Some exegetes see difficulty in likening the Majestic God to the unjust judge. There is no difficulty here because the similarity is not in the injustice of the judge, but rather in his conceding to the widow's cry and avenging her because of her persistence. If persistence affected the unjust judge who hates people, how much more will it touch God's heart that is full of mercy, justice, and goodness, who loves His chosen ones and promises to answer their prayers?

After the Savior declared that God avenges His elect very quickly, He continued: "Nevertheless, when the Son of Man comes, will He really find faith on the earth?" He is pointing to the second coming to judge the world, and yet His words could refer to His coming in the Spirit from time to time to save the saints and punish the wicked. Since *faith* has two meanings—the first is faith in one God and in the Trinity, and the second is faith in His promises—the Master pointed to both simultaneously. At His second coming, the number of believers will be very small, their faith in God's promises will be very little, and the number of those who endure hardships and difficulties will decrease. The Savior asks because the elect will be in danger due to their weak faith in the effectiveness of prayer, not due to God withholding vengeance for them.

There is another opinion to explain the parable: some see the unjust judge as the antichrist, the widow as the Jewish nation, and the adversary as the church. This would mean the Jews complain to the antichrist against the church because she takes their best people, and so the antichrist takes these people from the church and returns them to the defiled community. Some other exegetes see the unjust judge as the Roman Caesars and the widow as the ancient church. A third group sees that the purpose of this parable is to clarify the need for persistent fervent heartfelt prayers by the faithful in the present church, assuring them that if they persist, God will send them deliverance, look to their suffering, and grant them victory at the right time.

SECOND WEEK – TUESDAY
STRUGGLING TO CONTRIBUTE
(Charity: a cornerstone of the struggle)

Linking the Readings:

All the readings of this day center on one theme: **Being charitable**—as a cornerstone of the struggle

The first prophecy **reveals to the charitable that they will see God on Judgment Day**, as Job declared concerning himself to his friends; and the second prophecy reveals the **destruction of the greedy**, as Isaiah warned.

In the Matins Gospel, the Savior commands believers **not to worry about food and clothing** as do the Gentiles, but to be concerned with the Kingdom of God; and in the Liturgy Gospel, He exhorts them to **give from their possessions**, as He suggested to the rich youth.

In the Pauline Epistle, Paul appeals to them to **give liberally and cheerfully—coupled with humility**—as James says in the Catholic Epistle. And Peter reveals in his address in the Acts reading that **charity is the spirit of faith**, as he revealed to the Jews after healing the man lame from his mother's womb who sat begging for alms.

PROPHECIES

First Prophecy   Job 19:1–26

The charitable will see God on Judgment Day: This passage mentions that righteous Job, who was "blameless and upright, and one who feared God and shunned evil," a wealthy man who had offered many sacrifices to God, took to recounting to his friends all that had befallen him during his hard times, yet finally Job understood and said: "For I know that my Redeemer lives, and He shall stand at last on the earth; and after my skin is destroyed, this I know, that in my flesh I shall see God" (vv. 1:1; 19:25–26).

Second Prophecy   Isaiah 5:7–16

Destruction of the greedy: In this passage, the Divine Revelation calls down to Isaiah with woes, desolation, and great events: "Woe to those who join house to house; they add field to field, till there is no place," showing the punishment [to the greedy] in this life: "Truly, many houses shall be desolate, great and beautiful ones, without inhabitant," and revealing their end in the age to come: "Therefore Sheol has enlarged itself and opened its mouth beyond measure; their glory and their multitude and their pomp, and he who is jubilant, shall descend into it" (vv. 8–9, 14).

PSALMS AND GOSPELS

Matins Psalm   Psalms 41:4, 13

This psalm alludes to the believers (mentioned in the accompanying Gospel passage) who care about providing food and clothing for their bodies while leaving their souls in spiritual starvation—the illness of sin—and entreats God on their behalf to heal them, and then blesses Him for satisfying their souls and bodies: "I said, Lord, be merciful to me; heal my soul, for I have sinned against You. Blessed be the Lord God of Israel from everlasting to everlasting! Amen and Amen."

Matins Gospel   Luke 12:22–31

In this passage, the Savior urges His people to seek first the Kingdom of God, and not food and drink: "And do not seek what you should eat or what you should drink... But seek the kingdom of God, and all these things shall be added to you" (vv. 29, 31).

Liturgy Psalm   Psalm 41:1

This psalm encourages the believers to give charity (in accordance with the Savior's word to the rich youth in the accompanying Gospel passage), showing that charity saves from trouble: "Blessed is he who considers the poor; the Lord will deliver him in time of trouble."

Liturgy Gospel   Mark 10:17–27

In this passage, the Savior urges believers to give charity from their possessions, as He told the rich youth: "Go your way, sell whatever you have and give to the poor, and you will have treasure in heaven; and come, take up the cross, and follow Me" (v. 21).

EPISTLES

The Pauline Epistle   2 Corinthians 9:6–15

Giving liberally and cheerfully: In this passage, the apostle declares, "He who sows sparingly will also reap sparingly, and he who sows bountifully will also reap bountifully," then clarifies, "God loves a cheerful giver." Finally, he shows the reward to the charitable: "Now may He who supplies seed to the sower, and bread for food, supply and multiply the seed you have sown and increase the fruits of your righteousness" (vv. 6–7, 10).

The Catholic Epistle   James 1:1–12

Charity coupled with humility: In this epistle, James mentions that God

"gives to all liberally and without reproach," then encourages the rich to be humble: "Let the lowly brother glory in his exaltation, but the rich in his humiliation, because as a flower of the field he will pass away" (vv. 5, 9–10).

The Acts   Acts 4:13–22

Charity is the spirit of faith: This passage shows Peter and John

proclaiming to the Jews about faith in Christ the Master and the Resurrection. This is subsequent to their charity to the man, lame from his mother's womb, who was laid by the gate called Beautiful asking for alms. When they healed him, the leaders of the people and the elders of Israel were disturbed concerning Peter and John and the conversion of many to their teachings. They asked them not to mention the name of Jesus, but the two disciples responded: "Whether it is right in the sight of God to listen to you more than to God, you judge. For we cannot but speak the things which we have seen and heard" (vv. 19–20).

Matins Gospel
Luke 12:22–31
Seeking the Kingdom of God
See First Week Sunday Liturgy Gospel (Matthew 6:25–33) of the Great Fast.

Liturgy Gospel
Mark 10:17–27
The Rich Young Man
See Second Week Thursday Liturgy Gospel (Matthew 19:16–26) of the Great Fast.

SECOND WEEK – WEDNESDAY
STRUGGLING FAITHFULLY

Linking the Readings:

All the readings of this day center on one theme: **Struggling faithfully**, without hypocrisy

The first prophecy speaks of **God's support for the faithful**, as the priest of Midian invited Moses to eat because of his faithfulness; the second prophecy reveals **His punishment to the unfaithful**, as Isaiah warned; and the third prophecy reveals **His reward to the faithful**, as Malachi promised Christ's light shining on them.

In the Matins Gospel, the Savior commands them to **be faithful in fulfilling the precepts of His new commandments** that declare the need to reconcile with all adversaries before offering gifts to God. In the Liturgy Gospel, He gives to them His aid by **satisfying them with the nourishment of His Gospel**, as He fed the multitudes from the seven loaves and the fish.

In the Pauline Epistle, Paul reveals that **God's faithfulness to the faithful is equivalent to His faithfulness to others**; the Catholic Epistle points to **His reward to them—the Father and the Son being their share**; and the Acts reading points to **His retribution on the unfaithful**, as occurred to Ananias and Sapphira.

PROPHECIES

First Prophecy   Exodus 2:11–20

God's support for the faithful: This passage mentions Moses' faithfulness. While visiting his own countrymen, he killed the Egyptian who was beating one of them. The following day, in trying to reconcile between two of them, when the offender threatened to expose the incident with the Egyptian, Moses escaped. Finally, he rescued the daughters of the priest of Midian, who told his daughters at their return: "Why is it that you have left the man? Call him, that he may eat bread" (v. 20).

Second Prophecy   Isaiah 5:17–25

His punishment of the unfaithful: In this prophecy, Divine Revelation calls out, "Woe to those who call evil good, and good evil... Woe to those who are wise in their own eyes... Who justify the wicked for a bribe, and take away justice from the righteous man"; and then reveals their punishment: "Therefore, as the fire devours the stubble, and the flame consumes the chaff, so their root will be as rottenness, and their blossom will ascend like dust; because they have rejected the law of the Lord of hosts, and despised the word of the Holy One of Israel" (vv. 20–23, 24).

Third Prophecy   Malachi 1:6–4:6[66]

God's reward to the faithful: In this prophecy, Divine Revelation reveals how the children of Israel despised the name of God, since they offered on His altar the stolen, lame, and sick. He promises that He will make them contemptible and base because they have strayed from the way and offended many by [their hypocritical observance of] the law. Then, He calls them to return to Him and so He will return to them. He concludes His speech by telling the faithful among them about the coming of His kingdom: "But to you who fear My name the Sun of Righteousness shall arise with healing in His wings; and you shall go out and grow fat like stall-fed calves. You shall trample the wicked, for they shall be ashes under the soles of your feet on the day that I do this, 'Says the Lord of hosts'" (vv. 4:2–3).

---

[66] This prophecy was removed in the new edition to the Katameros, published 1953.

PSALMS AND GOSPELS

Matins Psalm   Psalms 18:17–18

This psalm alludes to the accompanying Gospel passage that reveals the scribes and Pharisees' disobedience of the Mosaic Law while the Savior accepts the offerings of believers and admits them into His kingdom—if they faithfully fulfill the commands of His law, which peacefully reconcile all adversaries and therefore says: "For they were too strong for me. They confronted me in the day of my calamity, but the Lord was my support."

Matins Gospel   Matthew 5:17–24

In this passage, the Savior urges believers to be faithful to His law and obey His commandments, which can reconcile all adversaries: "Therefore if you bring your gift to the altar, and there remember that your brother has something against you, leave your gift there before the altar, and go your way. First be reconciled to your brother, and then come and offer your gift" (vv. 23–24).

Liturgy Psalm   Psalms 18:1–2

The start of this psalm shows the multitude's love for Jesus which leads them to trust Him and follow Him for three days (having nothing to eat, as shown in the accompanying Gospel passage [of the feeding of the multitude]); then it shows His support for them by satisfying them with seven loaves and the fish—pointing to the nourishment of the Gospel: "I will love You, O Lord, my strength. The Lord is my rock and my fortress and my deliverer; my God, my strength, in whom I will trust."

Liturgy Gospel   Matthew 15:32–38

This passage shows the Savior's support for the faithful of His people, by satisfying them with the nourishment of the Gospel, as He said to His disciples about the multitude: "I do not want to send them away hungry, lest they faint on the way." He satisfied them with the seven loaves and the fish, symbolic of the nourishment of the Gospel (v. 32).

EPISTLES

The Pauline Epistle   Romans 3:1–18[67]

God's faithfulness to the faithful is equivalent to His faithfulness to others: In the start of the passage, the apostle shows the advantage of the Jews over the Gentiles: "Because to them were committed the oracles of God." He continues that, despite the unfaithfulness of some, God's faithfulness cannot be negated: "Indeed, let God be true but every man a liar." Then, he asks on the tongue of believers: "What then? Are we better than they?" and responds, "Not at all," supporting his words by the inspired words: "There is none righteous, no, not one" (vv. 2, 4, 9, 10).

The Catholic Epistle   2 John 1:8–13

His reward to them: John alerts believers: "Whoever transgresses and does not abide in the doctrine of Christ does not have God. He who abides in the doctrine of Christ has both the Father and the Son." Then he warns them: "If anyone comes to you and does not bring this doctrine, do not receive him into your house nor greet him" (vv. 9–10).

---

[67] [The author had this passage ending at verse 17, but the reading actually ends at verse 18.]

The Acts   Acts 5:3–11

R etribution on the unfaithful: This passage speaks of punishing the unfaithful, represented by what happened to Ananias and Sapphira (as explained on Monday of this week).

Matins Gospel
Matthew 5:17–24
Reconciling Adversaries

RECONCILING ADVERSARIES

Overview

A fter Christ the Master selected His 12 disciples (during the second of His three circuits of ministry in Galilee), He began to present His new law—the Law of Christian Goodness and Perfection—for the first time from atop the mountain. This law, known as the Sermon on the Mount, occupies three full chapters in Matthew's Gospel. In the Matins Gospel, which is part of this sermon, the Savior indicates He came to fulfill the law and not to destroy it. He also exhorts the need to teach it to the people and commands reconciling adversaries for the causes of evil to cease.

J esus Fulfills the Law

> 17 Do not think that I came to destroy the Law or the Prophets. I did not come to destroy but to fulfill. 18 For assuredly, I say to you, till heaven and earth pass away, one jot or one tittle will by no means pass from the law till all is fulfilled.

17 – Christ the Master knew the Jews exalt and respect the law publicly, yet do not actually keep it. Therefore, He said to them that He did not come to destroy the law but to fulfill it. By fulfilling it, He means He would complete it and add to His commandments. For example, He said, "You have heard that it was said to those of old, you shall not murder, and whoever murders will be in danger of the judgment" (verse 21), and also, "You have heard that it was said to those of old, you shall not commit adultery. But I say to you that whoever looks at a woman to lust for her has already committed adultery with her in his heart" (verses 27–28).

By fulfilling the law, He means shedding light on the prophecies and symbols mentioned in the Old Testament and bringing them into being. By saying "I did not come to destroy but to fulfill," He wants to prepare the minds of the Jews to accept the additions He will mention, so they do not think He is contrary to God's commandments.

Some exegetes see that by "I came to fulfill," He is indicating that He will apply the laws to Himself. While "I did not come," indicates His greatness and the difference between Him and the prophets, who, sent by God, did not come on their own. To negate something, one does the contrary; to negate, "Do not kill," one contradicts by saying, "Kill." As for following through with something, such as "do not be angry," it does not negate the original command, but changes it from one status to a more honorable status—keeping the original command intact.

Overall, all the commandments were physical, but they became psychological. The soul is more honorable than the body, and the body fights against the soul. By His words, Christ the Master wanted to establish the laws, not to destroy them. He did not say He was going to fulfill the law by destroying it, but rather that He will change its status from incomplete to complete; changing it from merely physical to psychological, from being specific for a certain era to being good for all times. The change is two-dimensional: a change in the nature and a change in the natural status— transforming it from an inferior to a superior condition. The Lord of Glory kept things as is (therefore He is right in saying He did not destroy), and yet He changed its condition from incompleteness to honor, and thus He did fulfill the law.

Paul the apostle reiterated the same meaning intended by the Savior: "Do we then make void the law through faith? Certainly not! On the contrary, we establish the law" (Romans 3:31). He explained: "For Christ is the end of the law for righteousness to everyone who believes" (Romans 10:4). He sums up by saying, "Therefore the law was our tutor to bring us to Christ, that we might be justified by faith" (Galatians 3:24).

18 – The Savior continued to confirm that the law would not fail: "For assuredly, I say to you, till heaven and earth pass away, one jot or one tittle will by no means pass from the law till all is fulfilled." *Even if heaven and earth pass away and change at the [general] resurrection, no part of the law will be abolished; all will be kept, because in the age to come there is no need for the law.* Heaven and earth passing away does not mean they will cease to exist, but rather that they will be changed and purified. Heaven and the four elements will not cease in the resurrection, but will become serene and obsolete, because the people were the ones who had effected change in them.

Some exegetes believe the Savior's words were hyperbolic. *Just as the earth will not be destroyed or perish, likewise the smallest commandment in the law will not fail, change, or be overturned in this world.* Another group of exegetes thinks His words mean nothing of the law written about Him will be left unfulfilled.

In explaining how the heaven and earth will "pass away," some exegetes see that the current world will cease to exist at the [general] resurrection, being renewed as a new spiritual world. This is evident from the Savior's words in the current verse. This is also supported by David's words, "Of old You laid the foundation of the earth, and the heavens are the work of Your hands. They will perish, but You will endure" (Psalm 102:25–26). A more correct explanation of "pass away" in this passage would mean the actions will pass away but the souls will be renewed, not destroyed.

Others think that since the *world* includes the higher heaven, firmament, sun, moon, planets, angels, demons, elements, animals, and plants, these components (except the angels, demons, animals and plants) will remain intact. Furthermore, the sun and the moon will not move. As for the planets, they will fall and return to their origin, and the elements will perish and cease to exist. Another group of exegetes said the stars will fall and the sun and moon will no longer emit light, and all will return to its origin, as the Gospel says, "The sun will be darkened, and the moon will not give its light" (Mathew 24:29).

Exhortation towards His Teachings

> 19 Whoever therefore breaks one of the least of these commandments, and teaches men so, shall be called least in the kingdom of heaven; but whoever does and teaches them, he shall be called great in the kingdom of heaven. 20 For I say to you, that unless your righteousness exceeds the righteousness of the scribes and Pharisees, you will by no means enter the kingdom of heaven.

19 – After Christ the Master announced that He had come to fulfill the law and not to destroy it, He went on to show, first, the penalty for those who break the law, and second, the reward to those who preach it. He said about the first, "Whoever therefore breaks one of the least of these commandments, and teaches men so, shall be called least in the kingdom of heaven." He called His commandments *least* out of humility, because the people were not accustomed to these commandments, since sins for the Israelites were only concerned with actions, such as killing and adultery.

For our Savior, however, sin concerned first the thoughts and the will (which are the sources of actions), and second, the action itself, of which He warned and forbade. He is decreeing that whoever teaches people that His forthcoming commandments are nothing, whoever teaches that sin is about the action not the will, or whoever disobeys and teaches people to disobey his commandments, "shall be called least in the kingdom of heaven," and shall be cast out of this kingdom. The kingdom of heaven refers to the age to come.

Regarding those who teach these commandments, He said, "Whoever does and teaches them, he shall be called great in the kingdom of heaven." *Whoever follows these commandments and encourages people to do the same will be honored and considered righteous at the resurrection and in the kingdom of heaven.*[i]

20 – The Savior continues talking to His hearers: "Unless your righteousness exceeds the righteousness of the scribes and Pharisees, you will by no means enter the kingdom of heaven."[68] *Unless you surpass the scribes' and Pharisees' righteousness by severing evil from your thoughts and will, by loving human beings, and by repaying good for evil, you will not inherit the kingdom of heaven.* To the Pharisees and scribes (as we mentioned above), righteousness is related to actions only, such as keeping the Sabbath, not committing adultery, or stealing, but for the Savior, righteousness is related to the will *and* action— neither desiring *nor* doing anything.

It should not be assumed from this verse that none of the Israelites would enter the kingdom of heaven. The Lord of Glory said this to those who obey His law, but this does not apply to those who lived before His coming. The children of Israel whom the Savior meant are the very ones

---

[68] Based on this verse, to the established prohibitions of marriage in the Jewish laws, the Holy Orthodox Synods added degrees of restriction on marriage (in an endeavor to seek Christian perfection) even though these restrictions are not specified in the Holy Bible.

Paul the apostle was referring to when He said, "But Israel, pursuing the law of righteousness, has not attained to the law of righteousness. Why? Because they did not seek it by faith, but as it were, by the works of the law. For they stumbled at that stumbling stone... For they being ignorant of God's righteousness, and seeking to establish their own righteousness, have not submitted to the righteousness of God" (Romans 9:31-33; 10:3).

Commandment to Reconcile with Adversaries

21 You have heard that it was said to those of old, you shall not murder, and whoever murders will be in danger of the judgment. 22 But I say to you that whoever is angry with his brother without a cause shall be in danger of the judgment. And whoever says to his brother, "Raca!" shall be in danger of the council. But whoever says, "You fool!" shall be in danger of hell fire. 23 Therefore if you bring your gift to the altar, and there remember that your brother has something against you, 24 leave your gift there before the altar, and go your way. First be reconciled to your brother, and then come and offer your gift.

21 – After the Savior explained the reward to those who obey His commandments, He began to put in place those commandments and precepts that fulfill the first law. His precepts, like any others, contain do's and don'ts. Some of them are to pluck out the roots of evil from the souls. He said "that whoever is angry with his brother without a cause shall be in danger of the judgment" *because anger is the root of murder.* Others are to plant good in the souls; He said, "Love your enemies." Some others are to control lusts, such as preventing the love of boasting, money, self-conceit, and hoarding.

The Savior's law is concerned with the psychology, the subconscious behavior, and rejecting the unconscious will, whereas the old law is concerned with the actions, the appearance, and its rewards—the will is the cause of the action.

The Savior did not begin teaching from the first commandment because He meant to fulfill the incomplete law first. Had He started with the first commandment, which exhorts to love God, He would have had to complete it by saying, "Love Me too," subjecting Himself to their objections and accusations of insanity. He began with the commandment about killing, because killing is the greatest of evils, and because the law originated from it. Thus, the relationship between the two laws is revealed.

He began by saying, "You have heard that it was said to those of old, you shall not murder." He mentioned this commandment in the passive voice, because had He attributed it to the Father or to Himself, the Jews would not have heeded Him. He repeated the original words to show how He will fulfill the law—it needs to be completed; He did not come to destroy the law but to fulfill it. Saying, "Whoever murders will be in danger of the judgment" means the murderer shall be murdered.

22 – The Savior continued to show the difference between Himself, the prophets, and those who preceded Him. He is sovereign, not a subject; the lawgiver is not a mere human. He said, "But I say to you that whoever is angry with his brother without a cause shall be in danger of the judgment." He fulfilled the law that said the murderer would be murdered—this amputates the root from which the evil originates, because anger is a source that leads to murder. He designated the type of anger that deserves judgment—anger without a cause. Anger in its proper place deserves appreciation.

A *brother* is a biological brother, near of kin, or of the same faith. The punishment for the person who is angry with his brother without cause is that he "shall be in danger of the judgment" on the day of judgment. Only God knows the intentions and will mete out the reward.

Punishment for the apparent actions belongs to the rulers, judges, and kings. John the apostle revealed the type of punishment awaiting someone who is angry with his brother without a cause: "Whoever hates his brother is a murderer, and you know that no murderer has eternal life abiding in him" (1 John 3:15).

The Lord of Glory continued His speech on this subject: "And whoever says to his brother, 'Raca!' shall be in danger of the council." *Raca* is an expression of disdain. One uses it to belittle another's body. It is like saying a person is unclean or ugly. To John Chrysostom, *Raca* is addressing a person in an informal derogatory manner.[ii] The leaders and scholars are the *council* in this verse. This means if someone curses his brother by saying something related to his body, he would deserve punishment from the leaders, but if his curse is about the soul, such as saying, *Fool*, calling him incapable or inept, then his punishment will be Hell, since the soul is more dignified than the body. The Savior wants believers to be virtue-loving, even in their conversations. Whoever fails to do that, the council will rule on his punishment and correction.

23 – Human nature may have overdone this in such ways as one person expressing anger against another or deriding him about what is shameful in his body or soul. Here, the Lord shows how to avoid or overcome this: "If you bring your gift to the altar, and there remember that your brother has something against you," *if you want to partake of the Holy Mysteries, but then remember that your brother is angry with you, justly or unjustly...*

24 – "...Leave your gift there before the altar, and go your way. First be reconciled to your brother"[iii] *because the intentions will not be sincere in the presence of hatred, and the offerings are not accepted without pure intentions*. It is very compassionate of our Savior to insist, for our benefit, that we leave His holy body—which is the most holy aspect of worship—to reconcile the hearts first, and then return to partake of Him! Truly, peace is the root of all good.

In like manner, the Apostles Paul and Peter wrote about prayer, considering it an uplifted sacrifice to God. Paul said, "I desire therefore that the men pray everywhere, lifting up holy hands, without wrath and doubting" (1 Timothy 2:8). And Peter said, "Husbands, likewise, dwell with them with understanding, giving honor to the wife, as to the weaker vessel, and as being heirs together of the grace of life, that your prayers may not be hindered" (1 Peter 3:7).

Liturgy Gospel
Matthew 15:32–38
Feeding the Crowd from the Seven Loaves and Fish
See Wednesday Liturgy Gospel (Matthew 15:32–38) the Ninevites Fast.

SECOND WEEK – THURSDAY
CREDO OF THE STRUGGLE
(Needing to obey the Gospel as the law)

Linking the Readings:

All the readings of this day center on one theme: **The credo of the struggle**—the Holy Bible needs to be obeyed as the guideline for the struggle

The first prophecy speaks of **God giving His laws to His people of old**; the second prophecy reveals **His threats to those who reject the credo**, as Isaiah warned the Israelites; and the third prophecy reveals **His inheritance to those who obey the credo**, as He had given the Promised Land to the children of Israel.

In the Matins Gospel, the Savior calls His people to **bear the yoke of the Gospel** to find rest for their souls; and in the Liturgy Gospel, He promises them **eternal life if they forsake all and follow Him**.

In the Pauline Epistle, Paul charges believers to **reject all who teach contrary to the Gospel**; in the Catholic Epistle, James commands them to **control their tongues while [the Word is] being taught**; and the Acts reading shows His **retribution on those who oppose the Word's preachers**, as occurred with Herod when he withstood Peter.

PROPHECIES

First Prophecy   Deuteronomy 5:15–22

God gives His laws to His people of old: In this prophecy, Moses speaks to the children of Israel, revealing to them that God gave him the law on the mountain[69] from the midst of the fire. Then, he mentions to them the famous Ten Commandments, concluding the conversation: "These words the Lord spoke to all your assembly, in the mountain from the midst of the fire, the cloud, and the thick darkness, with a loud voice; and He added no more. And He wrote them on two tablets of stone and gave them to me" (v. 22).

Second Prophecy   Isaiah 6:1–12

His threats to those who reject the credo: Here, Isaiah describes the throne of the Lord of Hosts surrounded by the heavenly hosts. He mentions one seraph coming with a coal in his hand with which he touched Isaiah's lips, and thus Isaiah's iniquity was removed. Then, the Lord said to him: "Go, and tell this people: keep on hearing, but do not understand... Make the heart of this people dull, and their ears heavy, and shut their eyes... until the cities are laid waste and without inhabitant" (vv. 9–11).

Third Prophecy   Joshua 2:1–6:27[70]

His inheritance to those who obey the credo: This prophecy takes up five whole chapters from the book of Joshua speaking of the children of Israel crossing the Jordan, the fall of Jericho into their hands (because the Ark of the Covenant was with them), and their entry into the Promised Land—symbolic of God's people entering Heavenly Jerusalem.

---

[69] Located at the apex of Mount Sinai (the mount on which Saint Catherine's Monastery in Sinai stands) is a church after the name of the Holy Trinity, which has reportedly been established on the spot on which God gave Moses the Ten Commandments.
[70] This prophecy was removed in the new edition of the Katameros.

PSALMS AND GOSPELS

Matins Psalm   Psalm 28:9

Speaking with the tongue of babes, to whom the Lord revealed His

Gospel (hiding it from the wise and prudent, who are also heavy laden
with sin), and whom He called to Himself to give rest, this psalm begs
God to give them salvation, blessings, and exaltation: "Save Your
people, and bless Your inheritance; shepherd them also, and bear them
up forever."

Matins Gospel   Matthew 11:20–30

In this passage, the Savior calls those who are heavy laden with sin, to

bear the yoke of His Gospel and find rest for their souls: "Come to Me,
all you who labor and are heavy laden, and I will give you rest" (v. 28).

Liturgy Psalm   Psalms 48:10–11

The start of the psalm alludes to the just reward that the Savior gives

to those who leave everything and follow Him (as comes in the
accompanying Gospel passage), and then He urges them to rejoice in
the Gospel commandments—the ones to which the Savior directed the
attention of the rich young man: "Your right hand is full of
righteousness. Let Mount Zion rejoice, let the daughters of Judah be
glad, because of Your judgments."

Liturgy Gospel   Matthew 19:16–30

This passage speaks of the life the Savior gives to those who forsake

all and follow Him, as He said to His disciples: "And everyone who has
left houses or brothers or sisters... for My name's sake, shall receive a
hundredfold, and inherit eternal life" (v. 29).

EPISTLES

The Pauline Epistle   Romans 16:17–27

Rejecting all who teach contrary to the Gospel: In this epistle, Paul commands believers to avoid anyone who teaches anything other than the message of the Gospel: "Now I urge you, brethren, note those who cause divisions and offenses, contrary to the doctrine which you learned, and avoid them." Then, after sending some greetings to the brethren, he entreats God to confirm them in the Gospel: "Now to Him who is able to establish you according to my gospel and the preaching of Jesus Christ... be glory through Jesus Christ forever. Amen" (vv. 17, 25, 27).

The Catholic Epistle   James 3:1–12

Controlling the tongue while teaching: In this passage, James commands believers to control their tongues while [the Word is] being taught, so as not to offend anyone: "My brethren, let not many of you become teachers, knowing that we shall receive a stricter judgment. For we all stumble in many things." He proceeds to show that the tongue "is an unruly evil, full of deadly poison," continuing, "these things ought not to be so" (vv. 1–2, 8, 10).

The Acts   Acts 12:12–23

His retribution on those who oppose the Word's preachers: This passage shows the believers' shock at seeing Peter return to them (after the angel released him from the prison into which Herod the king had thrown him). Herod gave the order to kill the prison guards because Peter had escaped, then he arrayed himself in royal apparel and addressed the people from his throne, until they cried out, "'The voice of a god and not of a man!' Then immediately an angel of the Lord struck him, because he did not give glory to God" (vv. 22–23).

Matins Gospel
Matthew 11:20–30
Calling on the Weary
See Wednesday Matins Gospel of the Ninevites Fast.[iv]

Liturgy Gospel
Matthew 19:16–30[71]
The Rich Young Man[v]

THE RICH YOUNG MAN

Overview

While Jesus was on His way to Jerusalem for the last time, a rich young man met Him and asked what he must do to attain eternal life. This pericope, which deals with the answer the Savior gave to this question, points first to the true path to eternal life, then to the love of money (which stands in that path) and its dangers, and concludes by pronouncing that eternal life awaits those who leave everything for the sake of the gospel.

---

[71] Commentary on this entire Gospel reading is taken from the Fourth Sunday of Hathor Liturgy Gospel (Mark 10:17–31). The numbers in brackets refer to the verses in Mark.

Way of life

16 Now behold, one came and said to Him, "Good Teacher, what good thing shall I do that I may have eternal life?" 17 So He said to him, "Why do you call Me good? No one is good but One, that is, God. But if you want to enter into life, keep the commandments." 18 He said to Him, "Which ones?" Jesus said, "'You shall not murder,' 'You shall not commit adultery,' 'You shall not steal,' 'You shall not bear false witness,' 19 'Honor your father and your mother,' and, 'You shall love your neighbor as yourself.'" 20 The young man said to Him, "All these things I have kept from my youth. What do I still lack?"

16 [17] – It is clear from the story that this young man possessed several good qualities: he was a young man (Matthew 19:20) with much money; a leader (Luke 18:18), probably the head of the Jewish council; upright because he kept the commandments, seeking the means to eternal life; keen to acquire his desire as seen in him eagerly running to ask the Savior; polite because he knelt before Him in honor and regard (not because he considered Him the Son of God); and humble because he knelt in the presence of the crowd. His only drawback was his preoccupation with the possessions of the world. He heard the Lord of Glory calling for eternal life everywhere, so he came to seek the way to it by saying, "Good Teacher, what shall I do that I may inherit eternal life?"

17 [18] – Since it was the Savior's custom to answer people according to their intention, not according to the apparent meaning of their words, He said to him, "Why do you call Me good? No one is good but One, that is, God." The young man considered Jesus not divine, but human—a teacher of the law. Perhaps the Savior wanted to alert him to the contradiction between his words and his belief because he called Him *good* (which belongs only to God) while he believed that He is only a human. Perhaps the Savior's intention behind His response to the

young man was to alert the Jews to their bad habit of customarily calling their religious leaders with attributes of perfection specific to God, since these leaders were seeking glory and honor.

Some atheists rely on the verse that states "no one is good but One, that is, God," to deny the divinity of Christ. In reality, He did not deny attributing goodness to Himself; He did not say, "I am not good," but rather, "No one is good but One, that is, God." Actually, at another occasion He attributed goodness to Himself by saying, "I am the *good* shepherd" (John 10:11, 14). At a different occasion, He praised His disciples for sincerely calling Him Teacher and Lord: "You call me Teacher and Lord, and you say well, for so I am" (John 13:13). Therefore, we see Him rebuking the rich young man because he spoke without faith.

18–19 [19] – Matthew continues that the Lord said to the rich young man, "If you want to enter into life, keep the commandments."[72] The rich young man asked Him about the commandments, hoping to gain some new ones he was unaware of, but the Lord cited to him the well-known commandments (Exodus 20).

20 [20] – The rich young man answered, "Teacher, all these things I have kept from my youth."

Offense of Possessions

21 Jesus said to him, "If you want to be perfect, go, sell what you have and give to the poor, and you will have treasure in heaven; and come, follow Me." 22 But when the young man heard that saying, he went away sorrowful, for he had great possessions.

---

[72] [Matthew 19:17].

21 – Seeing this persistence, the Savior turned to him, loved him, and said, "If you want to be perfect, go, sell what you have and give to the poor,[73] and you will have treasure in heaven; and come, follow me."[74] By saying "If you want," He gave him the freedom to choose, because one cannot gain virtue forcibly since each person has complete freedom and an absolute will. The Savior considered one who sells the belongings and gives their price to the poor in exchange for a treasure in heaven obedient to His earlier words that said: "Do not lay up for yourselves treasures on earth, where moth and rust destroy... Sell what you have and give alms; provide yourselves money bags which do not grow old, a treasure in the heavens that does not fail ... For where your treasure is, there your heart will be also" (Matthew 6:19–20; Luke 12:33–34). Paul the apostle advises the rich to be "ready to give, willing to share, storing up for themselves a good foundation for the time to come, that they may lay hold on eternal life" (1 Timothy 6:18–19).

After the Savior asked the young man to sell his possessions and give the price to the poor, He said to him, "Come, take up the cross, and follow Me" *bearing misery and poverty for Me.* By saying, "Follow Me," He did not mean the young man should join the clergy, but to hear His teachings, rely on and obey Him, follow His example, work in His vineyard, and deny himself for His sake. Note that many followed Jesus, but He did not command them to do what He ordered the rich young man to do. The secret is that He knew this rich young man's weakness—his attachment to his money—so He demanded that he leave it. Were

---

[73] Saint Anthony the Great, the founder of monasticism in Egypt, applied to himself the principle of voluntary poverty. Entering the church, He once heard the Gospel reading which included the Lord's words to the rich young man about selling what he had and distributing its value to the poor. Exiting the church, he applied this and went out into the wilderness to worship. Many people followed him, so he built monasteries for them; thus, he became the founder of monasticism in Egypt (See Synaxarion 22 Tobe). Note that the Van Dyke Arabic Bible (AVD) abridges the phrase "If you want to be perfect."

[74] [Matthew 19:21].

he attached to secular scholarship, bodily pleasures, or leadership, He undoubtedly would have ordered him to leave them. It is noticeable here that it is not enough for a person to give his money to the poor without giving his heart to God. Without sanctifying the heart, it is useless to leave the possessions.

22 – As soon as the rich young man heard the Savior's words, "He was sad at this word, and went away sorrowful, for he had great possessions." His love for money diverted him from the path to eternal life. The sin is not in earning money, whether it is a small or large amount, but in the excessive love for it, "For the love of money is a root of all kinds of evil" (1 Timothy 6:10). The Savior let the rich young man go his way without inviting him to return [or] by relaxing His commandments, to teach us that the invitation should be answered without hesitation, that the whole heart should be devoted to God, and that our treasures should be in heaven, not on earth.

Danger of Possessiveness

23 Then Jesus said to His disciples, "Assuredly, I say to you that it is hard for a rich man to enter the kingdom of heaven. 24 And again I say to you, it is easier for a camel to go through the eye of a needle than for a rich man to enter the kingdom of God." 25 When His disciples heard it, they were greatly astonished, saying, "Who then can be saved?" 26 But Jesus looked at them and said to them, "With men this is impossible, but with God all things are possible."

23 [23] – When the rich young man left sorrowful, the Savior explained to His disciples that the entry of those with money into the kingdom is not easy—a statement that does not focus on the nature of the possessions themselves, but on those who abuse them. This statement presumes an exhortation to meekness and abandoning attachment to earthly matters.

[24] – When the disciples seemed confused at His words, the Savior further elaborated by stating that it is difficult for the rich who rely on their money to enter the kingdom. Reliance on money is a difficult snare to escape, and its victims do not feel their need for spiritual richness; many of them content themselves with their materialistic wealth, setting aside godly piety.

24 [25] – Reliance [on money] is the reason why the Savior told them it is easier for a camel to go through the eye of a needle than for a rich man to enter the kingdom of God. We see the righteous, the prophets, and the apostles themselves calling for people to desist from it. Job states, "If I have made gold my hope, or said to fine gold, 'You are my confidence'; if I have rejoiced because my wealth was great, and because my hand had gained much... This also would be an iniquity deserving of judgment, for I would have denied God who is above" (Job 31:24, 28). The psalmist says, "If riches increase, do not set your heart on them" (Psalm 62:10). Sage says, "He who trusts in his riches will fall" (Proverb 11:28). And Paul addresses his disciple saying, "Command those who are rich in this present age not to be haughty, nor to trust in uncertain riches but in the living God, who gives us richly all things to enjoy" (1 Timothy 6:17).

The poor have this consolation, that they are not as vulnerable to destruction as the rich. Although their poverty does not save them, it protects them from the temptations of iniquity that afflict the rich. We must pray for the rich, not envy them.

Some exegetes believe the money-dependent affluent have difficulty entering the kingdom because they have already received their consolation in this world, according to the principle that says, whoever receives his share in this world, shall receive the opposite in the world to come. This is deduced from Abraham's words to the rich man: "Remember that in your lifetime you received your good things, and likewise Lazarus evil things; but now he is comforted and you are tormented" (Luke 16:25–26). Also from the words of the Savior, "But woe to you who are rich, for you have received your consolation. Woe to you who are full, for you shall hunger. Woe to you who laugh now, for you shall mourn and weep" (Luke 6:24–25).

25 [26] – The disciples, astonished at hearing these words from the Savior, said, "Who then can be saved?" *All people are busy with mundane matters, and it is difficult for them to give them up!* Even the hearts of the Jews were attached to their money; they believed that victory was in inheriting the promised land. The Sadducees did not believe in reward and punishment; in their opinion, nothing is better than the materialistic things they can enjoy.

26 [27] – That is why the Master replied that whatever they think is impossible with men is possible with God. *So long as My gospel has not yet spread, I have not ascended to heaven, and My Father has not yet sent the Holy Spirit, it is difficult for them to leave their old habits. However, after those events, people shall leave their attachment to the world, gladly accept My words, and live by them to win the kingdom of heaven.*

Reward of the Gospel

27 Then Peter answered and said to Him, "See, we have left all and followed You. Therefore what shall we have?" 28 So Jesus said to them, "Assuredly I say to you, that in the regeneration, when the Son of Man sits on the throne of His glory, you who have followed Me will also sit on twelve thrones, judging the twelve tribes of Israel. 29 And everyone who has left houses or brothers or sisters or father or mother or wife or children or lands, for My name's sake, shall receive a hundredfold, and inherit eternal life. 30 But many who are first will be last, and the last first."

27 [28] – Here, Peter directs a question to Jesus in a boastful tone over their reward since they left everything and followed Him. He had personally left his profession and his boat (Luke 5:11), his desires, and the guidance of the Jewish leaders who propagated rejecting Jesus.

28 [29] – The Lord answered him, according to Matthew: "Assuredly I say to you, that in the regeneration, when the Son of Man sits on the throne of His glory, you who have followed Me will also sit on twelve thrones, judging the twelve tribes of Israel" (Matthew 19:28).[vi] Then He said to them that everyone who has left a house or brothers or sisters or a father or a mother or a wife or children or lands for His sake shall receive a hundredfold. He did not mean completely leaving the family and the relatives, but rather to love Him more than them. Some exegetes see that we should leave them if they are in a state of faithlessness.

29 [30] – The hundredfold mentioned in this verse does not mean that he who left a brother will receive in his place a hundred brothers. Rather, Christ rewards the believers for what they have lost by increasing what would increase their happiness by a hundredfold, such as peace of the conscience, consolation in distress, joy in the Holy Spirit, confidence in forgiveness of sins, and reassurance in the hour of death—heavenly rewards. It may also mean the one who leaves his physical relatives will gain additional spiritual fathers, brethren, and relatives. The reward believers receive in this world will be accompanied by persecutions, but God's consolations make them tolerate them patiently, and in the age to come their share will be eternal life.

Note that in this verse, "houses, brothers, sisters, and fields" are plural, while "father, mother, and wife" are singular. This is an indication that polygamy is unlawful, since Christ the Master mentioned the persons who could not be plural, in the singular form. Just as the father is one and the mother is one, so too is the wife; polygamy in the eyes of the church is consistently clearly adultery.

30 [31] – The Master concluded His words: "Many who are first will be last, and the last first." The *first* might be those who believed and then became unbelievers, and the *last* those who had been infidels and then believed. The first could also refer to the Pharisees and priests while the last could refer to the apostles.

Some believe those who enjoy authority in this world are the first, as they will receive the opposite in the hereafter. Those who are last are those who are poor and despised here, who will be with the Lord in His glory and eternal kingdom. This supports the Lord equating the pay for the eleventh-hour workers with that of those who came early, "so the last will be first, and the first last" (Matthew 20:16). Similarly with the two sons, the first of whom refused to go to work in his father's vineyard, but finally regretted and went, while the second who agreed to work, did not go to work. Accordingly, the first was preferred over the second. Regarding this, the Lord told the chief priests, "Assuredly, I say to you that tax collectors and harlots enter the kingdom of God before you" (Matthew 21:31).

SECOND WEEK – FRIDAY
STEADFASTNESS IN STRUGGLE
(Confirming those who keep the Gospel)

Linking the Readings:

All the readings of this day center on one theme: **Steadfastness in the struggle**, the steadfastness of those who keep the credo of the struggle—the Holy Bible

The first prophecy speaks of **God's inheritance for those who cling to His commandments**, as He promised Israel with the Promised Land; the second prophecy speaks of their **victory over their enemies**, as David overcame Goliath; the third prophecy **assures them**, as Ahaz was assured against his adversaries; and the fourth prophecy speaks of **God's grace to them**, as Zophar the Naamathite revealed to Job.

In the Matins Gospel, the Savior **warns against teachings contrary to the Gospel**, as He warned against the teachings of the Pharisees; and in the Liturgy Gospel, He **empowers those keeping the Gospel** until they become solid, as the house built on the rock.

In the Pauline Epistle, Paul commands them to **stand firm in the grace of the Gospel**; in the Catholic Epistle, Peter encourages them to **endure its sufferings**; and the Acts reading urges them to **heed its restrictions**, as the apostles commanded the believers to keep themselves from "things offered to idols, from blood, from things strangled, and from sexual immorality."

PROPHECIES

First Prophecy   Deuteronomy 8:1–9:4

God's inheritance for those who cling to His commandments: At the start of this passage, God orders the children of Israel to keep His commandments to them, "that you may live and multiply, and go in and possess the land of which the Lord swore to your fathers," and describes the land to them: "A land of wheat and barley, of vines and fig trees and pomegranates, a land of olive oil and honey." Then He warns them against forgetting the Lord in their satiety with food: "Lest—when you have eaten and are full... your heart is lifted up, and you forget the Lord your God." Finally, He commands them concerning their enemies: "Do not think in your heart, after the Lord your God has cast them out before you, saying, 'Because of my righteousness the Lord has brought me in to possess this land'" (vv. 8:1, 8, 12, 14; 9:4).

Second Prophecy   1 Samuel 17:16–54; 18:6–9

Victory over their enemies: This passage speaks of David's victory over Goliath (the Philistine giant who defied Israel for forty days), and that Saul took David that day and did not allow him to return to his home, and that the dancing maidens' song of his glory and honor sparked Saul's envy.

Third Prophecy   Isaiah 7:1–14

Assuring the believers: This prophecy shows how King Ahaz of Judah was terrified at the arrival of the forces of the king of Syria and the king of Israel who came to fight against Jerusalem, yet the Lord responded on the tongue of Isaiah the prophet: "Take heed, and be quiet; do not fear or be fainthearted for these two stubs of smoking firebrands... It shall not stand, nor shall it come to pass." Then, He comforted the king with the sign—the promise of the Messiah: "Behold, the virgin shall conceive and bear a Son, and shall call His name Immanuel" (vv. 4, 7, 14).

Fourth Prophecy   Job 11:1–20

God's grace to them: In this passage, Zophar the Naamathite responds to Job's grievance against life, censuring him for justifying himself, and showing him that God's wisdom is unfathomable, then advises him: "If you would prepare your heart, and stretch out your hands toward Him; if iniquity were in your hand, and you put it far away, and would not let wickedness dwell in your tents; then surely you could lift up your face without spot; yes, you could be steadfast, and not fear... And you would be secure, because there is hope... You would also lie down, and no one would make you afraid" (vv. 13–15, 18–19).

PSALMS AND GOSPELS

Matins Psalm   Psalms 116:7–8

Alluding to the accompanying Gospel passage in which the Savior reminds His disciples that He fed them with bread twice, assures them, and warns them of the teachings of the Pharisees who contradict the Gospel, this psalm says, "Return to your rest, O my soul, for the Lord has dealt bountifully with you. For You have delivered my soul from death, my eyes from tears, and my feet from falling."

Matins Gospel   Matthew 15:39–16:12

In this passage, the Savior warns His disciples of the teachings of the Pharisees who contradict the Gospel, as the evangelist says, "Then they understood that He did not tell them to beware of the leaven of bread, but of the doctrine of the Pharisees and Sadducees" (v. 12).

Liturgy Psalm   Psalms 29:10–11

Alluding to the accompanying Gospel passage in which the Savior commands that those who preach the Gospel must first keep it, then promises to establish them, until they become as the house built on the rock, this psalm says: "The Lord sits as King forever. The Lord will give strength to His people; the Lord will bless His people with peace."

Liturgy Gospel   Luke 6:39–49

This passage shows that the Savior empowers those who obey His Gospel, as He said to His disciples: "Whoever comes to Me, and hears My sayings and does them, I will show you whom he is like: he is like a man building a house, who dug deep and laid the foundation on the rock. And when the flood arose, the stream beat vehemently against that house, and could not shake it, for it was founded on the rock" (vv. 47–48).

EPISTLES

The Pauline Epistle   Hebrews 12:28–13:16

Standing firm in the grace of the Gospel: In the start of this epistle, Paul commands believers who have gained the Gospel's grace to cling to it, then he charges them to remember their rulers and imitate their faith, warns them of strange teachings, and commands them to remain steadfast in the grace of the Gospel: "Do not be carried about with various and strange doctrines. For it is good that the heart be established by grace, not with foods which have not profited those who have been occupied with them" (v. 9).

The Catholic Epistle   1 Peter 4:7–16

Enduring suffering for the Gospel: Here, Peter encourages believers

not to be surprised by the fiery trial occurring among them (to try them), commanding them to rejoice for having shared in the sufferings of Christ the Master, so that they may rejoice at the revelation of His glory: "But let none of you suffer as a murderer, a thief, an evildoer, or as a busybody in other people's matters. Yet if anyone suffers as a Christian, let him not be ashamed, but let him glorify God in this matter" (vv. 15–16).

The Acts   Acts 15:22–31

Heeding the restrictions of the Gospel: This passage shows that the

apostles, priests, and the whole church were pleased to send Judas and Silas to Antioch with Paul and Barnabas, to inform them that: "It seemed good to the Holy Spirit, and to us, to lay upon you no greater burden than these necessary things: that you abstain from things offered to idols, from blood, from things strangled, and from sexual immorality. If you keep yourselves from these, you will do well" (vv. 28–29).

Matins Gospel
Matthew 15:39–16:12
Warning the Disciples from the Leaven of the Pharisees

WARNING THE DISCIPLES FROM THE LEAVEN OF THE PHARISEES

Overview[vii]

After the Savior healed the daughter of the Canaanite woman, near the area of Tyre and Sidon (at the beginning of His third circuit of ministry in Galilee, after He moved from there and came alongside the sea of Galilee where He healed many who were lame, blind, and mute), He had compassion on the crowd who followed Him and fed them from the bread, as the Gospel records. This passage speaks about the Savior's love and compassion on the hungry crowds (who symbolize sinners seeking forgiveness), about Him feeding them from the seven loaves and the fish, and finally about Him refusing to give the Pharisees a sign other than that of Jonah the prophet, because they are, as He said, "A wicked and adulterous generation."

Refusing the Request of the Wicked[viii]

> 39 And He sent away the multitude, got into the boat, and came to the region of Magdala. 1 Then the Pharisees and Sadducees came, and testing Him asked that He would show them a sign from heaven. 2 He answered and said to them, "When it is evening you say, 'It will be fair weather, for the sky is red'; 3 and in the morning, 'It will be foul weather today, for the sky is red and threatening.' Hypocrites! You know how to discern the face of the sky, but you cannot discern the signs of the times. 4 A wicked and adulterous generation seeks after a sign, and no sign shall be given to it except the sign of the prophet Jonah." And He left them and departed.

39 – Then He dismissed the multitude, got into the boat, crossed the lake to the western side, "and came to the region of Magdala."[ix] Mark

gave the exact location by saying He "came to the region of Dalmanutha."[75]

1 – Thereafter, the Pharisees and Sadducees asked the Savior for a sign from heaven. The desire behind this request was not to believe in Him but rather to antagonize Him. Theirs was not an honest request made in good faith, but a deceptive attempt to catch Him in their snares, and make the people doubt Him. Perhaps, by specifying a sign from heaven, they sought a likeness to the halting of the sun and the moon during the days of Joshua when the Lord delivered the Amorites to the children of Israel (Joshua 10:12–14).

2 – Mark adds here that the Savior "sighed deeply in His spirit."[76] He showed His sadness over their blasphemy, obstinacy, and hardness of heart, since by this hardness they brought misery upon themselves. He asked, "Why does this generation seek a sign?" This reveals that they were not oriented toward faith with their request. Next, Matthew says the Savior, in His answer, reproached them for their ugly deeds by saying, "When it is evening you say, 'It will be fair weather, for the sky is red.'"

3 – "And in the morning, 'It will be foul weather today, for the sky is red and threatening.' Hypocrites! You know how to discern the face of the sky, but you cannot discern the signs of the times." By, "the signs of the times," He means the signs of His first and second coming. Those signs specific to His first coming, such as raising the dead and healing the sick, are meant to attract the people to Himself. Those specific to His second coming are the judgment and sentencing, and His coming in divine glory with the angels.

---

[75] [Mark 8:10].
[76] [Mark 8:12].

Several exegetes remark that, "You know how to discern the face of the sky," means, *You know the signs indicating clear weather or rain,* and, "But you cannot discern the signs of the times," means, *you cannot distinguish the signs of My coming. Understand what I need to do now, and what I will do at My second coming. You assume I do whatever is convenient; you might appear right in your earthly perceptions, but you are fatally ignorant in your religious judgment.*

4 – In order to show that He knew their malicious thoughts in asking for a sign, He reproached them: "A wicked and adulterous generation seeks after a sign, and no sign shall be given to it except the sign of the prophet Jonah."[x] Next, the Gospel says the Savior "left them and departed," because they did not ask Him to elucidate His words, and because He only saw in them stubbornness, arrogance, and resistance to understand whatever contradicts their will and desire.

W arning [the Disciples] against the [the Pharisees'] Deception

> 5 Now when His disciples had come to the other side, they had forgotten to take bread. 6 Then Jesus said to them, "Take heed and beware of the leaven of the Pharisees and the Sadducees." 7 And they reasoned among themselves, saying, "It is because we have taken no bread." 8 But Jesus, being aware of it, said to them, "O you of little faith, why do you reason among yourselves because you have brought no bread? 9 Do you not yet understand, or remember the five loaves of the five thousand and how many baskets you took up? 10 Nor the seven loaves of the four thousand and how many large baskets you took up? 11 How is it you do not understand that I did not speak to you concerning bread? —but to beware of the leaven of the Pharisees and Sadducees." 12 Then they understood that He did not tell them to beware of the leaven of bread, but of the doctrine of the Pharisees and Sadducees.

5 – Heavenly matters preoccupied the feelings of the disciples to the point that they forgot to concern themselves with the earthly matters. Proof of this is that they forgot to take bread with them when they came "to the other side."

6 – Here, the Savior told them to "take heed and beware of the leaven of the Pharisees and the Sadducees," and as Mark added, "and the leaven of Herod" (Mark 8:15), *the leaven of their teachings, their deceptions*. He did not explicitly declare to them His meaning, to [take the opportunity and] remind them of the two miracles of the bread and that He is able to repeat what He did the first and the second times.

7 – They reasoned within themselves saying, "It is because we have taken no bread."

8 – Here, the Master rebuked them privately for keeping to the Jewish tradition concerning food but neglecting the remembrance of His miracles.

9 – He reminded them of their previous experience during the first time in feeding 5,000 from five loaves when 12 full baskets remained (Matthew 14:20; John 6:13).

10 – He also reminded them of the second occasion when He fed 4,000 people from seven loaves when seven baskets full of fragments were collected (Matthew 15:37–38).

11 – He told them plainly in His rebuke that He was not warning them against bread.

12 – Only then did the disciples realize He was not talking about bread but meant the leaven of teaching. In addition, His admonition alerted them and strengthened their faith and so set aside their concern over the lack of bread.

Liturgy Gospel
Luke 6:39–49
Steadfastness in the Holy Bible

STEADFASTNESS IN THE HOLY BIBLE

Overview

After Christ the Master chose His 12 disciples (at the beginning of His second circuit of ministry in Galilee), He gave His famous Sermon on the Mount. In this pericope, which is part of that sermon, the Savior wanted to show His disciples: firstly, the importance of observing the commandments of the Gospel, so they do not become like the blind leading the blind; secondly, the necessity of reinforcing their calling by good works; and thirdly, the stability God gives them until they become like a house built on the rock.

Observing the Commandments of the Gospel

39 And He spoke a parable to them: "Can the blind lead the blind? Will they not both fall into the ditch? 40 A disciple is not above his teacher, but everyone who is perfectly trained will be like his teacher. 41 And why do you look at the speck in your brother's eye, but do not perceive the plank in your own eye? 42 Or how can you say to your brother, 'Brother, let me remove the speck that is in your eye,' when you yourself do not see the plank that is in your own eye? Hypocrite! First remove the plank from your own eye, and then you will see clearly to remove the speck that is in your brother's eye."

39 – By giving the disciples the parable of the blind leading the blind (as part of His famous Sermon on the Mount), Christ the Master wanted to incite them to keep the commandments of the Gospel, so they are not like the blind leading the blind. When a blind person leads another blind person, both are subject to the danger of falling into every ditch along the road. What applies to physical blindness applies to spiritual blindness—a much graver evil.

40 – The Savior continued: "A disciple is not above his teacher." *A disciple does not rise above his teacher; he is not expected to know more than his teacher. If the teacher is blind, his disciple will likewise be blind.*

41 – He marveled at those who look at the speck in their brother's eye without realizing the plank in their own eyes. By speck, the Savior is referring to a small sin, while the plank represents a great sin, such as apostasy, murder, or injustice.

42 – He further wondered how a person could possibly demand the removal of the speck from his brother's eye while the plank remains in his own eye.

He reproached this individual's hypocrisy, for pretending to be just while being internally corrupt: "Hypocrite! First remove the plank from your own eye, and then you will see clearly to remove the speck from your brother's eye." He does not thus overrule rebuke, or call for those who reproach their brethren to be free from sin (if this were the case then all teaching and preaching would have been eliminated from the world), as "There is none righteous, no, not one" (Romans 3:10). This would result in the ungodly remaining wicked without anyone reproaching them, which contradicts the teaching of the Holy Bible.

The Savior's intention was to clarify to the guides and teachers the importance of behaving honorably and not contradicting with their lives and deeds what they preach with their mouths, like the scribes and

Pharisees of whom He warned the people: "The scribes and the Pharisees sit in Moses' seat. Therefore whatever they tell you to observe, that observe and do, but do not do according to their works; for they say, and do not do" (Matthew 23:2–3). The teacher, regardless of the honorable job, prestigious position, abundance in knowledge, or correct convictions, cannot have any influence in the souls of his listeners if they see him corrupt, worldly, or controlled by his desires— his deeds contradict his speech.

We see Paul the apostle strongly reproach saying, "You, therefore, who teach another, do you not teach yourself? You who preach that a man should not steal, do you steal? You who say, 'Do not commit adultery,' do you commit adultery? You who abhor idols, do you rob temples? You who make your boast in the law, do you dishonor God through breaking the law? For 'the name of God is blasphemed among the Gentiles because of you,' as it is written" (Romans 2:21–24). This admonition is not directed only to the church servants but to all the people, and to all those who object to teaching and instruction.

Accordingly, we see Paul the apostle command his disciple Timothy: "Take heed to yourself and to the doctrine. Continue in them" (1 Timothy 4:16). He likewise instructs the bishops: "Take heed to yourselves and to all the flock, among which the Holy Spirit has made you overseers, to shepherd the church of God which He purchased with His own blood" (Acts 20:28). Peter the apostle likewise advises them to be examples to the flock: "Shepherd the flock of God which is among you, serving as overseers, not by compulsion but willingly, not for dishonest gain but eagerly; nor as being lords over those entrusted to you, but being examples to the flock" (1 Peter 5:2–3).

Importance of Good Deeds

> 43 For a good tree does not bear bad fruit, nor does a bad tree bear good fruit. 44 For every tree is known by its own fruit. For men do not gather figs from thorns, nor do they gather grapes from a bramble bush. 45 A good man out of the good treasure of his heart brings forth good; and an evil man out of the evil treasure of his heart brings forth evil. For out of the abundance of the heart his mouth speaks.

43 – The Savior gave supporting evidence for keeping the Gospel: "For a good tree does not bear bad fruit, nor does a bad tree bear good fruit." *The virtuous person brings forth good fruit, while the evil person brings forth evil fruit.*

44 – "For every tree is known by its own fruit" —these are instructions for us not to honor a person based on appearances or embellishments but on actions. Obedience leads to the action that is in line with God's will. Obviously, "men do not gather figs from thorns, nor do they gather grapes from a bramble bush." *There is a strong relationship between a person's character and his teachings. If he is a good person, then he cannot teach errors; if evil, then he cannot teach the truth.*

45 – After the Master declared that "a good man out of the good treasure of his heart brings forth good; and an evil man out of the evil treasure of his heart brings forth evil," He placed this great standard: "For out of the abundance of the heart his mouth speaks." Here He symbolized the heart with a spring and the words as the running waters; the heart can be known from the words just as the spring is known by its water.

Stability of the Doers

> 46 But why do you call Me "Lord, Lord," and not do the things which I say? 47 Whoever comes to Me, and hears My sayings and does them, I will show you whom he is like: 48 He is like a man building a house, who dug deep and laid the foundation on the rock. And when the flood arose, the stream beat vehemently against that house, and could not shake it, for it was founded on the rock. 49 But he who heard and did nothing is like a man who built a house on the earth without a foundation, against which the stream beat vehemently; and immediately it fell. And the ruin of that house was great.

46 – Since the Lord of Glory hates those who claim to belong to Him but disobey His teaching, He asked them, "Why do you call Me 'Lord, Lord,' and not do the things which I say?"

47 – Then He started to reveal the destiny of those who are doers, likening them to...

48 – "...a man building a house, who dug deep and laid the foundation on the rock." Every Christian knows that doing what is pleasing to the Lord is not an easy task; rather, it is full of difficulties, hard work, and continual strenuous warfare. This requires labor, seriousness, and struggle, just like the person who builds his house on the rock needs self-denial, steering away from pride, being adorned with humility, crucifying the will and desires, clinging to the mind that is in Christ, and considering everything as nothing and rubbish for His sake. A person whose religion is as such has true faith that is solid as a house built on the rock.

He symbolized His law with a rock for its stability and solid stand against evil opinions, stubbornness, or resistance. The Savior continues, "The flood arose, the stream beat vehemently against that house, and could not shake it, for it was founded on the rock." *If a flood of disasters or the shock of persecutory quakes struck that religion, it would not be shaken or destroyed, but rather will resemble a protective fortified fortress.* This is the religion where upright faith and good works meet.[xi]

49 – Finally, the Lord of Glory spoke about those who listen and do not do, likening them to a person "who built a house on the earth without a foundation." This house might appear good and stable, akin to a person who listens to the Gospel and appears to be good and truthful. People who see him would not be able to differentiate between him and one who hears and does (both of them attending the same church and carrying out the religious rituals in the same manner), just as there appears to be no difference between the house built on the rock and that built on the earth without foundation. However, when the winds of misfortune and hardships hit the house with no foundation, its decorated walls that appeared strong during the gentle times come crumbling down and its flawed foundationless structure is revealed. Such is anyone whose religion suffices with listening, researching, and knowing, without pairing it with good works; this leads to failure. Instead of turning a profit or benefit, it leads him to the most insurmountable loss. Is there a greater loss than the loss of the soul? This loss is the one the Savior is pointing to: "The ruin of that house was great," leading to hell.

SECOND WEEK – SATURDAY
TRIALS OF THE STRUGGLE
(Difficulties in the Holy Life)

Linking the Readings:

All the readings of this day center on one theme: **Trials of the struggle—** the trials accompanying the holy life

In the Matins Gospel, the Savior **instructs believers to avoid causes of offenses**; and in the Liturgy Gospel, He **encourages them to enter through the narrow gate**, to endure the difficulties of the holy life until they gain salvation.

In the Pauline Epistle, Paul urges believers **not to judge or offend each other**; in the Catholic Epistle, James charges them **not to be only hearers of the word, but also doers**; and the Acts reading reveals that it is necessary to **suffer in order to spread the Word**, as Paul suffered from the Jews and was driven to the examination.

PSALMS AND GOSPELS

Matins Psalm   Psalms 25:7, 8, 11

Speaking for believers, who are instructed to avoid offenses in the accompanying Gospel passage, this psalm confesses their many iniquities and pleads with God to forgive them: "According to Your mercy remember me, for Your goodness' sake, O Lord. Good and upright is the Lord. For Your name's sake, O Lord, pardon my iniquity, for it is great."

Matins Gospel   Mark 9:43–50

This passage shows that the Savior commands believers to avoid the causes of offenses, as He says: "If your eye causes you to sin, pluck it out. It is better for you to enter the kingdom of God with one eye, rather than having two eyes, to be cast into hell fire" (v. 47).

Liturgy Psalm   Psalms 118:19–20

This psalm points to the commands of the Gospel, which it calls the gate of righteousness (the narrow gate mentioned in the accompanying Gospel passage) and encourages believers to enter it: "Open to me the gates of righteousness; I will go through them, and I will praise the Lord. This is the gate of the Lord, through which the righteous shall enter."

Liturgy Gospel   Matthew 7:13–21

This passage shows that the Savior gives life to all who enter through the narrow gate: "Narrow is the gate and difficult is the way which leads to life, and there are few who find it" (v. 14).

EPISTLES

The Pauline Epistle   Romans 14:1–18

Not judging or offending one another: In this epistle, Paul urges believers to accept those who are weak in faith without meddling into their affairs, and charges them not to judge or despise the brethren, then commands them: "Therefore let us not judge one another anymore, but rather resolve this, not to put a stumbling block or a cause to fall in our brother's way" (v. 13).

The Catholic Epistle   James 1:22–27

Not to be only hearers of the word, but also doers: Here, James directs the believers to "be doers of the word, and not hearers only, deceiving yourselves... He who looks into the perfect law of liberty and continues in it, and is not a forgetful hearer but a doer of the work, this one will be blessed in what he does" (vv. 22, 25).

The Acts   Acts 22:17–30

Suffering in order to spread the word: This passage shows that the Jews rioted against Paul when he told them that God told him to: "Depart, for I will send you far from here to the Gentiles... [and] ...the commander ordered him to be brought into the barracks, and said that he should be examined under scourging, so that he might know why they shouted so against him." Yet, he was saved from scourging when he proved that he was a Roman citizen, and was later presented (by the commander's order) before the chief priests and the council for examination (vv. 21, 24).

Matins Gospel
Mark 9:43–50
Avoid the Causes of Sin
See First Week Monday Liturgy Gospel of the Great Fast.

Liturgy Gospel
Matthew 7:13–21
The Narrow Gate

THE NARROW GATE

Overview

After Christ the Master selected His 12 disciples (at the beginning of His second circuit of ministry in Galilee), He gave His famous Sermon on the Mount. In the pericope, which is part of this sermon, the Savior wanted to show to the faithful the importance of entering through the narrow gate (tolerating the hardships of the sacred life) and avoiding the hypocritical believers whose deeds contradict their words. He concluded by saying the kingdom of heaven will be awarded to those who do according to what they hear.

Tribulations of the Faithful

> 13 Enter by the narrow gate; for wide is the gate and broad is the way that leads to destruction, and there are many who go in by it. 14 Because narrow is the gate and difficult is the way which leads to life, and there are few who find it.

13 – Christ the Master concluded His famous Sermon on the Mount by saying, "Enter by the narrow gate." This phrase is borrowed from wedding traditions where guests would enter the wedding through a short narrow gate where the gatekeeper would bar the entry of uninvited guests. By the narrow gate, the Lord of Glory is referring to His laws. He called it a *gate* because it leads to the kingdom of heaven. He called this gate *narrow*, not because it is narrow in and of itself (it is a question of what is possible and what is doable), but because its narrowness is proportional to the person passing through the gate, since the hardships of the holy life challenge our fallen nature.

He elucidated His wisdom in this commandment: "Wide is the gate and broad is the way that leads to destruction." He called the way that leads to destruction *wide* because the person who enters through it is loaded with desires and pleasures. These physical desires prevent entry through the narrow gate. He said there are many who enter through the wide gate. This indicates that we commit these actions willfully, not being coerced by anyone.

14 – He went on to talk about the narrow gate: "Narrow is the gate and difficult is the way which leads to life" *because it is fenced in by God's Ten Commandments. It is the gate of faith and obedience.* A person needs to have unshakable faith and follow the Divine Economy. A person also needs to live with a clean conscience, to be patient in hardships, and to reach a high level of virtues. Having its fair share of persecution and difficulties, the narrow gate is a safe gate with a clear conscience.

It is narrow in the world and wide in eternity; it "leads to life" *not only remaining in the kingdom of heaven but moreover enjoying it.* The wicked will also remain, but in eternal torment. He also said "few" would find the gate. *The few keep the precepts of the Gospel and have an unshakable faith during hardships and difficulties. Rather, they have fortitude during trials and temptations with a strong will that does not submit to desires.*

Avoiding Hypocritical Believers

15 Beware of false prophets, who come to you in sheep's clothing, but inwardly they are ravenous wolves. 16 You will know them by their fruits. Do men gather grapes from thornbushes or figs from thistles? 17 Even so, every good tree bears good fruit, but a bad tree bears bad fruit. 18 A good tree cannot bear bad fruit, nor can a bad tree bear good fruit. 19 Every tree that does not bear good fruit is cut down and thrown into the fire. 20 Therefore by their fruits you will know them.

15 – After Jesus encouraged the faithful to endure the hardships of the holy life and live by His commandments, He began to warn them of hypocritical believers: "Beware of false prophets." Some exegetes believe *prophets* refers to those called Christians but have another belief system. Others respond that although their doctrines are bad, they may have actions that are compatible with virtue. The best theory is that by "false prophets," He means those who have the correct faith and know the religion but do not walk according to it. On the contrary, they seek to oppress the people and kill the truth in their hearts.

He called them *prophets*, like the prophets of the Old Testament among whom appeared false prophets. He warns of them here, as He did in the past: "If there arises among you a prophet or a dreamer of dreams, and he gives you a sign or a wonder, and the sign or the wonder comes to pass... saying, 'Let us go after other gods'... you shall not listen to the words of that prophet... for the Lord your God is testing you to know whether you love the Lord your God" (Deuteronomy 13:1–3). He warned against them on the tongue of Jeremiah saying, "Do not listen to the words of the prophets... They speak a vision of their own heart, not from the mouth of the Lord" (Jeremiah 23:16). Such examples, are the false prophets who appeared before the destruction of Jerusalem (Matthew 24:11).

The disciples of our Savior repeated this same theme. Paul writes to the Romans, "Now I urge you, brethren, note those who cause divisions and offenses, contrary to the doctrine which you learned, and avoid them. For those who are such do not serve our Lord Jesus Christ, but their own belly, and by smooth words and flattering speech deceive the hearts of the simple" (Romans 16:17–18). He also advises the people of Ephesus, "Let no one deceive you with empty words, for because of these things the wrath of God comes upon the sons of disobedience" (Ephesians 5:6).

Peter chimes in, "But there were also false prophets among the people, even as there will be false teachers among you, who will secretly bring in destructive heresies, even denying the Lord who bought them, and bring on themselves swift destruction. And many will follow their destructive ways, because of whom the way of truth will be blasphemed" (2 Peter 2:1–3). Likewise, John advises, "Beloved, do not believe every spirit, but test the spirits, whether they are of God; because many false prophets have gone out into the world" (1 John 4:1).

Speaking to the believers, the Master described false prophets as those "who come to you in sheep's clothing, but inwardly they are ravenous wolves." *They show humility but their insides are as ravenous wolves.* Micah the prophet expressed this: "Thus says the Lord concerning the prophets who make my people stray; who chant 'Peace' while they chew with their teeth, but who prepare war against him who puts nothing into their mouths: 'Therefore you shall have night without vision, and you shall have darkness without divination; the sun shall go down on the prophets, and the day shall be dark for them'" (Micah 3:5–6).

To his disciple, Paul describes the false prophets as "having a form of godliness but denying its power. And from such people turn away" (2 Timothy 3:5). He also says, "For I know this, that after my departure savage wolves will come in among you, not sparing the flock. Also, from among yourselves men will rise up, speaking perverse things, to draw away the disciples after themselves" (Acts 20:29–30).

16 – The Lord of Glory pinpointed their corruption: "You will know them by their fruits." This is a warning against honoring people because of their outward appearance instead of their deeds. We should judge based on *fruits* only, as only God knows the contents of the heart. Backing that their evil deeds reflect the contents of their hearts, and that

"an evil man out of the evil treasure of his heart brings forth evil,"[77] He asked, "Do men gather grapes from thornbushes or figs from thistles?"

17 – As a good tree bears good fruits, a virtuous individual produces beautiful fruits. Evil fruits come out of the evil person as long as he continues in his evil.

18 – It is impossible for a good tree to bear bad fruits or for a bad tree to bear good fruits.

19 – The natural destiny for the tree that does not produce good fruit is to be cut down and thrown into the fire. We are familiar with this fate from the unfruitful fig tree, where the keeper of the vineyard asked the owner to "let it alone this year also... And if it bears fruit, well. But if not, after that you can cut it down" (Luke 13:8–9). The fire, into which the tree is thrown is metaphorical of the eternal torment and remoteness from God that awaits the wicked.

20 – "Therefore by their fruits you will know them." Here, the Savior reiterates His earlier statement that a person's actions, not appearance, indicate what is within his soul.

Heavenly Kingdom is for the Doers

21 Not everyone who says to Me, "Lord, Lord," shall enter the kingdom of heaven, but he who does the will of My Father in heaven.

21 – The Savior concludes: "Not everyone who says to Me, 'Lord, Lord,' shall enter the kingdom of heaven, but he who does the will of My Father in heaven." *If an individual pretends to be just, while his deeds contradict this, he has no relationship with Me and will not inherit the*

---

[77] [Luke 6:45].

kingdom of heaven. This occurred to the foolish virgins who stood at the door knocking and saying, "'Lord, Lord, open to us!' But he answered and said, 'Assuredly, I say to you, I do not know you'" (Matthew 25:11–12). Doing God's will is by working according to His laws of truth. He said, "He who does the will of My Father," instead of, "My will." Indeed, They have one will, yet those who were listening were too weak to accept this.

SECOND WEEK – SUNDAY
VICTORY OF THE STRUGGLE[78]

Linking the Readings:

All the readings of this day center on one theme: **Victory of the struggle**—the Savior's victory for true believers over Satan's temptations against them

The four Gospels of this day mention the story of the devil tempting the Savior in the wilderness; in each, a passage highlights one of the meanings specific to this topic. In the Vespers Gospel, the Savior **urges tempted believers to repent of the sins that lead to temptations**. The three remaining Gospel readings each point to one of Satan's three temptations of the Savior: lust of the flesh, lust of the eyes, and pride of life, as John mentions (1 John 2:16). In the Matins Gospel, the Savior **preserves those who are tempted with the pride of life**. Satan said, "Throw yourself down from here," and He responded, "It has been said, 'You shall not tempt the Lord your God.'" The Liturgy Gospel speaks of **aiding those tempted by the lust of the eyes**. Satan said, "All these things I will give you if you will fall down and worship me," to which the Savior responded, "It is written, you shall worship the Lord your God." The Evening Gospel speaks of Him **rescuing those tempted by the lust of the flesh**. Satan said, "Command this stone to become bread," to which He responded, "Man shall not live by bread alone."

In the Pauline Epistle, Paul warns believers against **offending the brethren by the lust of the flesh** (eating and drinking); in the Catholic Epistle, James charges them against **offending the brethren by the lust of the eyes** (partiality to the rich); and the Acts reading points to the **pride of life** (represented by the difference of opinion between the Pharisees and Sadducees regarding Paul's address).

---

[78] This Sunday is known as Temptation Sunday, as all the Gospel readings display the story of the devil tempting the Savior.

PSALMS AND GOSPELS

Vespers Psalm   Psalms 51:1, 9

Speaking for believers enticed by their sins, this psalm begs God to flood them with His mercy and erase all these sins (as the Savior urges them in the accompanying Gospel passage, "Repent and believe in the Gospel"): "Have mercy upon me, O God, according to Your lovingkindness; according to the multitude of Your tender mercies blot out my transgressions, hide Your face from my sins, and blot out all my iniquities."

Vespers Gospel   Mark 1:12–15

In this passage, the Savior urges tempted believers to repent of their sins that led them into temptation: "Repent and believe in the gospel" (v. 15).

Matins Psalm   Psalm 57:1

Alluding to the accompanying Gospel passage, in which Satan addressed Christ the Master: "If You are the Son of God, throw Yourself down from here. For it is written: 'He shall give His angels charge over you, to keep you,'" this psalm speaks for those enticed by the pride of life and begs God to have mercy on them, showing that they have relied on Him: "Be merciful to me, O God, be merciful to me! For my soul trusts in You; and in the shadow of Your wings I will make my refuge, until these calamities have passed by."

Matins Gospel   Luke 4:1–13

This passage speaks of the Savior preserving believers who rely on His care without testing Him, as He answered Satan: "It has been said, 'You shall not tempt the Lord your God'" (v. 12).

Liturgy Psalm   Psalms 27:8–10

Speaking for believers who are enticed by the lust of the eyes, this psalm pledges that their worship is to God alone, and not to riches (alluding to the accompanying Gospel passage in which Satan asks the Savior to worship him, after showing Him all the kingdoms of the world). Then it begs God to bestow upon them His help: "Your face, Lord, I will seek. Do not hide Your face from me; You have been my help; do not leave me nor forsake me, O God of my salvation."

Liturgy Gospel   Matthew 4:1–11

This passage shows that Jesus helps believers enticed by the lust of the eyes, who direct their worship to Him alone, as He answered Satan: "Away with you, Satan! For it is written, 'You shall worship the Lord your God, and Him only you shall serve'" (v. 10).

Evening Psalm   Psalm 41:1

This psalm encourages believers to consider the poor and the needy, so that God may rescue them from the temptation of the lust of the flesh (this is what is meant by "in time of trouble"), alluding to the accompanying Gospel passage in which Satan tempts the Savior with bread: "Blessed is he who considers the poor; the Lord will deliver him in time of trouble."

Evening Gospel   Luke 4:1–13

This passage shows that the Savior rescues believers enticed by the lust of the flesh, as He said to Satan, "It is written, 'Man shall not live by bread alone, but by every word of God'" (v. 4).

EPISTLES

The Pauline Epistle   Romans 14:19–15:7

Offenses related to the lust of the flesh: In this epistle, Paul warns believers not to offend others by the lust of the flesh: "It is good neither to eat meat nor drink wine nor do anything by which your brother stumbles or is offended or is made weak." Then he shows that the offense is not from faith: "But he who doubts is condemned if he eats, because he does not eat from faith; for whatever is not from faith is sin." Then he also calls for their unity of opinion: "Now may the God of patience and comfort grant you to be like-minded toward one another, according to Christ Jesus" (vv. 14:21, 23; 15:5).

The Catholic Epistle   James 2:1–13

Offenses related to lust of the eyes: Here, James charges believers not to esteem the rich and scorn the poor, showing that this is a sin: "If you show partiality, you commit sin, and are convicted by the law as transgressors" (v. 9).

The Acts   Acts 23:1–11

Offenses related to pride of life: This passage shows that a great dissension occurred between the Pharisees and the Sadducees in the Jewish council as a result of Paul's address, and his life was placed in danger, yet the Lord's words to him by night were: "Be of good cheer, Paul; for as you have testified for Me in Jerusalem, so you must also bear witness at Rome" (v. 11).

Vespers Gospel
Mark 1:12–15
The Temptation[xii]

THE TEMPTATION

Overview

After John the Baptist baptized Christ the Master, the Spirit drove Him into the wilderness to be tempted by the devil. The pericope that speaks about His Temptation on the Mount includes two points: first, the Lord of Glory's victory over the tempter (as Mark narrated here succinctly, while Matthew and Luke described in detail), and second, His coming to Galilee to preach repentance and faith in the Gospel, after John was delivered.

Jesus' Victory

12 Immediately the Spirit drove Him into the wilderness. 13 And He was there in the wilderness forty days, tempted by Satan, and was with the wild beasts; and the angels ministered to Him.

12 – Mark began narrating the events of the temptation by saying, "Immediately the Spirit drove Him into the wilderness." This verse has four phrases, each of which needs further elucidation.

First, "Immediately," means this happened right after the Savior's baptism mentioned in the previous verses. Here, the exegetes ponder why our Savior presented Himself to Satan for temptation *after* baptism, not before. They answer with the following reasons:

1) Baptism beckoned Satan to struggle against Him. When Satan saw the glory with which He was crowned in the Jordan (the voice of the Father saying, "This is my beloved Son," and the descent of the Holy Spirit on Him like a dove), his envy coerced him to struggle against Him with the hope of making Him fall.

2) Christ wanted to alert us and teach us to approach the struggles Satan stirs up against us after baptism without fear or dread.

3) After uniting with His church (His community) in the Jordan, He fought for her sake and prevailed over Satan who had overcome her.

4) Just as at Adam's creation (as he first started to inhale the Spirit of life) Satan initiated the struggle against him and defeated him—and by so doing defeated the entire human race—when the second Adam, the Master of All, began the new life after baptism, the devil launched an attack against Him, but Christ conquered Satan—and by so doing He defeated the satanic forces and scored a victory for the entire human race.

For the second[79] phrase, [Mark] the evangelist records that the Spirit "drove Him," and Matthew records that He was "led up" by the Spirit, while Luke records that He "was led" by the Spirit. Exegetes ponder, "How could the Lord of Glory go on His own to be tempted by Satan although He commands us to pray 'do not lead us into temptation'" (Matthew 6:13; Luke 11:4)? He did not go on His own accord, but was caught up by the Spirit, as the three Gospels record. Naturally, the Spirit mentioned here refers to the Holy Spirit. The Holy Spirit caught Him suddenly, as it caught up Philip from Jerusalem to Azotus (Acts 8:39–40). The Holy Spirit led Him to fight the evil spirit, to teach us that we

---

[79] [In the Arabic translation, here the verb comes before the noun; thus the reversal of phrase ordering.]

should not place ourselves in the way of temptation (to show off our strength in warring against Satan), but if we are pushed to fight him, we need to fight with all diligence and stamina. When the Savior went, He did it to be tempted by Satan, conquer Satan, and make his defeat evidence that it is in our nature to resist Satan and conquer him. Moreover, He entered the temptation to prove His incarnation.

For the third phrase, all three evangelists concur that immediately "the Spirit" drove Him. As we mentioned earlier, the Spirit mentioned here refers to the Holy Spirit. How sweet are the words of Luke: "Jesus, being filled with the Holy Spirit, returned from the Jordan." This indicates that when the first Adam fell, the Holy Spirit departed from him, and secondly, it points to "Him being full of the grace that is about to be poured out abundantly upon those who are born by the grace of the new birth."[xiii]

Fourth and last, the Spirit led Him to the "wilderness." The wilderness mentioned is a barren deserted location in the land of Judea where John the Baptist started his ministry, near the Mount of Olives. The wisdom behind our Savior going to the wilderness (not to the city, the market, or the streets) to fight Satan is, first, to entice Satan to fight Him because isolation intrigues Satan and compels him to fight the human race. This is why people avoid isolation and prefer gathering with virtuous people, to check Satan's dominion over humans. Perhaps our Master intended, by going to the wilderness, for the entire host of demons to recognize and fear Him. This would explain why one of them said to Him once, "Let us alone! What have we to do with You, Jesus of Nazareth? Did You come to destroy us? *I know who You are*—the Holy One of God!" (Mark 1:24). Second, His wisdom is also in wanting to conquer the devil in both the city and in the wilderness, so as not to give him an opportunity to say (if he is defeated in one of them) that he could have had victory in the other. Thus, He eased the way for humanity in both arenas through His struggle. His struggle in the city was when "the devil took Him up into the holy city, set Him on the pinnacle of the temple" (Matthew 4:5).

13 – The evangelist continues: "He was there in the wilderness forty days, tempted by Satan." Exegetes agree that the duration of His fast was exactly 40 days (not more, not less) for the following reasons:

1) The human embryo does not reach the embryonic stage until after 40 days. Since our Savior intended to create us anew, He fasted instead of humanity for 40 days, the number of days it takes the protoplasm to reach the embryonic stage.

2) He imitated the prophets of His forefathers, such as Moses and Elijah who fasted 40 days, to show that He is not estranged from them.

3) He wanted to renew our nature that had been destroyed by sin and corrupted by Satan. Since our nature is composed of the four elements, He fasted ten days for each element because the number ten is a perfect number.

4) Since our five senses caused us to fall into sin, the Savior fasted eight days for each sense. Since seven is symbolic of the current world, the number eight is the mystery of the eternal world.

5) The number 40 is a noble number in the Holy Bible. The earth was cleansed from the flood in 40 days, Noah opened the door of the ark after 40 days, Moses remained in Egypt for 40 years, and after 40 days Elijah was worthy to ride the fiery chariot and join the spirituals.

Mark writes that the Master was tempted by "Satan," while Matthew and Luke say that He was tempted by the "devil." The devil has many names, each of which bears a specific meaning. He is called Satan, devil, slanderer, deceiver, and the fallen. A slanderer because he slandered God by telling Eve "You shall not surely die" (Genesis 3:4). He is called Satan because he deviated from his duties, the fallen because he fell from his rank, and the deceiver because he fills hearts with evil thoughts.

During the temptation, Satan presented himself to the Savior as the deceiver and the slanderer. He exposed himself as the slanderer by saying, "If You are the Son of God, command this stone to become bread" (Luke 4:3), and as the deceiver by saying, "If You are the Son of God, throw Yourself down from here" (Luke 4:9). During the 30 years of our Savior's private life, *Satan* would approach Him trying to turn Him from being good, as the Savior Himself said, "The ruler of this world is coming, and he has nothing in Me" (John 14:30), and saying of Himself, "Which of you convicts Me of sin?" (John 8:46).

Among all the evangelists, Mark alone says the Master "was with the wild beasts" (Mark 1:13). This indicates He was in a desolate place in the wilderness, far from human dwellings or aid. The evangelist mentioned this to show the harshness of that wilderness in which Satan thought he could score a victory over Christ.

When Satan was conquered during the temptation (as this day's Liturgy Gospel clearly shows), he left the Savior, and, as Mark continues, "angels ministered to Him." Some exegetes interpret this as angels brought Him food, while others believe the angels came to worship Him, while still others believe some angels brought Him food while some angels worshipped Him.

His Call for Repentance

> 14 Now after John was put in prison, Jesus came to Galilee, preaching the gospel of the kingdom of God, 15 and saying, "The time is fulfilled, and the kingdom of God is at hand. Repent, and believe in the gospel."

14 – Mark agrees with Matthew that our Savior, after hearing about the imprisonment of John, left Nazareth, went to Galilee and came and dwelt in Capernaum (Matthew 4:12–13). Luke was less specific as he said Christ went to Galilee after the temptation (Luke 4:14). The Savior meant to leave Judea for Galilee, to give us an example of fleeing the source of danger. Because of the lack of faith of the people of Nazareth, He

preferred to reside in Capernaum, where He can select His disciples from its fishermen and where a variety of people reside.

The evangelist continues writing that the Savior began "preaching the gospel of the kingdom of God." His good news (His gospel) is "the kingdom of God." It is worth noting that our Savior decided not to begin His ministry (and the miracles it entails) while John was still preaching, to avoid splitting the people into two camps (one siding with Him while the other sides with John) and to give John the opportunity to prepare the souls to receive Him through preaching and chastising.

15 – After John's imprisonment, the Master began preaching, "The time is fulfilled, and the kingdom of God is at hand." The fulfilled time is a reference to Jacob's prophecy to his son Judah: "The scepter shall not depart from Judah, nor a lawgiver from between his feet, until Shiloh comes; and to Him shall be the obedience of the people" (Genesis 49:10), and Daniel's words: "Seventy weeks are determined for your people and for your holy city, to finish the transgression, to make an end of sins, to make reconciliation for iniquity, to bring in everlasting righteousness, to seal up vision and prophecy, and to anoint the Most Holy" (Daniel 9:24).

This time period is what the apostle was pointing to when he said, "When the fullness of the *time* had come, God sent forth His Son, born of a woman, born under the law, to redeem those who were under the law, that we might receive the adoption as sons" (Galatians 4:4–5). This fullness of the time also points to the completion of the first law and attaining the second law. While the Master proclaimed, "The kingdom of God is at hand," He was calling for repentance saying, "Repent, and believe in the gospel." He used John's terminology to sway the hearts and to avoid repelling people from Him if He introduces strange terminology. He *did* avoid using the threats John had used to warn his listeners.

Matins Gospel
Luke 4:1–13
The Temptation
See Liturgy Gospel of this day.

Liturgy Gospel
Matthew 4:1–11
The Temptation[80]

THE TEMPTATION

Overview

After Christ the Master was baptized by John, He was immediately led by the Spirit to the wilderness to be tempted by the devil. Today's Gospel reading deals with the three weapons the devil used to attack our Savior—the same weapons he previously used to conquer our race.[81] These evils run through the veins of all races. John the apostle summed them up in his first epistle, "For all that is in the world—the lust of the flesh, the lust of the eyes, and the pride of life" (1 John 2:16). The first temptation, as written by Matthew, is the lust of the flesh, and it includes the desire for food, drink, sexual immorality, and fornication. The second (which Luke mentions as the last temptation) is the pride of life, and it includes arrogance, pride, envy, and hypocrisy. The third

---

[80] Jesus' temptation is also covered in Mark 1:12–13 and Luke 4:1–13.

[81] Satan overcame Adam and Eve through the lust of the flesh when he tricked them into eating from the tree, overcame them by the pride of life when he said to them, "In the day you eat of it your eyes will be opened, and you will be like God, knowing good and evil," and overcame them by the lust of the eye when he lied to them saying, "You will not surely die" (just like he lied to our Savior saying, "This has been delivered to me"), and when Eve saw that the tree was "fair to the eyes, and delightful to behold" [DRA Genesis 3:6].

(which Luke mentions after the lust of the flesh) is lust of the eyes—the love of money—and the recklessness, stealing, and lying that it entails.

Lust of the Flesh

> 1 Then Jesus was led up by the Spirit into the wilderness to be tempted by the devil. 2 And when He had fasted forty days and forty nights, afterward He was hungry. 3 Now when the tempter came to Him, he said, "If You are the Son of God, command that these stones become bread." 4 But He answered and said, "It is written, Man shall not live by bread alone, but by every word that proceeds from the mouth of God."

1 – Matthew begins the narrative of the temptation by saying, "Jesus was led up by the Spirit into the wilderness to be tempted by the devil." We elucidated on this in the Vespers Gospel. Here, we would like to add that our Savior allowed the devil to tempt Him in order to destroy the authority the devil had gained after conquering Adam. When Satan overcame Adam, he assumed the human race was unable to withstand him; the Master of All withstood him and showed us the way to conquer Satan. The Savior withstood him, not through His divinity, but through His humanity. Had His struggle against Satan been through His divinity, none would have been able to stand, neither Satan nor the whole of creation. This would have been of no benefit because the intended gain was for a human to conquer Satan, who had defeated humanity in the past; otherwise, Satan would have said his defeat was unavoidable and that it would have been fairer for a human to challenge him.

Exegetes ponder how the disciples learned of the location of the temptation since they were not with their Master in the wilderness. They answered that the disciples learned this through the Spirit and divine revelation, as Moses knew of Adam's struggle and the victory of Satan over him in paradise. Others see that the Lord told His disciples about the temptation before it began and promised to return to them. Still others believe that He did not reveal this to them until the day of Pentecost.

2 – Matthew continues the narrative: "When He had fasted forty days and forty nights, afterward He was hungry." Luke was more precise: "He ate nothing." Christ was not in need to fast, but He did that to encourage us to fast. He started His struggle by fasting, not by prayer or other similar virtues, for the following reasons:

1) Satan conquered Adam through food, so the Savior decided to conquer Satan by refraining from food.

2) Fasting was the bait that drew Satan into tempting Him. When Christ fasted, Satan assumed He was hungry and drew closer to Him to entice Him with what would fill His stomach.

3) He wanted to teach us to avoid gluttony after baptism and to cling to fasting, which will help us conquer Satan who had conquered the human race of old through the love of food.

4) The righteous of old depended on fasting, and through it they reached their goal: Moses' face shone when he fasted, Elijah was taken up to heaven, Daniel shut the mouths of the lions, and the three youth quenched the fire.[82]

Fasting means preventing the body from food, and preventing the soul from tumbling in evil and pursuing desires. This second meaning satisfies the true purpose of fasting. Our Master did not conquer Satan by simply abstaining from food but by preventing him from reaching his goal.

Some commentators think Christ the Master did no miracles before His fast even until after His temptation and until John the Baptist was thrown into prison. Yet, John's Gospel indicates that when He returned to

---

[82] Our Savior fasted in January (Tobe). The disciples and Moses fasted in June (Paone). Daniel fasted in April (Parmoute). The time of Elijah's fast, however, is unknown.

Galilee to select His disciples after His baptism, He changed the water into wine before going out to struggle against Satan.

Some exegetes ponder why the face of the Savior did not shine, as did the faces of Moses and Elijah after they fasted. They answer: 1) Had Satan seen His luminous face, he would have panicked and withdrawn from tempting Him; 2) Christ insisted on walking on the path of humility; and 3) He chose to use the illumination at its appropriate time—during His transfiguration on the mountain.

Matthew continues that after the Savior fasted for 40 days and 40 nights,[83] "Afterward he was hungry." He hungered to show that He is of our race and to give Satan a way to tempt Him. Some exegetes say He did not hunger at the beginning of fasting or in the middle but only at the end, according to His own discretion. They also say He did not gradually experience hunger as we experience, and as Moses and Elijah experienced, but He hungered all at once as He chose; His hunger was voluntary and natural. We feel hunger [to prompt us] to replenish our bodily loss, but His hunger was according to the Economy of His incarnation. Exegetes ponder how Satan knew our Savior was hungry. Some answer that he realized this when he saw Christ picking some plants to eat, while others see that the signs of hunger started to show on Him. It is worth noting that all three temptations happened on the last day of fasting, otherwise the fast would have lasted more than the 40 days.

3 – Matthew expands on the first temptation by saying that after the Savior was hungry, "the tempter came to Him." This indicates Satan talked to Christ verbally, not in a vision of sleep, or by planting thoughts in His mind, as he is inclined to do. Satan's approach to Christ after His hunger reveals that by fasting we can deflect Satan's attack and

---

[83] We explained the wisdom behind the Savior's 40 days fast, no less no more, in the Vespers Gospel under verse 13.

abandoning fasting entices him to attack us. Some exegetes see that Satan approached and talked to Christ as a counselor and helper, as one sent to fill His hunger. Others see that Satan appeared to Christ as a hungry traveling stranger, to entice Him to change the stone into bread so that both would eat.

The exegetes ponder if Satan tempted Christ knowing that He is God, or assuming Him a man. One group sees that he tempted Him as a man with the hope of conquering Him as he did Adam in paradise; Satan does not force people to commit sin but only places the snares in their way to trap them. Satan assumed that by encouraging Christ to eat bread to satisfy His hunger he would conquer Christ the same way he did with Adam after six hours had passed without food—the natural amount of time after which a human needs to feed.[84]

A second group thinks Satan tempted Christ as if He is God, because Satan makes a habit of contradicting God. Although Satan knew God since the fall, he does not relent nor care nor repent, but continues resisting God and leading people astray to idolatry and the abandonment of worshiping God. However, this opinion is not correct because Satan knows there is no chance for any creature to overcome the Creator.

A third group, including Chrysostom, sees that Satan approached Christ unsure if He was God or human.[xiv] When he saw the annunciation of His birth, the presentation of gifts to Him, Simeon carrying Him on his arms, and the voice of the Father at the Jordan, he assumed He is God, but when he saw that He has a body and senses that need to eat and drink, he thought He was human. Their claim is supported by Satan's unsure words: "*If* You are the Son of God, command that these stones become bread."

---

[84] [The notion of six hours is taken from the apocryphal books.]

When Satan approached the Savior, he said to Him, "If You are the Son of God, command that these stones become bread." He intended to deceive the Savior with praise: "If You are the Son of God," instead of saying, "If you are hungry." Satan (like Pilate) did not try to substantiate if Christ was the Son of God for the following reasons:

1) Satan wanted to abase Him, as he did Adam and Eve when he had told them, if you eat of this tree "you will be like God, knowing good and evil" (Genesis 3:5). Therefore, he told Him, "If You are the Son of God, command that these stones become bread."

2) In asking Him to create bread, Satan was asking Him a trick question: either He obeys the request, in which case Satan has conquered Him and shown that he can lead Him to fulfill His desire like the first Adam, or he leads Him to doubt His father. "If You are the Son of God," as was said at the Jordan, then the Father would listen to You and turn these stones into bread, but if the Father does not hear you and does not change the stone, then that claim is impossible and false.

3) Satan wanted to lure Him by presenting himself as a loving, caring advisor who is compassionate over His hunger. (Although mercy never found its way into Satan's heart, even for a single day!)

4) Satan was curious if He is a human or a God; if He listens to his command, then Satan would verify that He is a human.

4 – The Savior answered Satan, "It is written, Man shall not live by bread alone, but by every word that proceeds from the mouth of God." This quote points to Moses' words to the children of Israel: "Every commandment which I command you today you must be careful to observe, that you may live... remember that the Lord your God led you all the way these forty years in the wilderness, to humble you and test you, to know what was in your heart, whether you would keep His commandments or not. So He humbled you, *allowed you to hunger*, and fed you with manna which you did not know nor did your fathers know, that He might make you know that man shall not live by bread

alone; but man lives by every word that proceeds from the mouth of the Lord" (Deuteronomy 8:1–3).

In addition to this incident with the children of Israel, humans, through divine power, can live without bread as did Moses on the mountain for 40 days without eating anything (Exodus 34:28). And as did Elijah when "he arose, and ate and drank; and he went in the strength of that food forty days and forty nights as far as Horeb, the mountain of God" (1 Kings 19:8). Likewise, Adam could have remained without food had he kept from disobeying the commandment and committing transgression. The power of God is unlimited, and He who made bread a source of sustenance for us is able to make another fulfill this function.

Exegetes searched for the reason why the Savior answered Satan with passages from the Holy Bible instead of a typical answer. They came to the following conclusions: 1) To show Satan that He is not a stranger from His Father, as His answers came from the books of His prophets; 2) To rebuke Satan because he sought what he should not according to Holy Scriptures; and 3) To teach us to rely primarily on Holy Bible verses (which are infallible) in defending ourselves against the enemy of the human race, and then secondarily on typical answers.

If we contemplate the answers given by the Savior, two main points shine forth: first, Christ's persistent patience in cutting the strings of *desire* urging Him to change the stones into bread to satisfy His hunger, as Adam had done; and second, Satan's ignorance—not realizing that humans can live without bread and not being aware that this is written in the Holy Bible.

Exegetes give many reasons as to why the Savior did not change the stone into bread although He could (as He is the one who fed thousands thereafter from a few loaves of bread):
   1) He did not want Satan to realize that He is the Son of God, and so lose his drive to tempt Christ for the two upcoming times.

2) He did not want to give Satan the desire of his heart. Some might object that Christ did listen to him in allowing the Legion to enter the swine (Mark 5:9). The response is the Lord of Glory allowed this in order to reveal His power in the land of the Gadarenes and draw people to Himself.

3) Here, He wanted to undo Adam's obedience to Satan's will in Paradise.

4) Satan did not ask Him for a miracle in order to believe, but to tempt Him; one should not listen to a tempter. Christ likewise did not give the Pharisees what they wanted when they asked Him for a miracle to test Him, but answered, "An evil and adulterous generation seeks after a sign, and no sign will be given to it except the sign of the prophet Jonah" (Matthew 12:39).

5) He wanted to teach the necessity of not paying attention to the advice of the enemy of our race.

6) He does not want us to seek miracles for all our issues and requests.

Here we need to notice the difference between the behavior of Adam and of Christ: Adam was conquered by the devil while Christ was victorious over him; Adam followed his desire while Christ overcame His; Adam could not wait more than six hours to eat[85] while Christ waited 40 days and conquered the desire for food; Adam was defeated in paradise while Christ was victorious in the wilderness; and Adam was conquered by the devil through the serpent while Jesus conquered the devil with no mediator.

Pride of Life[86]

5 Then the devil took Him up into the holy city, set Him on the pinnacle of the temple, 6 and said to Him, "If You are the Son

---

[85] [Again, the notion of six hours is taken from the apocryphal books.]
[86] As we have already mentioned, Luke does not mention this temptation as second in order, but as third. The ordering is not significant here.

of God, throw Yourself down. For it is written: 'He shall give His angels charge over you,' and, 'In their hands they shall bear you up, lest you dash your foot against a stone.'" 7 Jesus said to him, "It is written again, you shall not tempt the Lord your God."

5 – When Satan's first arrow missed the target, being conquered by the Savior, he resorted to his second weapon in warfare: the pride of life, the love of boasting, which overpowers all humans. He purposefully transferred the war-venue from the wilderness to the city. Matthew says, "Then the devil took him up into the holy city."[87] "Took him up" does not mean the devil took Christ against His will (this would be impossible since the Master is the One who exorcises demons). What is meant is that the devil wanted Him to be in the holy city, Jerusalem, as Luke wrote, so the Savior went to Jerusalem of His own free will. Thus, this makes it seem as if the devil snatched Him to Jerusalem. Some exegetes think the devil changed his appearance here and appeared as the High Priest. Matthew continues that Satan "set Him on the pinnacle of the temple," the upper outer ledge of the temple. Satan chose this particular spot to set fear in His heart from the very high altitude when he says, "Throw Yourself down."

6 – Once the stage was set, the devil shot his second arrow to entice Christ by saying, "If You are the Son of God, throw Yourself down." His aim was to accomplish one of his four goals: 1) The Savior would die, elating Satan's joy; 2) Christ would suffer, making Satan laugh at Him; 3) Christ would not suffer, wherein Satan will have conquered Him with pride; or 4) Christ would not answer him (and here is the biggest prize), for Satan would denounce Him for not daring, for being afraid [to jump].

---

[87] [Matthew 4:5].

Obviously, had Christ thrown Himself from the pinnacle, no harm would have come to Him, just as later when the Jews led Him to the brow of the hill on which their city was built, wanting to throw Him over the cliff, "passing through the midst of them, He went His way" (Luke 4:30). Christ refrained from fulfilling the desire of Satan for the same reason He refrained from changing the stones into bread.

In an attempt to imitate the Lord of All in responding by a verse from the Holy Bible and to encourage Him to throw Himself, Satan told Him, "For it is written: 'He shall give His angels charge over you,' and, 'In their hands they shall bear you up, lest you dash your foot against a stone.'" This verse comes from the psalmist: "Because you have made the Lord, who is my refuge, even the Most High, your dwelling place, no evil shall befall you, nor shall any plague come near your dwelling; for He shall give His angels charge over you, to keep you in all your ways. In their hands they shall bear you up, lest you dash your foot against a stone" (Psalm 91:9–12). This verse is not specific to Jesus, but for every good man; on this basis Satan used it, assuming Christ was simply a good man.

7 – It is true that "The angel of the Lord encamps all around those who fear Him, and delivers them" (Psalm 34:7), and that "The steps of a good man are ordered by the Lord, and He delights in his way. Though he fall, he shall not be utterly cast down; for the Lord upholds him with His hand" (Psalm 37:23–24). It is also true that it is a human's responsibility to cry out to God asking for help at the time of need, and God will rescue him, but if a person exposes himself to danger voluntarily and then asks God for help (or if he is careless), God will abandon him and not respond or help him. For this reason, Jesus replied to Satan, "It is written again, you shall not tempt the Lord your God." This verse is from Deuteronomy where God addressed the children of Israel: "You shall

not tempt the Lord your God as you tempted Him in Massah" (Deuteronomy 6:16).[88]

Lust of the Eyes

> 8 Again, the devil took Him up on an exceedingly high mountain, and showed Him all the kingdoms of the world and their glory. 9 And he said to Him, "All these things I will give You if You will fall down and worship me." 10 Then Jesus said to him, "Away with you, Satan! For it is written, 'You shall worship the Lord your God, and Him only you shall serve.'" 11 Then the devil left Him, and behold, angels came and ministered to Him.

8 – After being defeated twice, Satan did not lose hope that he might win, so he decided to launch the last arrow in his quiver against the Savior: the sword of desire, possessiveness, and control. In this regard, the evangelist writes, "Again, the devil took Him up on an exceedingly high mountain" to show Him the entire world, and to see if Christ is able to climb the mountain—if He is unable to climb, then He is human. Exegetes think the devil appeared in this temptation as a magnificent king surrounded by his soldiers (for Jesus to assume he is a god), speaking to Him in the manner of a god. Then, he "showed Him all the kingdoms of the world and their glory."

Exegetes pondered if he showed Him real kingdoms or a mirage—as he had done in Egypt with Moses and the rods that turned into

---

[88] Tempting God in Massah. The children of Israel contended with Moses while in the wilderness because of the lack of drinking water. They tried to tempt God saying, "Is the Lord among us or not?" Moses cried out to the Lord for them, and the Lord ordered Moses to strike the rock at Horeb. He did this, water came out, and the children of Israel drank, "So he called the name of the place Massah and Meribah, because of the contention of the children of Israel, and because they tempted the Lord, saying, 'Is the Lord among us or not?'" (Deuteronomy [sic Exodus] 17:7).

serpents. Had they been real kingdoms, a person would only be able to see a few Levant cities [from that vantage point]. In fact, Satan's deception cannot be hidden from the Lord of All. How can he deceive Him when he could not even deceive His servant Moses; the magicians turned the rods into serpents, but Moses saw simple rods, nothing more. Although Luke said he "showed Him all the kingdoms of the world in a moment of time,"[89] this is impossible and cannot be accomplished by humans except over a long period of time and with extreme difficulty. Some exegetes think he showed Him all the kingdoms by pointing his finger to the kingdoms of the world. Others think he brought all those kingdoms as a mirage in the air, displaying their splendor and glory.

9 – Matthew writes, "And he said to Him, 'All these things I will give You if You will fall down and worship me,'" but Luke writes, "The devil said to Him, 'All this authority I will give You, and their glory; for this has been delivered to me, and I give it to whomever I wish.'"[90] This is a false claim, since God never gave such authority to the devil. However, it is an expected claim for him to make, being a liar and the father of lies, as the Savior said of him (John 8:44). As he had lied to Adam and Eve by saying, "You shall not surely die" (Genesis 3:4), here again he lied to Jesus about having authority over the world. Had "it been delivered" to him, then he is no god, because he is receiving from another.

10 – When the devil exceeded the limit that could be tolerated from him, having slandered the Father by claiming all creation was given to him, he deserved to be censured by Christ: "Away with you, Satan!"[91]

---

[89] [Luke 4:5].
[90] [Luke 4:6].
[91] The church arranged for the baby being baptized to be undressed, carried by the father, mother, or godparent facing west with the right hand raised, while repeating their renunciation of Satan after the priest: "I renounce you Satan, and all your unclean works, and all your wicked angels... and all your abominable service, and all your evil cunning and error... I renounce you. I renounce you. I renounce you." This indicates

Christ did not rebuff Satan during the first two temptations, to keep him from quitting, but here He did, because he asked Christ to worship him as God Almighty is worshiped, especially after he tried to claim the Father had lost His authority, no longer having control over anything. When the Savior rebuked Satan, He said to him, "You shall worship the Lord your God, and Him only you shall serve." By this, the Master is pointing to God's commandment to the children of Israel of old when He said, "You shall fear the Lord your God and serve Him, and shall take oaths in His name" (Deuteronomy 6:13).

11 – Satan thought the Master of All had not recognized him, and therefore he dared to tempt Him. When Christ called him by name, he fled defeated. This fall is the one pointed to by our Master when He said, "I saw Satan fall like lightning from heaven" (Luke 10:18). About leaving defeated, Matthew writes, "Then the devil left Him," while Luke writes, "Now when the devil had ended every temptation, he departed from Him until an opportune time."[92]

"An opportune time" indicates Satan returned to tempt the Savior thereafter. He enticed Judas to betray Him. The Savior pointed to his return to tempt Him by saying, "The ruler of this world is coming, and he has nothing in Me" (John 14:30). He told the Jews, on the night of His arrest, "Have you come out, as against a robber, with swords and clubs? When I was with you daily in the temple, you did not try to seize Me. But this is your hour, and the power of darkness" (Luke 22:52–53). Satan did not lose hope until after the resurrection when he found that all his arrows boomeranged onto himself.

The evangelist says once Satan left from the Savior's presence, "Behold, angels came and ministered to Him." The angels were close to Christ

---

the condition of the human before baptism. This is similar to the Savior's words to Satan: "Away with you, Satan!"
[92] [Luke 4:13].

expecting His victory, while the demons were next to their leader awaiting his victory. When the latter left conquered and depressed, the angels came to serve Christ. Some exegetes think the angels came to serve Christ by bringing Him food, others think they came to praise Him, while still others think some did this, and others did that.

Exegetes disagree as to which temptation is the hardest: is it desire, which includes abstaining from food, drink, adultery, and fornication? Or pride, which includes arrogance, haughtiness, envy, and hypocrisy? Or possessiveness, which includes extravagance, stealing, and lying? Some claim the love of money is the hardest, as per the apostle's words, "The love of money is a root of all kinds of evil" (1 Timothy 6:10), and therefore Satan used it as his last temptation. Others claim it is pride, and that is why Luke listed it last.

Some exegetes see the entire earthly life of Christ the Master centered on resisting these three temptations. He conceded for His bodily needs to be met by charity from people; Luke wrote that several women "provided for Him from their substance" (Luke 8:3). He refused to be an earthly king as indicated by His action after the miracle of the five loaves and two fish when He perceived that "they were about to come and take Him by force to make Him king, He departed again to the mountain by Himself alone" (John 6:15). He also refused to do any miracles for His personal gain, but did all the miracles to glorify God and to benefit people, as He said: "This is an evil generation. It seeks a sign, and no sign will be given to it except the sign of Jonah the prophet" (Luke 11:29).

Let all Christians be consoled knowing that we have in heaven a beloved Savior who mourns for our weaknesses and continually helps us. We should always be prepared to fight against our conniving enemy and put on the full armor of God, and there is no doubt that the devil will be conquered before us as the apostle said, "Resist the devil and he will flee from you" (James 4:7). Our Savior did not go out to fight against

Satan because He was unsure of the outcome of this fight—for the Lord of Glory was aware of His sure victory—but because He wanted to expose Satan's scandal and prove to us that we can confidently know that we are able to conquer him, just as He fully overcame him.

Evening Gospel
Luke 4:1–13
The Temptation
See Liturgy Gospel of this day.

---

[i] Godparents. *Ashbeen* is a Syriac-Chaldean word that means "guardian, charge, custodian" who is entrusted with caring for and guarding the baptized individual against deviating from Christianity until maturity. Children do not understand the essence of the faith, or the meaning of baptism, and cannot confess their sins, declare their repentance, and confirm their faith, therefore, the church saw a need to accept the declaration of their faith and baptism through their godparent's *vow* to raise them with a Christian upbringing.

The appointment of the godparents is very old in the church. It originated during the time of the apostles and comes from the Holy Bible. The Lord assigned Ananias to take care of and guide Paul in the way of truth before his baptism (Acts 9:10–19). He also entrusted Peter the apostle with teaching Cornelius the foundations of the faith and guiding him to salvation (Acts 10).

The Godparent must be: 1) Orthodox in faith; 2) A godly individual; 3) Well aware of the foundations of the faith; 4) An adult; 5) Appointed by the parent of the child, or by the church if the child is orphaned.

They are required to: 1) Provide the godchild with religious and proper upbringing until the child grows in the orthodox faith; 2) Plant in the child the spirit of the Christian magnanimity, moral courage, beautiful traits, and virtues; and 3) Plant in the child the spirit of loving the church.

If godparents raise the child on these principles, they will be counted great in the kingdom of heaven, as this verse indicates. If godparents are negligent, they will be condemned before God (Matthew 5:19) as is clear from the story of Eli the priest (1 Samuel 2).

Once the child reaches the age of maturity, the godparents take and entrust the child to the church, in front of God, to the servant of the Lord, and are relieved of their responsibility. It is the church's responsibility to prepare the child without the godparents, following the examples of the Apostles Paul and Philip (Acts 8:38; Philemon 1:10) or she enlists a deacon, cantor, or any church servant as a substitute godparent. The parents cannot be the godparents. All the Christian churches concur on the appointment of a godparent during the sacraments of baptism and marriage (*La-alekh El-Nafeesa* (2:19–26) [Arabic reference]).

[ii] John Chrysostom 1.16.10 (NPNF1 10:107).

[iii] The Ecclesiastical Kiss. The kiss in church nomenclature is given during the liturgical prayers by hand greeting as follows: 1) Before the Offering of the Lamb, the officiating priest kisses the hands of his brothers the priests and greets the congregation as a symbol of reconciliation and peace, fulfilling the verse we are explaining; 2) At the beginning of the liturgy, after reading the Holy Gospel and its interpretation, the priest bows down before the sanctuary, offers a prostration to his brothers the priests and kisses them, and greets the congregation, beseeching the acceptance of all, fulfilling this verse; 3) After the Prayer of Reconciliation, the priest says at the end of the prayer, "And make us all worthy, O our Master, to greet one another with a holy kiss," as an indication of the genuine Christian love and hearty union; 4) Before the Dismissal, the priests kiss each other, and the congregation bids the clergy farewell with a kiss before leaving, as the faithful fell on Paul's neck and kissed him (Acts 20:37). If Divine Providence does not allow for them to meet again, then the kiss is in hope of meeting in heaven.

As for the congregation kissing the hand of the priests when they enter the church (after prostrating before God), it is out of respect and out of submission to God who entrusted the priests with these mysteries, and to take the blessing from them. Therefore, the priest puts his hand on the head of those who greet him, as Jacob had placed his hands on the heads of Benjamin and Manasseh, the sons of Joseph, and blessed them.

The church forbids kissing on Wednesday and Thursday of the Passion Week so that it does not become a treacherous hypocritical superficial greeting like the kiss of Judas the traitor.

[iv] *[Actually the Archdeacon did not expound upon verses 20–25 anywhere!].*

[v] The Rich Young Man is mentioned in Matthew 19:16–30, Mark 10:17–31, and Luke 18:18–30.

[vi] The New Heavens. Christ the Master told His disciples who followed Him that in the regeneration, when He sits on His throne of glory, they will sit on twelve thrones to judge the children of Israel. Isaiah mentioned this regeneration: "For behold, I create new heavens and a new earth; and the former shall not be remembered or come to mind" (Isaiah 65:17). He also said: "'For as the new heavens and the new earth which I will make shall remain before Me,' says the Lord, 'So shall your descendants and your name remain'" (Isaiah 66:22). Peter refers to these new heavens God has promised to make: "Nevertheless we, according to His promise, look for new heavens and a new

earth in which righteousness dwells" (2 Peter 3:13). The book of Revelation also mentions, "Now I saw a new heaven and a new earth, for the first heaven and the first earth had passed away. Also, there was no more sea" (Revelation 21:1). It was described: "But there shall by no means enter it anything that defiles, or causes an abomination or a lie, but only those who are written in the Lamb's Book of Life" (Revelation 21:27).

The Savior's promise (made to the disciples to sit on twelve thrones judging the children of Israel) is what led the sons of Zebedee's mother to ask Jesus to seat her sons one on His right and the other on His left in His kingdom (Matthew 20:21). The Savior said: "But you are those who have continued with Me in My trials. And I bestow upon you a kingdom, just as My Father bestowed one upon Me, that you may eat and drink at My table in My kingdom and sit on thrones judging the twelve tribes of Israel" (Luke 22:28–30). Paul supports this by saying, "Do you not know that the saints will judge the world?" (1 Corinthians 6:2). Furthermore, He said in the book of Revelation: "To him who overcomes I will grant to sit with Me on My throne, as I also overcame and sat down with My Father on His throne" (Revelation 3:21). The judgment He is referring to is when His disciples will inquisition the truth out of the children of Israel, just as the queen of the South and the Ninevites are said to bear witness against their generation (Luke 11:31–32). As for the Judgment on the last day, it belongs to the Savior alone.

He designated the judgment of the children of Israel to be by the disciples, because they were of them and under the same law—they, and people like them who followed Christ, while the rest of the Jews rejected Him. His promise to seat them is proof of their high dignity with which He singled them out. The Lord included Judas, who betrayed Him, in this dignity because he was then worthy of that promise. When he betrayed Christ, this authority passed to the one elected in his place. Had the Master not shared this authority with him, Judas would have used this as a pretext to blaspheme Him. His promise was true, but, being provoked, he betrayed his Master and fell from his rank. This teaches us that God's promise should not lead us to negligence, and His warnings should not lead us to despair, for the door of repentance is open and God wants everyone's salvation.

One might object to the judgment of the tribes of Israel by the disciples saying, "If Christ will judge all creation, then when will the apostles judge the tribes (as He promised them), and are the tribes not part of the creation?" His promise (a true vow by the Most High) refutes this objection; if He promised them, then they will judge in a specific category, as could be understood from the thrones and ranks. God, who is incomprehensible and imperceptible, will not judge people in this fashion. His truthful judgment will be beyond our comprehension. By comparison, we find many events announced in ancient and modern times credited to an illustrious name, while in fact they are done by others. For example, we say the king wrote a book, while the king did not personally write it, but his scribe.

Saint Gregory the Great sees that human beings in the resurrection are divided into four categories: in the first category are those who judge but are not judged, like the great saints and apostles to whom the previous promise was made; in the second category are those who are judged and saved; in the third are those who are judged and condemned; and in the fourth are those who are not judged and perish since they did not believe, and transgressed the law imprinted in their conscience.

[vii] Overview taken from Wednesday of the Ninevites Fast.

[viii] Commentary on these verses taken from Wednesday Liturgy Gospel of the Ninevites Fast.

[ix] The word Magdala means tower. Mary Magdalene hails from this village. Dalmanutha is a smaller village near Magdala.

[x] This reproach was explained in the Ninevites Monday Liturgy Gospel (Luke 11:29–30).

[xi] The Protestant declaration that salvation is by faith only (not by faith and works as the apostolic churches believe) is a vain opinion. If their principal is applied, it produces a harmful result: the equality between those who respect the law and those who disdain it. This contradicts the words of the Savior that those who listen and do are likened to those who build the house on the rock, but those who listen and do not do are likened to those who build the house on the sand.

[xii] The Temptation of Jesus is also found in Matthew 4:1–11 and Luke 4:1–13.

[xiii] See Commentary of *Al-Meshriqi* (2:79) [Arabic reference].

[xiv] John Chrysostom 1.13.3 (NPNF1 10:78).

WEEK 2: NATURE OF THE STRUGGLE

DAY	PROPHECIES		PSALMS & GOSPELS		EPISTLES		
			Matins	Liturgy	Pauline	Catholicon	Acts
MONDAY: STRUGGLING TO PRAY	*1 Ex: God answers the prayers of those who fear Him*	*2 Is: He rejects the wicked's prayers*	God's mercy is on those who pray to Him with faith	Believers need to persist in their prayer	*God's wrath is on those who forsake prayer*	*They are condemned —a warning*	*Retribution for unfaithfulness in prayer*
TUESDAY: STRUGGLING TO CONTRIBUTE	*1 Job: The charitable will see God on Judgment Day*	*2 Is: The greedy are destroyed*	Believers seek first the Kingdom of God	Believers give from their possessions	*Give liberally and cheerfully*	*Charity is coupled with humility*	*Charity is the spirit of faith*
WEDNESDAY: STRUGGLING FAITHFULLY	*1 Ex: God supports the faithful*	*2 Is: He punishes the unfaithful*	Be faithful in fulfilling His commandments	He nourishes believers with His Gospel	*God is faithful*	*His reward to believers*	*His retribution on the unfaithful*
	3 Mal: God's reward to the faithful						
THURSDAY: CREDO OF THE STRUGGLE	*1 Duet: God gives His laws to His people of old*	*2 Is: He threatens those who reject the credo*	Bear the yoke of the Gospel	Eternal life for those who forsake all to follow Him	*Reject all who teach contrary to the Gospel*	*Control the tongue while teaching*	*His retribution on those who oppose its preachers*
	3 Josh: His inheritance is to those who obey the credo						
FRIDAY: BEING STEADFAST IN STRUGGLE	*1 Deut: God's inheritance for those who follow His commandments*	*2 1 Samuel: Victory over their enemies*	He warns against teachings contrary to the Gospel	He empowers those keeping the Gospel	*Standing firm in the grace of the Gospel*	*Enduring its sufferings*	*Heeding its restrictions*
	3 Is: Assuring the believers	*4 Job: God's grace to them*					
SATURDAY: TRIALS OF THE STRUGGLE			He commands believers to avoid the causes of offenses	He encourages them to enter through the narrow gate	*Not judging or offending one another*	*Not being only hearers of the word, but also doers*	*Suffering in order to spread the word*
SUNDAY: VICTORY OF THE STRUGGLE	**Vespers Gospel** He urges tempted believers to repent	**Matins Gospel** He preserves those tempted by pride of life	**Liturgy Gospel** He aids those tempted by the lust of the eyes	**Evening Gospel** He rescues those tempted by the lust of the flesh	*Do not offend others by lust of the flesh*	*Do not offend others through lust of the eyes by showing partiality*	*Do not cause dissension through the pride of life*

Appendix 1: THE HOLY GREAT FAST QUICK-REFERENCE GUIDE

(OVERALL THEME: SPIRITUAL STRUGGLE)

GENERAL TOPIC	WEEK	SPECIFIC TOPIC	WEEKDAYS — THE SPIRITUAL STRUGGLE					WEEKEND — THE SAVIOR'S GRACE	
			M	T	W	T	F	S	S
FIRST SECTION — FEATURES OF THE STRUGGLE	1	Preparing for the struggle	Forsaking Evil	Clinging to Good	Loving Others	Spiritual Growth	Reliance on God	Walking in Perfection	Leading to God's Kingdom
	2	Nature of the struggle	Struggling to Pray	Struggling to Contribute	Struggling Faithfully	Credo of the Struggle	Steadfastness in the Struggle	Trials of the Struggle	Victory of the Struggle
	3	Purity of the struggle (repentance)	Penitent Confession	Righteousness of Repentance	Trials of Repentance	Judgment of Repentance	Security of Repentance	Penitence Forgiveness	Accepting Repentance
	4	Credo of the struggle (the Holy Bible)	Spirit of the Gospel	Preaching the Gospel	Peace of the Gospel	Gospel Enlightenment	Faith in the Gospel	Keeping the Gospel	Strength of the Gospel
SECOND SECTION — FRUITS OF THE STRUGGLE	5	Goal of the struggle (faith)	Reliance on Faith	Faith-Ministry	Hope of Faith	Freedom of Faith	Vengeance of the Faith	Guidance of the Faith	Strengthening the Faith
	6	Anointing of the struggle (Baptism)	Repentance of Baptism	Confession of Baptism	Judgment of Baptism	Life of Baptism	Resurrection of Baptism	Salvation of Baptism	Enlightenment of Baptism
	7	Victory of the struggle (the Savior)	The Savior's witnesses	Confessing the Savior	Faith in the Savior	Resurrection of the Savior	The Savior's Judgment	Blessings of the Savior	The Savior's Redemption

www.ingramcontent.com/pod-product-compliance
Lightning Source LLC
Chambersburg PA
CBHW031944080426
42735CB00007B/261